OPINIONATED

THE WORLDVIEW OF A JEWISH WOMAN

OPINIONATED

THE WORLDVIEW OF A JEWISH WOMAN

Sara Reguer

Boston
2017

Library of Congress Cataloging-in-Publication Data:
A catalog record for this book as available from the Library of Congress.

Copyright © 2017 Academic Studies Press
All rights reserved.

ISBN 978-1-61811-645-1 (paper)
ISBN 978-1-61811-646-8 (electronic)

Cover design by Ivan Grave.
Book design by Tatiana Vernikov.
On the cover: "Giotto's Garden, no. 2", 2013, by Raphael Fodde.

Published by Academic Studies Press in 2017

28 Montfern Avenue
Brighton, MA 02135, USA
press@academicstudiespress.com
www.academicstudiespress.com

*To my special husband,
Raffaele Gershom Fodde*

Contents

Introduction	9
Part I	
Farewell Column	12
History	
The Purim Play	14
Women's Suffrage. Part 1	16
Women's Suffrage. Part 2	18
The Spanish Inquisition	20
Synagogue Decorum	22
American Jews	24
A Dress Code	26
The Entrepreneur	28
Sacred Music	30
The Field of Food	32
Roman Roads	34
The Traveler	36
The Blessing of Water	38
The Power of Poetry	40
Censorship	42
A Question of Art	44
Explaining Judaic Studies	46
Tribal Divisions	48
Kaifeng, China	50
Shanghai	52
Saying Good-Bye	54
Learning Languages	56
The Armies of Rome	58
Setting the Calendar	60
Dancing	62
Stereotyping	64
The Game of Chess	66
Tombstones	68
Biblical Women	
Noah's Wife	70
Childless Then and Now	72
A Husband's Obligations	74
Toldot	76
A Thread of Clothing	78
Bilha and Zilpa	80
Va-Yishlach	82
Tamar and Judah	84
A Matriarchal Legacy	86
Siblings	88
Midwifery	90
Some Thoughts on Miriam	92
Deborah the Judge	94
The Roles of Avishag	96
Some Lessons from Ruth	98
Kohelet	100
The Captive Woman	102

Jewish Women in History

Jewish Women	
of Turkey	104
Kiddush HaShem	106
Gluckel the Working	
Woman	108
The Lady Was a Spy	110
The First Woman	
Publisher	112
Ugav Rahel	114
Stereotypes and Jewish	
Women. Part 1	116
Stereotypes and Jewish	
Women. Part 2	118
A Modern Zealot	120
The Realities	
of Widowhood	122
Anna of Rome	124
Women and Synagogue	
Worship	126
Second Thoughts	
on Rahav	128

Holocaust Studies

The Holocaust Museum	130
Fifty Years Later	132
The Annual Conference	134
A Busy Week	136
Kristallnacht	
Seventy Years Later	138

Reviews

A Woman of Enterprise	140
Jewish Legal Writings	
by Women	142
Biblical Films	144
Intellectual Stimulation	146
The Jews of Brooklyn	148
The Story of Blood	150
Protecting Women	152

"Dr. Ruth"	154
Visions of Israel	156
Book Day	158
Minhagei Lita	160
Italy and the Holocaust:	
A Reappraisal	162

Part II

Jewish Law and Custom

The Modern Day *Aguna*	165
Love of Parents	168
The Proselyte	170
Decisions	172
Endless Summer	174
Local Custom	176
Ramifications	
of *Kashrut* Laws	178
The Synagogue Service	180
Social Justice	182
In Memoriam	184
Presentation	186
Blessings	188
A Moving Prayer	190
Tefillat Ha-Derech	192
A Special Relationship	194
The *Eruv*	196
My Brother's Death	198
The Glassmakers	200

Italian Jews

A View from Naples	202
Ghetto Jews	204
Jewish Symbols	206
Synagogue History	208
Completing a Course	210
Italian Journal. Part 1	212
Italian Journal. Part 2	214
Searching for Signs	216
Megillat Antiochus	218

Elul: A Lesson in Tolerance ... 220

Opinion
A Legacy ... 222
"Jewish" Food ... 224
The Cost of Being Jewish ... 226
Intertwining Links ... 228
A Personal Chana ... 230
In Defense of Vashti ... 232
Family Purity ... 234
Memories ... 236
Prenuptial Agreements ... 238
Jewish Self-Images ... 240
The Dog in Jewish History ... 242
A Question of Spirituality ... 244
Nechama: A Personal Comment ... 246
The Challenges Ahead ... 248
Letter Writing ... 250
Public Humiliation ... 252
David's Prayer ... 254
Two Concerts ... 256
Word Play ... 258
Minimalism ... 260
Limitations ... 262
Selective Memory ... 264
Rites of Passage ... 266
Jews of Arabia ... 268
Topics for Discussion ... 270
A New York Experience ... 272
Natan Sharansky ... 274
The Task of Translation ... 276
Tracing a Career through Primary Sources ... 278
Small Kindness ... 280
The Roles of Animals ... 282
Professor J. C. Hurewitz ... 284
Cruelty to Animals ... 286
Hebrew Language Instruction ... 288
A Dangerous Cult ... 290
A National Treasure ... 292
At Your Parent's Knee ... 294

Appendix ... 296

Index ... 300

Introduction

The ivory tower is a comfortable, lofty perch from which scholars can view the world and engage in research and writing which they can share with other occupants equally versed in the ins and outs of academe. To support this lifestyle, they must occasionally and sometimes disdainfully descend into the classroom, there to share the fruits of their learned labors with a new generation. This transmission of scholarship from the ivory tower to the classroom is, however, not an easy process. The professor must translate and communicate a vast body of sophisticated knowledge to students who may still lack the skills to operate on his or her level and do so without compromising intellectual integrity.

This process is even more daunting when a scholar enters the public arena and attempts to communicate with a broader audience of laypersons alien to the rarified atmosphere of the academy. A few decades ago, Prof. Sara Reguer was invited to undertake such a daunting task. An accomplished scholar with bona fides in Middle Eastern studies, Jewish history, Jewish religious studies, and women's studies, her task was further complicated by her chosen venue: a Jewish newspaper with a primarily Orthodox Jewish target audience. To her many skills she now had to add a balancing act, striving to prudently communicate sensitive themes without compromising her standards or offending her readers.

This collection of essays, culled from over twenty years of her columns, is testimony to Prof. Reguer's multiple skills and her ability to communicate and educate on a variety of levels. Her writing is alternately informative and inspiring, passionate and poignant, and ranges from the comic to the tragic, all frequently peppered with personal insights and anecdotes. Her readers learned about the preservation of Jewish tradition during the Spanish Inquisition and the challenge of synagogue decorum in the time of Maimonides. A visit to the Metropolitan Museum of Art prompts an essay on Jewish art and a timely recommendation to acquire a reproduction of an illuminated Haggada.

Critical family issues such as childlessness, a husband's duties to his wife, matriarchy, and much more are sensitively covered alongside issues of death and burial. The collection includes many charming—sometimes humorous, sometimes poignant—vignettes. The description of her Cousin Feigel is most touching, and her account of the funeral conducted by her youthful father for a bird he accidentally killed is just one of several humorous moments in the book.

In sum, this collection provides a sweeping overview of Jewish life and culture as viewed through the eyes of an academic, equally at home in the real world and the ivory tower.

Dr. Jonathan Helfand,
Emeritus Professor, Brooklyn College, CUNY

Part I

Farewell Column

June 8, 2012

Over twenty-five years ago, when I was a scholar-in-residence at the Homowack Hotel, I was approached by a smiling older woman, who complimented me on the lecture I had just delivered on one of the Biblical women. "Let me introduce myself," she said. "My name is Irene Klass. My husband and I own *The Jewish Press*, and I would like you to write a column for us." Taken aback at the offer, I responded: "I don't think you would want me to write for you." Even more taken aback, she said: "Why not?"

"Because I am a modern Orthodox feminist, with an educated Litvak approach to Judaism." She paused and said: "Let me get back to you." And she did. "The offer still stands, but we reserve the right to edit your column."

"No, you either accept it as is, or you reject the entire thing. No one is to touch what I write."

"I'll get back to you." She did, and we agreed.

Over the years, there were only five columns that were totally rejected [four of which are included in this volume], and many others were tweaked by me, after negotiating with then-editor Sheila Abrams. One rejected one was on the Rubashkin scandal, one was on Puah Rakovsky, one was on my admiration for Vashti, and one was on modern day *agunot*. It is interesting to note that about a year after my column on the last topic was rejected, Mrs. Klass telephoned me to ask if I could write a more in-depth work on this topic to be used as one of their feature articles. *The Jewish Press* is now a major advocate on this issue, and my article is still used in classes on Jewish women in colleges across the country.

Over the years I have moved from the typewriter and the fax machine to email attachments. I got tired of writing only about Jewish women, so my column morphed into "Perspectives." I sent them in from Israel, Turkey, Italy, China, Hawaii, England, and from Camp Yavneh in New Hampshire. You got to know about my research, my classes at Brooklyn College, and about my family.

But things change. For example, my department imploded this year with three retirements. We will be hiring new professors over the next two years. The profile of the Department of Judaic Studies will thus inevitably change. This paper is reworking itself, and so this column will end. In the next few months I will be putting the finishing touches on my book, *The Most Tenacious of Minorities: The Jews of Italy*, as it heads to the presses. Then I will be able to return to my next project, which is half done, entitled *My Father's Journey: A Memoir of Lost Lithuanian Jewish Worlds*, which will cover his experiences, especially during World War I, and his relationship with the family he left behind in Brest-Litovsk, until the Nazis murdered them all. I have memoirs, letters from my grandfather, the *dayan* of Brisk, photographs, interviews, and my own recollections. It will not be an easy job, but I am constantly encouraged to finish it. I will. [It was published in 2015 by Academic Studies Press.]

So I thank my readers, many of whom have sent me interesting comments over the years. I was constantly surprised as to who read my column, and actually paid attention to what I wrote.

History

The Purim Play
March 1, 1996

The laws of Purim focus on the reading of the Scroll of Esther, the two foods of *mishloach manot,* and the festive meal. The central idea of Purim, that God saves Jews from destruction in the Diaspora in hidden ways, manifests itself through Jewish history in more personal or special Purims such as the Purim of Cairo (1524) and the Purim of Syracuse (1425).

An interesting creative offshoot of the holiday is the Purim play or *Purimspiel,* which took two forms in the Middle Ages. One form was a parody called *Masechet Purim,* which could have included a Purim "rabbi." This tradition still exists in many *yeshivot* today. The second form of the *Purimspiel* was something much more elaborate, which evolved into the complex dramas of the Renaissance in the northern Italian Jewish communities. At one time it was thought that the Italian *Carnivale,* which precedes the Christian season of Lent and thus corresponds roughly with the timing of Purim, was the influence on the Jewish Purim plays. However, research points in the other direction, for there are many historical instances of attacks on the Jews because of Purim plays which date back to the eleventh century. These public plays, which were parodies of the Purim story in which Haman and his sons were hanged, were seen by the suspicious Gentiles as parodies of local kings, dukes, princes, or church figures. It did not take much to provoke an attack on the small Jewish communities, as a result.

As the Renaissance began, the Purim plays became complex dramas acted out by men, women, boys, and girls, using elaborate costumes, scenery, and props. Gentiles were invited to attend these plays, and in 1489, a Purim play using the theme of the story of Judith and Holofernes was performed at a wedding of the House of Sforza in Pesaro. Some scholars who deal with this subject have concluded that it was the *Purimspiel* that influenced modern theater.

Purim plays exist today as well, but not on the level of those produced in Renaissance Italy. Nowadays, they are performed by boys and girls in their various schools. The younger the children, the more likely the script will follow the actual Purim story, with most of the girls fighting over who should have the role of Esther. After all, how often is there a story in which the leading character is a woman? The boys, on the other hand, have a broader menu of leading characters—whether hero, villain, or stupid king. As the children get older the school plays—if they are still put on—become more sophisticated and may end up in the yeshiva-type parody of *Masechet Purim*, referred to above. I have some published variations of these parodies, and some are very creative indeed.

The only really public manifestation of Purim *a la Carnivale* is held in Israel and appropriately named *Ad De-Lo Yada*, in keeping with the custom that some Jews have of drinking liquor on Purim until the drinker does not know the difference between *"arur Haman u-barukh Mordekhai,"* cursed is Haman and blessed is Mordekhai.

History

Women's Suffrage
Part 1

March 28, 1997

Soon after the Balfour Declaration was issued, Jewish activists both inside and outside Palestine began trying to set up an elected body to represent the *Yishuv*. One of the questions that arose dealt with the eligibility of women to vote for, or to be elected to, that representative body.

At the second Constitutive Assembly meeting in June 1918, women were given the right to vote, with a minimum age of twenty-five set for those women who might be elected. At the third assembly, held in December 1918, the Ashkenazi Old Yishuv representative stated that the group would not actively resist women's suffrage, although it opposed it, but it could absolutely not accept the right of women to be elected. The assembly rejected this, and the next few months saw the issue hotly debated in the Old Yishuv. In March 1919, the Ashkenazi leaders of the Old Yishuv proclaimed that it forbade women both to elect and to be elected.

Not all Ashkenazi Orthodox Jews in Palestine agreed with this stance. The Mizrachi in particular was divided. As a compromise, after months of disputing whether or not to vote in the first general elections, the election date was postponed until October 1919, and the newly instilled Ashkenazi Chief Rabbi of Jerusalem, Rabbi Abraham Yitzhak Ha-Cohen Kook (1895–1935) was empowered to participated in a rabbinic forum, representing the "moderates." Yet, to the shock of these moderates, Rabbi Kook came out with an unequivocal rejection of women's suffrage. The Mizrachi again obtained a postponement of the elections, and the World Executive of that party came out in March 1920 with a decision in favor of the election as proposed, i.e., giving women the right to vote. Rabbi Kook stood his ground on *halakhic* reasons, and the debate continued until 1925.

Rabbi Kook wrote two Responsa (*teshuvot*) spelling out his *halakhic* principles. In his first Responsum, he stated that there were three aspects to the issue and that he was addressing all three. The first was the *halakhic* aspect, which was directed to the Jews, whose first loyalty was to Judaism.

The second was the national aspect, namely, what was best for the new Zionist national home. The third was the moral aspect, directed at those for whom this was their primary outlook.

He stated that Judaism opposed women's suffrage for two reasons. First, because the roles requiring initiative and action in Jewish tradition are only for men. This includes political roles, judicial office, and testifying in court. Also, the Torah always sought to separate the genders in public gatherings. Women entering politics would transgress both norms.

From the national aspect, it should be recognized that Great Britain's attitude to the Jewish homeland was based on her recognition of the Biblical connection. The Biblical role for women was that of homemaker. To prevent the enemies of Zionism from claiming that the Jews of today are no longer connected to the Bible, it required Zionists to reject women's suffrage, thus strengthening the world's positive perception of the Biblical tie.

Third, from the moral aspect, social relations between the sexes would not be free from immorality. This could only take place in the messianic period. Preempting the future by allowing women to become politically active now would delay the messianic coming.

In his second Responsum (April 1920), Rabbi Kook showed the essential difference between the centrality of the family in Jewish and Gentile Society. For the latter, the family was not the cornerstone of society as it was for the Jews. For the Gentiles, who have low regard for their women, the women must attempt to rectify the bad treatment through politics. But Jewish women were well treated and highly regarded; should they be thrust into the strife of politics, this would enter the home and destroy harmony.

History

Women's Suffrage
Part 2

April 11, 1997

The main opponent of Rabbi Kook's opinions against women's suffrage was Rabbi Benzion Meir Hai Uzziel (1880–1953). Born in the Old City of Jerusalem to an illustrious Sephardi family, Rav Uzziel eventually served as the Sephardi Chief Rabbi of mandatory Palestine and was the first Sephardi chief rabbi of the State of Israel, a post he held until his death.

Rabbi Uzziel divided his Responsum into two issues: women's right to vote, and their right to be elected to public office. With regard to the first issue, he stated that reason led to the recognition of women's right to vote and that without unequivocal proof that the Torah denied such a right, *halakha* subscribed to reason. Elections were nothing but the delegation of authority to representatives, enabling them to act in a binding manner in the name of the electors. Women would be expected to be bound by the results of an election. Reason states, thus, that if women are bound to obey those elected, they should not be denied the right to participate in the elections.

Some, he wrote, claim that women do not have the mental capacity to vote because their "minds are frivolous." But are not many men like this too? Women have always been as clearheaded and intelligent as men. *Halakha* itself recognizes this in civil law. As for voting leading to immoral public behavior, Rabbi Uzziel wrote that the genders mixed in public places, especially in commercial negotiations every day. What immorality could there be in casting a vote in a poll office? That voting would disrupt home tranquility was patently absurd, since differences of opinion among adults were not out of place and a loving family environment would not be damaged by such differences.

Rabbi Uzziel thus did not accept the norm of Rabbi Kook that what was done and said in the past is definitive of what should be done in the present. (Within this mind-set, "innovation" is a negative factor.) Rabbi Uzziel accepted the premise that present issues must derive from principle:

in the case of women's suffrage, from the self-evident principles of equity and human dignity. The basic unit of the modern polity is not the family but the adult individual, and women who were also "created in the Divine image" are included in the term "adult individual."

The assumption of most people, when coming to an issue such as women's suffrage, is that European rabbis would be open to such modern innovations, while "Oriental" traditionalism would be committed to the religious status quo. Yet, as we see, however original Rabbi Kook was in Jewish thought and Zionism, with regard to *halakha*, Rabbi Kook adhered to a right-wing, even reactionary genre. This may have been because European Jewry was threatened by changes in Judaism made by the Reform movement and so responded with fear to any "innovation." Middle Eastern and Sephardi Jews had no such experience and so felt free to continue to innovate, which to them was not a sign of modernism but of traditionalism. Rabbi Uzziel had many prominent adherents from both the Ashkenazi and Sephardi rabbis. The issue of women's suffrage became a moot point when the Yishuv's quasi-government enacted laws giving women both the vote and the ability to hold office. Mandated Palestine thus joined most northern European states and the United States in granting women suffrage. It is hard for us to imagine that this was one of the burning issues of the early twentieth century.

History

The Spanish Inquisition

May 22, 1998

The Inquisition, the special permanent tribunal of the medieval Catholic Church, was established to investigate and combat heresy. It was instituted by Pope Gregory IX in 1233 CE, and the mission of judging heretics was given to the Dominican order, which divided the duties with the Franciscan order. The tribunal directed its activities against Christian heretics, not against Jews. So, how did the Inquisition become almost synonymous with the torture of Jews?

In Spain, in the years 1391 and 1412 at the time of anti-Jewish riots, hundreds of Jews temporarily converted to Christianity in order to save their lives. In their minds this was temporary, however, in the minds of the church authorities, this was permanent. Thus, with the arrival of the Inquisition into Spain in 1481, one of its targets of possible heresy was this easily identifiable group of "New Christians" or *Conversos* (known pejoratively as *marranos*).

Starting in the province of Andalusia, the activities of the Inquisition against the *Conversos* spread to Aragon, Catalonia, and Valencia, under the able and fanatical leadership of Tomas de Torquemada, appointed Inquisitor General in 1483. These activities had the support of the rulers of Spain, Ferdinand and Isabella.

Arrested *Conversos* had a thirty to forty day "period of grace" during which time the Inquisition gathered evidence, and the person sat in prison in complete ignorance of his or her accusers and accusations. Torture was then used to extract "confessions," and punishments were meted out according to the Inquisitor's decision. The *Converso* could be sent to the galleys or to prison; his or her family could suffer; and property could be confiscated. Most serious of all would be the death penalty, and since this punishment had to be meted out "without blood," it was via the *auto-da-fe*, or burning at the stake. This was done in a very public manner, with a procession before a huge crowd, with the doomed person dressed in a *sanbenito* or long yellow robe with a black cross on it, and a tall miter.

Sermons were delivered as the crowd waited impatiently for the main attraction—the pyre.

The activities of the Inquisition are recorded in detail. But in reading these archives, not only do we find evidence of them but we also gain insight into the lives of the *Conversos*. Women's connections to Judaism are particularly strong, according to the records. In addition to the focus on the fast of Yom Kippur—a holiday easier to observe than Passover with the secret baking of matza and having a kind of *seder*—women were specifically involved in the preparation of Shabbat lamps, both in devising systems to keep the oil burning longer, as well as in preparing the wicks. The women cleaned the house and prepared food on Friday, changing clothing and linens as well as dressing festively. But gradually, intention often had to replace deed, as the Inquisition's spies checked all of these activities. The exception was women's lighting Sabbath lights; this continues in secret.

As the decades passed, women developed special *Converso* traditions such as immersion and bathing prior to the Sabbath. The ablutions were often performed in a group, when *Converso* women gather to visit among themselves. They had to choose safe ways in which to hide their ritual acts, and since many *Conversos* had pools in their homes, this could be done in relative privacy. Thus we see the merging of bathing before the Sabbath with ritual immersion for married women. We also know of ritual immersions performed by brides, since some were performed in streams and thus open to spying eyes.

A whole system for observing the rites connected with death and burial comes to light via the Inquisition documents, as does a special oath sworn by *Conversos* among themselves. There were Bibles and prayer books and books of Jewish laws in the early stages, when Hebrew was still read. But as years passed, these books were revered only for what they represented.

The expulsion of 1492 was directed mainly at separating the *Conversos* from the "bad" influence of the Spanish Jews. But the *Converso* practicing of Judaism continued, and those who could left the Iberian Peninsula for safer havens. Sometimes the long arm of the Inquisition followed them to these places, such as Italy and Mexico. Those who did not leave continued to practice secret rites and rituals until the connection with Judaism was almost totally forgotten.

History

Synagogue Decorum
June 18, 1998

Proper decorum in the synagogue is a constant topic of discussion in my house of worship. My rabbi tried everything he could think of to get the men to keep quiet during prayers. There is also a constant flow of people to and from in both the men's and women's sections. The only time when almost everyone is quiet and still is during the sermon.

Within the stream of history, my synagogue is not unique. During the Cairo Geniza period, the excessive length of the service, the reading by laymen of texts that had to be chanted according to fixed rules, the personal rivalries and public dissentions encouraged by specific synagogue procedures (such as who got which honor), and, in general, the fact that the synagogue also served as a courthouse and clubhouse where the men spent most of their free time—all must have seriously impaired the character of the synagogue as a house of worship. Moses Maimonides and his son Abraham decried the constant lack of decorum in the Cairo synagogues. Other Geniza documents even mention brawls in local synagogues on Shabbat, leading to cessation of the morning service. In a letter from Ramla, dated September 1052, a fistfight is reported in the synagogue between pilgrims from Tyre and Tiberias on Yom Kippur that was so fierce the police were called in.

In the early part of the service—certainly until well into the Torah reading—the women are not the focus of the rabbi's exhortation to be quiet. There is a simple reason for that: most are not there yet. Since women don't have a fixed time for saying the *Shema*—which is one of the seven time-bound positive commandments from which women are exempt—women are not obligated to be in the synagogue for it. Women with young children also have to dress them as well as themselves. Yet most women do go to the synagogue, and most do make it on time for the sermon and *Musaf*. Those who are more particular make it in time to hear the Torah portion. This is in keeping with what we know of the women's synagogue attendance in time of prosperity in medieval Cairo, Renaissance Florence, Muslim Cordoba, and nineteenth-century Frankfort. Similar, too, is the tendency for young men and women to "hang out" in the courtyard of the synagogues, talking to each other and "checking out" the scene. We know of this, in part, because of the content of some rabbinic sermons and from letters sent to rabbinic authorities.

It is very hard to concentrate on a long prayer service. It is hard to concentrate on a Torah portion like *Naso,* which is so repetitive. The only novel item is the sermon, and this is the opportunity for the rabbi to really have an impact on the community. This past Shabbat we were informed of a wonderful project geared toward problem teenagers in the Orthodox communities across the greater New York area. Yes, our communities also have to face the reality that there are teenagers with learning problems, with deep religious questions and crises, and with drug habits, all of whom can easily drop out of religious life as well as home life. The schools are finally beginning to work together to address these complex and sensitive issues. We were asked to let the heads of the schools know that we approve these projects and to wish them good luck.

History

American Jews
July 17, 1998

This Fourth of July we celebrated the 222nd birthday of the United States of America. On that day, I attended a lecture given by Prof. Jonathan Sarna of Brandeis University addressing the question of whether and how the American Revolution affected the Jewish community. There were only a few hundred Jews living in the Thirteen Colonies, and a majority of them sided with the revolution. Everyone should have heard of the activities of Haim Solomon in helping to finance George Washington's endeavors.

The Constitution of the United States brought into reality the separation of church and state, and eliminated any kind of religious test in order to hold public office. American Jews never had to be "emancipated" for they had never been anything but equal (more or less).

On the Jewish community level, synagogues began to draw up their own "constitutions"—not that there were so many synagogues at that time. What should be noted is that these "constitutions" reflected both the wording and the ideas of the American Constitution in that the ordinary members began to see themselves as equal to the *parnasim* or rich men. Nothing bound any member to stay within a synagogue if he did not like it, thus setting the ground for "breakaway" groups, as well as dissolving at the early stage any possibility for an official chief rabbi.

This type of thinking affected the women as well. Until the revolution there had been a special *bainch* or *banca* set aside in the too-small women's section of Congregation She'erith Israel in New York for the Gomez family's women. This was the wealthiest family of the congregation. After the revolution, this reserved seating was done away with.

Women did go to the synagogue on Saturdays and in much stronger numbers than in Europe. This probably reflected the church-going habit of the Protestant Christian neighbors. Thus the original building of synagogues like She'erith Israel, built along the traditional European lines, did not have enough room for its women. The second structure, usually in a new neighborhood, did.

Another change in the women's balcony of She'erith Israel was the removal of the highly decorative lattice work of the *mechitza*. It was decided that the separation of the women in the balcony sufficed for prayers, and that the lattice—while beautiful to look at but blinding to look through—should come down. The women wanted to be able to observe the service.

America became a unique country for a whole complex of reasons. Jews benefited from this, and American Judaism as well as Jews began a 200-year-old journey down a road that had never been traveled before. We are what our forebears made us in more ways than one.

History

A Dress Code
February 12, 1999

When the Israelites left Egypt, the text describes that they left *khamushim*. Most of the commentators define this to mean that they were armed. They did not have to be armed to fight the Egyptians, for that was within the power of God. So why were they armed? In his sermon on this topic, my rabbi stated that the men were dressed as free men, and in those days that meant being armed. In other words, they chose to express themselves in a visual way that they were no longer slaves.

For long periods of time in Jewish history, Jewish men suffered discrimination by being told what to wear in order to be singled out as Jews. There were special hats—"Jews' hats," which were assigned to them, and we can see what they looked like in illuminated manuscripts. That was in the Ashkenazi world.

In the Islamic world, there were dress codes of nonbelievers (Jews and Christians), both for men and for women. These developed over time and were enforced, or not enforced, depending on the ruler and the general religiosity of the time and place. The differentiating piece of clothing could be the size of the turban, its color, its fabric, the color of a man's shoes, or his outer cloak, or the shape of his beard, or the dangling of the *peyote* in front of the ears.

For women, the dress code could include forbidding the use of the veil, or mandating use of a dark outer cloak with a special collar decoration. The headgear of Jewish women was distinctive all over the Middle East, the most well-known example of which is the hood—like embroidered headgear of Yemenite women. In fact, there were variations in fabric and decoration according to locality, marital status, and occasion. One had to be educated into the local nuances of costume to pick up on these variants.

It is interesting to note that even when Jewish men and women used the public baths—a much looked-forward-to-luxury for all—in various periods of time and place, they had to wear a necklace from which dangled something symbolic of their religion. The public baths were among the only places where "nonbelievers" could socialize with Muslims, and

Muslim men feared the influence of Jewish women on their own women to this extent. As for Jewish men wearing a sign as well, this was to prevent Muslims from speaking too openly about politics, which could be reported to the authorities by the nonbelievers.

Modernization and secularization of society, in Europe and the Middle East, led to the dropping of these enforced dress codes. What happened in many parts of the Jewish world was total acculturation, with the exception of the Jews who remained traditional. In other words, if fashion dictated immodesty, fashion was bent or reshaped or ignored by the modest Jewish man and woman. If a hairstyle for men involved removing any remnant of *peyote*, the hairstyle was ignored.

Yet, in certain groups, Jews are also choosing to "dress Jewishly." There is almost a uniform among the young married women, in particular, let alone the young men. A large proportion of Jewish women have chosen to wear necklaces with stars of David dangling from them, or Hebrew names, or other obviously Jewish items. The difference between being forced to dress a certain way and choosing to do so is the difference between slavery and freedom. The Israelite men had to visually show that they were free, and they did so by arming themselves.

History

The Entrepreneur
March 12, 1999

Webster's Collegiate Dictionary defines "entrepreneur" as "one who organizes, manages, and assumes the risks of a business or enterprise." An entrepreneur often takes an old idea, uses the latest technology in developing this idea, and thus makes a profit. On the positive side, an entrepreneur can create new industries and new jobs; on the negative side, there can be an attempt to get rid of competition, which can lead to monopolies and higher prices for the consumer. The qualities of an entrepreneur include aggressiveness, self-reliance, and often self-education. Success may lead to an attempt to influence those in political power, but success can also lead to philanthropy.

When Americans are asked to list stereotypical "Jewish jobs" or professions, the most common list includes doctor, lawyer, retail manufacturer (especially in the garment industry), accountant, diamond dealer, jewelry manufacturer and dealer, and teacher. Landlord is usually on the list of New York minority groups. What is not listed is entrepreneur, and yet this is a field that is as old as the Jewish Diaspora. When a minority group is frozen out of the guilds or simply not hired or apprenticed, this group has to search for jobs, work, and professions that rely on innate talent or creativity. Jews have become experts at this. A twentieth-century example is the movie industry, from filmmaking to distribution, as well as the movie houses themselves. This holds true for early television, and it carries over into all the marketing taking place on the web.

Entrepreneurship of the twentieth century must make use of the major changes in technology, and thus you find that this is mainly in the hands of relatively young men and women who are at home with the computer and comfortable with virtual reality.

A traditional Jewish profession both in Europe and the Middle East was entertainment. Jewish men and women became singers, musicians, actors, vaudeville performers, and comedians because the focus was on talent. They already were in the peripheries of society, so there was nothing to lose by becoming performers. Entrepreneurship entered into this as well, as the jobs of manager, *impresario*, and agent were created. The agent's role is an old one—Spanish and Portuguese Jews were agents in the port city of Livorno, Italy, dealing with exporting and importing all kinds of goods, as well as matching up storage warehouses with shippers who needed storage. The agent could be an Esther Kiera, who supplied luxury items to the sultan's harem in Istanbul, or an Esparanza Malchi doing the same for the sultan's favorite wife. The agent could also have been an Estee Lauder of Helena Rubinstein, when they were just getting started in their cosmetics firms and not only had to manufacture but market their goods as well.

The general topic of entrepreneurship and Jews in economics is a fascinating one, and one that deserves more in-depth study, for earning a living is one of the basic needs of men and women, so basic that we even have blessing importuning God for success in this very important area of life.

History

Sacred Music
April 21, 2000

In order to make the book that I am working on with my two colleagues more "twenty-first century," we decided to include a CD utilizing a variety of musical forms of the Jews of the world of Islam. We will have comparative *trope,* reading in the various Jewish languages (Judeo-Arabic, Judeo-Persian, Ladino), examples of liturgy, as well as adaptations to cultural influences. Some songs will be those sung by women as they worked together preparing foods for holidays such as Pesach.

Music is one of the components of Jewish history and culture, and no general book can omit it. I was struck, recently by how important a yardstick of acculturation this is. I attended a recital on nineteenth-century sacred music of The Great Synagogue of Livorno, Italy, featuring compositions of David Garzia (ca. 1830), Moise Ventura (ca.1860), Giuseppe Pontercorboli (ca.1880), and Michele Bulaffi (1768–1842). The choir's sophisticated harmonies reminded me that not everyone likes Shlomo Carlebach's music. The choir's music was sublime, attracting Jews as well as non-Jews to this architecturally magnificent synagogue in this famous port city on the northwest coast of Italy.

Livorno, a stronghold of Sephardic Jews, mainly of Portuguese background, has a unique history in Italy, in which there was little competition from the original, highly sophisticated Italian Jews. Yet by the nineteenth century, the music was more Italian than Iberian, with the exception of the folk songs. These song, although sung in Hebrew at the recital, were also sung in Ladino by women at home. This sacred music reflected what was popular in Italy at the time, similar to the introduction of Israeli popular melodies (minus the words) into many traditional synagogues today.

I still have difficulty applying the melody of *Erev Ba*, for example, to *Kedusha* without playing out the dance steps in my mind.

Acculturation, therefore, manifests itself even in the realm of sacred music. The realm in which there seems to be the least outside influence is in *trope,* or cantillation. Yet, listening closely to the variations of *trope* from

Morocco eastward through Iran, and from Turkey southward through Yemen, the differences seem to lie in the pronunciation of the words, reflecting the pronunciation of the language of the country in which Jews found themselves. But the basic music remains stubbornly traditional; only the elaborations or flourishes seem to be culturally affected. This holds true for Italian *trope* as well, with the Sephardic sounds coming closer to the Italian than to the original Middle Eastern ones. Ashkenazic *trope* is a separate issue.

The recital of the *Musica Sacra di Livorno* was magnificent and uplifting, and makes me wonder why such sublime choral music is no longer popular in most Orthodox synagogues.

History

The Field of Food
December 1, 2000

A burgeoning field of research is that of the history of food. A subfield is the social history of immigrants to America., with scholars asking questions such as: "Why did this immigrant group retain its Old World foods, whereas that immigrant group dropped its food and rapidly Americanized?" Since women were and still are the main preparers of food in most societies, this is part of women's studies too.

How much of the retention of traditional foods is connected with holidays, in particular religious holidays? As people become more Americanized and secularized, does their taste in foods also Americanize or do they even more adamantly hold on to, in this case, "gastronomic Judaism?" Is there a gradual balance reached?

In doing research on the acculturation of Middle Eastern Jewish communities that moved to Italy in the late '60s and '70s, a group of questions that I asked the women interviewees had to do with food. In that case, I asked the Libyan and Iranian Jewish immigrants if they served pasta dishes. This question followed a series of protests that they only served Libyan or Irani dishes to their families. Of course they served pasta; that was part of their acculturation to Italy. But that "did not count" because it was for weekday meals; for Shabbat and holidays they would never dream of serving anything Italian.

The studies done on American Jewish immigrants cover longer periods of time, and are coming out with some fascinating observations. Some of it has to do with the actual quality of food coming from the Old World. For example, the Eastern European Ashkenazi Jewish of Poland and Lithuania, most of whom were very poor, had cooking traditions that included all kinds of boiled foods. No wonder they succumbed to the tastier roasts of America. Foods high in fats gradually disappeared as well—when was the last time you tasted *grivin* (chicken cracklings) or potatoes fried in *schmaltz* (chicken fat)? Thus we see that health issues also influence food preparation.

Another factor is the American mind-set against organ meats. Liver is about the only Ashkenazi organ meat that is still popular, and one can no longer easily find *miltz* or lungs or heart or even the unlaid eggs of chickens. My father used to entertain us with the details of how to *kasher* a cow's udder, part of his memories of Lithuania, and how delicious it was to eat, looking with disbelief at our disgusted facial expressions.

Italian immigrants to America retained most of their foods because Italian food is delicious and healthy. Their foods have so influenced America that even small towns have Italian-style restaurants. The most successful kosher restaurants for upscale New Yorkers are the Italian ones. Italian Jewish food, however, is limited to Jews of Italian descent who serve their traditional dishes on the holidays.

American Jews join America in general for that most American of all holidays, Thanksgiving, and most of us come to the table to feast on that most American of birds, the turkey. This is truly the ultimate Americanization of all immigrant Jews.

History

Roman Roads

March 23, 2001

In a recent news article, the reporter honed in on the fact that the Israeli army had closed the main roads leading from Gaza in Israel to lessen the incidence of terrorism and attacks.

Control over roads is an act of power as old as time itself. Roads are the main connectors within cities, states, and empires, and those masters of engineering of ancient times—the Romans—understood this perfectly well. Roman roads are still a topic of study, and there are many remnants of these roads in Israel. Scholars say that the Romans did not really build much in Israel until the Revolt of 66 CE; until then, they relied on earlier roads built and rebuilt by the various ancient empires, and kept in good order by the Jews of the Second Temple period in order to ease the thrice yearly pilgrimages to the Temple in Jerusalem from far off Babylonia and Egypt as well as from the Galilee.

Road building was one of the most important projects of the Roman imperial administration. The 1,500 kilometers of roads in Judea alone, included bridges, supporting terraces, and land leveling. The Romans adjusted road building to the surroundings, using local material, for example, but also employing all the engineering knowledge at their disposal, which included not putting roads in the direct path of winter flooding. The roads were built by the Roman army as well as by manpower recruited in the local provinces.

The main motivations of Roman road building were military and administrative. If there was growth of population and the economy, this was the result of their road network, not the reason for it. The army had to be able to reach all areas of the empire and as quickly as possible. Their methodical advance up to Jerusalem was one of the causes for the overthrow of the First Revolt of the Jews and of the Bar Kokhba Revolt (132–135 CE), for the roads carried the heavy Roman war machines and the supply convoys that utilized wagons.

When war was not the focus, but rather administration, the roads carried Roman tax collectors and mail as well as commerce. Road stations were erected as were *caravanserai*; wells and reservoirs were built as well as watchtowers to protect travelers from robbers. As an act of power and propaganda, as well as information, the Romans erected milestones along the roads, each one over five feet high and inscribed in Greek and Latin, praising the power of Rome as well as informing the traveler how much farther it was to Jaffa or Caesarea.

Jewish pilgrims, and then Christian ones, left us records of their experiences traveling to Jerusalem. With the Arab Conquest (starting in 634 CE) many Roman milestones were gradually replaced by new ones carved in Arabic. But the Roman roads remained in use well into the British mandate period when new roads, using new technology, began to replace the Roman roads. Yet Roman roads played an unusual role in the history of modern Israel: during the 1948 war and again in 1967, knowledge of the existence of these ancient roads enabled some Israeli military leaders—most notably Yigael Yadin, who was also a professor of archaeology—to come behind Arab contingents, utilizing the important military factor of surprise.

If the Israeli military today retains control of the major land arteries, they are only doing what any army that wants to remain in power must do.

History

The Traveler
April 6, 2001

The medieval traveler prepared for a long trip by organizing everything in his domain, instructing his family what to do in case he did not return, and packing his wagons, or his saddlebags, or his cases. If the traveler was a Jew, he did all of the above but included his *siddur*, his *tefillin*, his holiday ritual objects if necessary, kosher candles or oil and wicks, at least two pots and utensils, and possibly kosher wine or grape juice. He also would try to travel with other Jews.

Traveling then was slow, and a pilgrimage from Paris to Jerusalem could take months. Depending on the political situation, traveling could also be dangerous. There were brigands in the mountains, there were pirates on the sea, and there could be local bands of marauding peasants. There was also always the possibility of an accident or a storm at sea. To protect Jewish women travelers, we have Responsa that allowed them to dress as men. And Jewish women did travel, both on short journeys to trade to important fairs and on long journeys such as pilgrimages to Israel.

Today's traveler tends to take his safety for granted. Yet bad things can happen even in this age of advanced technology, such as accidents, sabotage, and terrorism. The plane can be seen as a flying petri dish for disease incubation. Because air travel now reaches formerly isolated areas, health officials are increasingly worried about widespread transmission of diseases such as bubonic plague from India, meningococcal disease from Mecca, and especially tuberculosis. How many of us have come down with influenza after an international trip! This give new meaning to reciting the Traveler's Prayer.

Traditional Jews today need not travel with two pots and utensils, for kosher food is available on every airline—some even give you a choice of chicken, meat, or vegetarian. Most of us do not know how to slaughter a chicken anyway, something that was common knowledge in earlier times, which enabled the traveler to eat fresh fowl during the months on the road. Today, the maximum time of a flight would be a trip to Australia from North America—not enough time to really miss a meal of grilled chicken.

(I can't imagine bring the utensils needed to actually *kasher* a chicken on a medieval voyage, thus the preparation of grilled chicken.)

However, not all of us end up spending Shabbat with a family or in a kosher hotel. Thus, even today, the traveler packs a box of matza, two candles, and a small bottle of grape juice or wine. Most big cities around the world do have synagogues, but not all communities are geared to house and feed all Jewish travelers. This is very different from the Middle Ages when this was considered obligatory on the community. The Cairo Geniza refers to the special hostel to accommodate travelers, as does the material on Baghdad at the time of the Abbasids. But today this would be almost impossible; just picture all the Jews who come to visit Rome or Paris. The smaller the Jewish community, the more apt it is to stick to traditional Jewish hospitality.

So, life for the Jewish traveler has not changed that much over the centuries except for the technological advances. Shabbat comes every week as it always has, and how the traveler deals with this is still a matter for some anxiety. As for the issues of accidents, terrorism, and illness, those—as always—are in the hands of God.

History

The Blessing of Water
July 13, 2001

Years ago, while working on my doctoral dissertation on Winston S. Churchill and the shaping of the Middle East, I came across references to Pinchas Rutenberg. There were very few people who made a deep impression on Churchill, and as Rutenberg was one of these few, I was determined that when I had time, I would delve further into this man's activities. Little did I know that this search would lead me into the convoluted world of the politics of the Jordan River, both in mandated Palestine, as well in post-independence Israel.

Israel only has one river system to exploit for all of its needs. Other sources of water include rain, wells, and, according to some, dew. Once the Cross-Israel Water Carrier was completed in 1964, and the Hashemite Kingdom of Jordan completed its East Ghor Canal in 1980, the Jordan River was, in effect, turned into a drainage ditch except during the winter rains. So what could Israel do to obtain more water, what with its growth in population and higher demands on water resources? The last Water Commissioner stated to me many years ago that there were two alternatives: one was a major technological breakthrough, and the other was war to gain control over other rivers. The major technological breakthrough has recently occurred. It has taken the form of affordable water desalinization plants.

Water desalinization has been in existence for decades. Kuwait built its first desalinization plant in 1957, but Israel could not do so, not because of lack of knowledge, but because of the enormous energy costs involved in starting up the plant, which is based on heating and distilling the salt water. Israel had even less available energy than it did water. But the new plants use a different process. This is a reverse osmosis system in which the desalinization plants strain salt out of seawater with synthetic membranes.

The Israeli government is now taking bids first for a plant at Ashkelon and then for Ashdod. This is coming just on time, as the water levels in Israel's reservoirs and aquifers have dropped precipitously. The Kineret, which is the storage place for most of the fresh water, has receded to its lowest level in history, and the country is importing water in huge plastic floating tanks from Turkey. Rainfall has not been good and the government has to cut back on water usage in farming area. The new technology will be able to provide drinking water at $2 per thousand gallons, and the experts forecast that there will be further reductions in the near future.

The construction of new desalinization plants will not ease the political tensions in Israel, but it will certainly ease the stress on those who have to make important water-related decisions in the country. We in the United States take water availability for granted, which we should not; we used to take electricity availability for granted, and look at what is going on all around the country. Be that as it may, let us raise our glasses to drink a *L'Chaim* to what technology can produce—pure affordable drinking water.

History

The Power of Poetry
July 27, 2001

When Balak sent for Bil'am to "cast a spell" or to curse Israel, the latter ended up blessing Israel instead. These blessings are superb examples of the use of poetry in the ancient Middle East. Poetry was the most admired art form then as well as in the Islamic Middle East; it was held in very high esteem in ancient and medieval Europe as well.

For Jews, the majority of the poetry was religious. We have selections of David's poetry (Psalms), Moshe's Song of Triumph after crossing the Sea of Reeds, and Bil'am's *Ma Tovu* in our daily prayer book. *Piyyutim* (prayers in poetry form) composed in the Talmudic period and later are also religious poetry, some of which were included in the prayer books as well. The *Piyyut* continued a long and healthy existence in the culture of Middle Eastern Jews long after it ceased to be popular in the northern Mediterranean shore as well as in the Rhineland.

It is under the rule of Islam that we see the beginning of secular poetry. This is a perfect example of the profound influence of the environment on Jews. The Arab poets of Spain wrote on themes such as praise of a respected person (their patron), friendship, joyous occasions, sorrow, love, wine, reflections, human aspiration, and human failures. So did the Jewish poets of Spain such as Samuel ha-Nagid, Solomon Ibn Gabirol, Moses Ibn Ezra, Judah ha-Levi, and Dunash Ibn Labrat. But they also wrote on religious themes, and those poems were always in Hebrew.

Poetry was written at the same time by the Jews north of the Pyrenees, in the area of France/Germany known as the Rhineland. But these Jews, as far as we know, wrote only on religious themes, and they usually hid their identities. They wrote on Israel's plight, hopes, and sinfulness. They pleaded for mercy. They fused their own religious yearnings and emotions with those of the entire Jewish people.

Not so the Spanish poets who expressed their own feelings toward God, even interweaving their names into the stanzas of their poems. This had a profound influence on the Jews of Italy both before and during the Renaissance. We have selections from these poets in the liturgy of the High

Holy Days, as well as in the more specific prayer books of the Ashkenazim, Sephardim, Italians, and Middle Eastern Jews.

The power of Hebrew poetry revived with the rebirth of Hebrew as part of Jewish nationalism, also known as political Zionism. But few poets wrote on religious themes, as the secular world bulldozed Jewish life. Today the Jewish world—similar to the larger world—gives only token recognition to the power of pure poetry.

Yet we study poetry in school and in college. If we are lucky, we will have a teacher who can inspire us and lead us into a deeper understanding of the poem, as well as into a deeper appreciation of the power of words. My father was such a teacher. Bible was his specialty, but, as a passionate Hebraist, he managed to inculcate love of Hebrew as well into his students over the span of the forty years that he spent in Yeshiva University. Everywhere that I go I meet former students, who begin to recite selections from Amos, Isaiah, or Jeremiah. In my memory, I can hear him declaiming—rolling the consonants in that deep voice of his—as well as chanting the poetry of the *Haftarot* as only he could. What an inspiration!

History

Censorship

October 16, 2002

A new interpretation of the life of Galileo will open at the Brooklyn Academy of Music this week. The opera, composed by Philip Glass and produced by Mary Zimmerman, is reviewed in the *New York Times* of September 29. What struck me was the photograph of the Chicago performance, for in it Galileo is appearing before the Inquisition. He tried to defend his belief that the earth orbits the sun, but he also recanted the belief so as not to face dire Inquisitorial punishment. This is one of the most infamous examples of church censorship, and is still described in most textbooks.

The Catholic Church saw that its duty was to protect man from endangering eternal salvation through exposure to heretical books and ideas. Its long arm reached into the books of the Jews as well as into those of scientists, and anything deemed blasphemous had to be excised. The infamous Index issued by the Popes listed the Talmud in 1559, and by 1595 there was a special section for Hebrew books. Official revisers were usually Jewish apostates, and objectionable passages or expressions were deleted, altered, inked, out or even torn out. Jewish museums house books with signs of the censors' work and censors' signatures at the end of the volumes.

Russia and Poland imposed governmental censorship in the nineteenth century, and, of course, Nazi Germany did so in the 1930s. But there also was Jewish censorship. In Italy, during the height of papal control, the Jews practiced self-censorship to prevent the Catholic censors from taking action. But the Italian Jews also established a system of internal control for the printing of Hebrew books (followed by the Council of the Four Lands, Frankfort, and Amsterdam) to prevent the publication of salacious material, incorrect *halakhic* decision, and apostate authors. Ideological struggles played a role in what was banned—for example, philosophical tracts, Sabbatean books, Hasidic works, *Haskala* ideas, Reform movement literature, and Zionist pamphlets.

Two colleagues and I have just completed the massive undertaking of coediting and cowriting a 500-page manuscript. As editors, we not only had to read the chapters looking for errors in grammar and spelling, but also we were looking to see if our authors had followed our instructions of what to include. We were trying to end up with a unified whole, and, knowing that some of our authors have very strong political views, we also had to ensure that their chapters did not become harangues or platforms. It was not easy. But, in keeping with the ethics of scholarship, we would never censor an author, and any changes that we made had to be sent back to the author for approval. E-mails and attachments were a great boon, but sometimes—in part because the original language of an author was French, or German, or Hebrew, or Hungarian—we had to resort to the telephone to clarify the issue. Some authors were cooperative, and others fought each change tooth and nail. The argument that finally won over each contributor was that the change was necessary for the overall cohesion of the book.

The galleys went back to the publisher the first week of August. We now await the final proofs and to cover. It has been a long haul, but *The Jewish of the Modern Middle East and North Africa* is due to come to the bookstores in December.

History

A Question of Art
March 21, 2003

In the midst of all of the busyness of my life, it is a good thing to remember that I live in New York City, a world center of art and creativity. Last week, I took time off to go to the Metropolitan Museum of Art to view the latest exhibitions. One exhibition on view for a very short period of time is "Leonardo da Vinci, Master Draftsman." Leonardo was the embodiment of the universal Renaissance genius, and these 120 works demonstrate his contribution as artist, scientist, theorist, and teacher. Everyone has his or her favorite pieces—mine include the study for the head of a soldier in red chalk, and the blueprint of a technique to destroy an army attacking a walled city.

While at the museum, I also walked through the other two new exhibitions, one devoted to Thomas Struth, the pioneering German photographer, and the second devoted to African American artists, 1929–1945. I actually recognized one of the portraits in the last exhibit, that of Robert Blackburn, who also has five of his own works on display. At this exhibit, the questions raised by the curators included: How "black" were the artists in term of their themes? What defines "African American" artists?

The same questions are raised with regard to Jewish artists: Is the artist a "Jewish artist" if he or she is Jewish, or if the themes are Jewish? The debate continues, not only in the plastic arts, but also in the fields of literature and philosophy.

Throughout Jewish history, most of the creative impulse was directed at producing ritual objects either for the synagogue or for sacred use at home. The recently read Torah portion describes the activities of Bezalel ben Uri and Ahaliav ben Akhisamakh in building the Tabernacle. The detailed orders given to the two artists did not leave much room for independent creativity, but artists manage to put their own stamp on whatever is created. The Biblical activity gave rise to the artistic tradition in decorating synagogues, tradition being modified by local artistic styles and tastes which Jews observed in the surrounding cultures.

Could there have been a Jewish Leonardo da Vinci? Leonardo was unique; there was no one like him. The flip side of that is, could there have been a non-Jewish Albert Einstein? Genius is individual. The more appropriate question would be, did Jewish life encourage artistic expression? The answer to that is, it depends where and when. During the Renaissance, in Italy, Jews too were artistically inspired, but in true Jewish tradition, this was manifested mostly in ritual art.

To produce secular art or to design war technology required a patron, and Jews were too small in number and were not Christian. The competition was fierce, and only the most talented or the best connected won out. Jews were too involved with survival, and this included fear of expulsion from a town or a city, let alone from a province.

You wanted something beautiful? Purchase an illuminated manuscript or a masterfully printed Haggada, easily transportable should you have to move in a hurry. If any area of creativity during the Renaissance lent itself to Jewish expression, it was the art of the book. How appropriate a field it was for the "People of the Book"!

History

Explaining Judaic Studies
June 13, 2003

I was presented with a difficult task last week. In ten minutes I was to present an overview of what Jewish history has to contribute to global studies. This was not in a forum of professors well versed in Judaic Studies, but a forum of interested colleagues who came with the preconceived notions (and prejudices) as to what the field is.

I decided to focus on two main points and see where the questions from the audience would take us. The first lesson to be learned from Jewish history is techniques for survival. These began as far back as Biblical times, when, at the destruction of the First Temple and the exile to Babylon, the Jews were not severed from their religion. Unlike ancient cults, which were geographically connected to a place and temple worship, the Jews created a portable place of worship—the synagogue. They also created a verbal manner of addressing their invisible deity, namely, prayer. When they returned to the land of Israel, these new creations did not disappear, but coexisted with the newly rebuilt Temple and the reinstated priesthood.

When the Second Temple was destroyed, these tools of survival accompanied the Jews to the imperial capital of Rome and eastward into the Persian Empire. But now the synagogue expanded into a general community center, with the added tasks of provider of all community needs, which stressed education above all things, but also included kosher meat, charity, and a *miqve* (ritual bath). There is no society that stressed literacy as much as Jewish society did.

The second lesson is that Jewish history is by definition global. Jews are dispersed all over the world, and acculturation connected Jews to their geographic locus while Judaism connected Jews to all other Jews. A good example of this is the languages spoken by communities across the globe. They spoke the local language. How well they spoke it depended on the challenge of the outside society: if the society was on a high intellectual level, Jews quickly adopted this language and became creative, contributing to literature and intellectuality. Good examples of this are German, Arabic, and English. If the surrounding culture was not challenging, Jews spoke only the basics needed in the marketplace, e.g., Ukrainian and Polish. They then continued to speak the language of their earlier place of residence. Some Jews also spoke a Jewish variant of a language such as Judeo-Spanish, Judeo-German, Judeo-Persian, and Judeo-Arabic. In addition, Jews also were literate in Hebrew; how well they knew it depended on a variety of factors.

These were the two basic lessons that I presented on Faculty Day to my colleagues under the title "From Periphery to Academic Center: Ethnic and Minority Studies and Emerging Global Studies." Public discussion was interesting and the private comments were illuminating. It really is important for Judaic Studies professors to do this kind of thing.

History

Tribal Divisions

June 27, 2003

June means summer school, which, for me, means switching gears from teaching Judaic Studies courses to teaching Middle Eastern studies courses. I have ten two-hour periods to teach my half of Brooklyn College's mandatory core course on non-Western cultures. My teammate then covers Latin America, and in the end, we compare and contrast the two world areas.

In preparing my lecture on the rise of Islam and Muhammad's attempts to forge the tribes of Arabia into one people, I saw a comparison to the Biblical Exodus, which occurred about two millennia before that. Tribal organization is as old as the Middle East. The logical smallest unit is the family, which expands over time into a clan, and from there, into the largest feasible organizational unit, the tribe. Members of a tribe owe allegiance, along a clearly spelled-out hierarchy of patriarchal power, to the tribal leader.

As the Israelites marched into the Sinai, Moshe was given clear orders about how the tribal groups were to be placed. There were to be three tribes marching together on the four sides of the Tabernacle, to the east, to the west, to the north, and to the south. Each tribe thus was individuated, yet united with at least two other tribes. But the most important new element introduced here is that each of the twelve tribes looked inward to the Tabernacle, the spiritual focal point of this setup. Thus, the tribes learned at a very early stage that the focus of their lives, the locus of their spirituality, was God, and that took precedence over all else.

Muhammad forged the tribes of Arabia into an *'Umma*, a people, but according to tribal law, the contract of loyalty outside the tribe lives only as long as the two contracting parties are alive. Thus, with the death of Muhammad in 632 CE, the contract ended, and the tribes were poised to disappear, heading back into the desert of Arabia. This crisis of leadership led to the hurried invention of the caliph as deputy to the dead leader, for no one could actually replace him, for as according to Islam, Muhammad was the seal of all prophecy. The idea of the *'Umma* was thus saved.

However, the realities of life are that tribal organization remained in the Middle East and exists down to today, causing problems for modern, nationalistic leaders. It is one of the factors to be taken into consideration by the United States in dealing with Iraq, let alone Afghanistan.

For the Israelites, the tribal organization did continue into the conquest of Canaan and the settling down into geographic units. Fights did occur between various tribes, as did alliances. But with the destruction of the Northern Kingdom, and then, the Babylonian exile of the Judean Kingdom, tribal identity disappeared. That, of course, does not mean an end to division among the Jewish people. History simply moved the Jews into a different line, so that we identify ourselves as Ashkenazim, Sephardim, Middle Easterners, Italians, Iranians, Lithuanians, Germans, Yemenites, *Mitnagdim*, *Hasidim*, Israelis, and Americans.

History

Kaifeng, China
February 6, 2004

Many people are fascinated with the saga of the Jews of Kaifeng, located in central China. The story of their discovery and the sadness connected with their disappearance have piqued people's interest for decades. Where did they come from? Where did they go? If they did not go anywhere, why did they assimilate? The latest book on this topic, *The Jews of Kaifeng, China: History, Culture, and Religion* by Professor Xu Xin of the University of Nanjing (Ktav, 2003), attempts to answer all of these questions.

He concluded that this community originated from the region of Persia, perhaps via Bukhara, probably during the Song dynasty (960–1279 CE). It lasted 900 years, and the rise and decline of the Jewish community of Kaifeng parallels that of Chinese society and the city of Kaifeng itself. The Chinese emperors permitted the Jews to settle in Kaifeng and to observe their own laws and customs; they could own property and would be treated equally. The Jews were part of the city's merchant class. It took a while before the first synagogue was built, ca. 1163; it was rebuilt and enlarged in 1279.

During the Mongol rule, called the Yuan dynasty (1279–1368), the Jews were treated like other minorities and allowed to practice Judaism, engage in commerce, and even serve in the army. Some became financial advisers and tax collectors. The original group was also supplemented by Jews arriving from the Middle East.

It is surmised that one of the factors contributing to the continuity of the Kaifeng community is the Chinese concept of lineage, basic to its culture, which emphasizes family bonds. This in turn strengthened Jewish family values, intensifying Jewish communal bonds. Integrated with Jewish traditions, this contributed to the stability of the Kaifeng Jewish community even after the closing of the Silk Route.

The "Golden Age" was during the early Ming dynasty (1368–1644). It was at this time that the Jews adopted Chinese surnames, which reflects both acculturation and acceptance of the Jews by Chinese society. Jews were allowed to take the prestigious civil service examination, which provided a ladder by which to rise in Chinese society; they were no longer outsiders. But the flip side of this is that by passing these examinations, the young men would be sent to the far reaches of the empire, losing touch with home and gradually assimilating. The Jews thus gradually lost the best brains of the community. By this time they spoke Chinese (although they retained a knowledge of Hebrew), dressed like the Chinese, and even adapted ceremonies of ancestor worship to Judaism by setting up ancestral halls. They also included the mandatory imperial tablet in honor of the emperor in front of the synagogue but added the *Shema* inscribed directly above it in order to avoid the appearance of idolatry. Philosophic expressions combined the wisdom of Judaism and Confucianism by expanding "honor your father and mother" into the concept of Chinese filial piety.

Two major events contributed to the decline of Kaifeng's Jews—the Yellow River flood of 1642, which was the worst in its history, killed over half of the Jewish population, and only 200 families survived. The second event was the rise of a new dynasty, the Qing (1644–1911), which was hostile to other ethnic groups and isolationist. The Jews became increasingly marginalized and poor, losing their critical mass. More floods and political upheavals, along with lack of leadership, provided the last push toward disappearance. The Kaifeng Jewish community ceased to function as a viable entity by the middle of the nineteenth century.

History

Shanghai

February 20, 2004

The final stop on our four-week "Brooklyn College in China Winter Program" was Shanghai. From the perspective of Jewish history, it was appropriate to visit this bustling westernized city last since its Jewish community was one of the last to be founded.

Shanghai was opened up to western merchants after China's 1842 defeat at the hands of the British, during the Opium Wars. An international settlement was established there in 1863 where the Europeans, especially the British and the French—but also the Italians, American, and Japanese—set up their businesses and their homes. These autonomous settlements were extraterritorial and therefore did not follow Chinese law. The population of the city jumped to over one million by 1900, including some 60,000 foreign residents. Starting with trade in silk, tea, and opium, the city gradually became a center of finance.

The first Jewish merchants to arrive came from Baghdad via India, and, while they founded a cemetery by 1862, a synagogue was not established until 1887. The Jews met, until then, in the homes of some of the wealthiest merchants. Many of the Baghdadi Indian Jews had British papers, since India had become the "jewel" in Great Britain's imperial crown.

The second Jewish group to arrive came from Russia as a result of the Bolshevik Revolution. Escaping to the Far East, the Ashkenazi Jews found the thriving, although small, Middle Eastern Jewish community and for many years prayed in their synagogues before breaking away to form their own. They were supplemented in 1938 with the arrival of German and Austrian Jews escaping from Hitler.

The fourth Jewish group had a harrowing history. It was also escaping Nazi control, but it was from eastern Poland and Russia, fleeing in 1941 after Hitler broke his pact with the Soviet Union in his major offensive aimed at Stalingrad, known as "Operation Barbarossa."

This last group included about 300 young men from the Mir Yeshiva. Traveling across Siberia, they landed in Kobe, Japan, but as a result of Japan's joining the Axis and Hitler demanding that Japan also enact his anti-Semitic goals, this group ended up being sent to Shanghai. The Jews were ensconced in the International Zone, which became the ghetto. Gradually, even the local rich Jews were ghetto-ized as well.

Life in the ghetto was harsh, food was scarce, and disease was rampant. But Shanghai was a refuge, and most of the Jews who landed there survived. I have a paternal first cousin—Rabbi Chaim Ber Gulewski—who used to entertain us with stories of life in Shanghai during World War II. He was part of the Mir Yeshiva.

So, when I visited the city I took the entire Brooklyn College group (one-third of which was Jewish) to see the synagogue in the ghetto. It now houses a memorial hall paid for by many of the Jewish refugees, recognizing with gratitude the actions of the Chinese in saving their lives. The records list some 10,000 names.

Shanghai is going to take the place of Hong Kong, according to China's plans. If this is so—and the city certainly has an incredible vitality—then the tiny Jewish community that is there today will expand again. It shrank after World War II for two reasons. First was the reunification of Jewish families. For example, my father worked tirelessly to get an American visa for his nephew, with the cooperation of a wealthy cousin who sponsored him financially, and Yeshiva University, which guaranteed him a job.

The second reason it shrank was the Communist takeover. But China today, while remaining Communist, is involved in developing a market economy. That is bound to attract investors, and the Chinese market is incredibly huge. Shanghai, with its history and resources, is therefore going to see the growth of its Jewish community in the near future.

History

Saying Good-Bye
July 22, 2005

As usual, as the months of *Tammuz* and *Av* approach, I become reflective. Perhaps the somberness of the seventeenth of *Tammuz*, which leads inevitably to *Tisha B'Av*, spills over into my personal life. Perhaps, it is that the *yahrzeits* for both of my parents arrive along with these two summer months. Perhaps it is a result of the oppressive and seemingly endless summer heat. It may be a combination of all of these factors.

It comes as a bit of a shock to realize just how many years ago my parents died—twenty years for my father, twenty-six for my mother. On top of that realization of the passing of time comes the beginning of the "empty nest syndrome." I am the one sending off one daughter to China for her intensive summer course in Mandarin Chinese, and one daughter to Italy for her research on nineteenth-century synagogue architecture. How many times did my parent see me off on my junkets to Europe and my research projects to the Middle East! Now I'm the one staying home while my children go off on their exciting new adventures, and I worry as all good Jewish mothers (and fathers) do. I also reflect on how my parents must have felt to see me going off. Those were not the days of email connections and relatively cheap telephone calls. They had to await letters, and if calls came through, it usually meant bad news, like a hospital stay in Madrid, or a robbery in Venice, or the consulate calling from Moscow. How they must have worried.

I recently participated in an intensive seminar in Hebrew College, which is located just outside of Boston. One of the primary sources that I read through and analyzed for the participants, was a segment from Rabbi Benjamin of Tudela's writings. His long voyage, lasting from 1165 to 1173, searching out Jewish communities, led him from Spain across Provence, down through Italy, and into the Balkans to visit the Romaniot, or Greek, Jews in Salonika and Constantinople before the Ottoman Turkish conquest, before the arrival of the Sephardi Jews in large numbers. He traveled through Anatolia, down the Mediterranean coast to Israel and Egypt, and on to Arabia and Yemen. One of his main goals was to reach

Iraq and see for himself the great Academies of Baghdad, as well as the scion of the House of David, the Exilarch. But he did not stop there, and continued both east to Persia and Khorasan, and southeast to India. Wherever he went, he described not only the Jewish community, but also the surrounding societies. His travels are a wonderfully enlightening primary source and all of use parts of this wherever we can.

But did anyone ever think of his wife and family left behind in Tudela, Spain? Which wife would agree to let her husband go off alone on a voyage lasting eight years? The answer is either a wife who had a wonderful relationship with Rabbi Benjamin and understood his deep need to travel, or a wife who was really glad to see him go. We will never know.

Saying good-bye in the Middle Ages meant the possibility of never seeing that person again. The same held true in the early twentieth century as Jews left Eastern Europe in the tens of thousands. My father described his tearful farewell when he left Brest-Litovsk for Mandated Palestine in 1926. My mother was too young to remember the wrenching farewell to her grandparents who stayed behind in Poland.

So, all in all, I guess that if one has to see one's children off on their adventures, I have to be grateful to know that after winging her way over the Pacific Ocean, my China-bound daughter will either email or call. My daughter in Italy has already done so. I miss them both, but we live in an age where we take it for granted that we will see each other again, and soon.

History

Learning Languages
May 13, 2005

There are new sounds in my house. My older daughter, visiting for Pesach, is deeply immersed in her newest language, and she comes out with translated words and usually with a literal explanation of them as well. So we are all sort of learning Chinese. The term for Westerners is "white men"; the term for Asians is "yellow men." The term for Jews has no color.

My daughter is doing what Jews have done for millennia, and we can trace some of our successes in international trade, and some of our contributions to world cultures, to this knowledge of many languages. Sometimes, it even gave us political power, as multilingual Jews rose to positions of advisors to heads of state.

Jews always learned Hebrew—it was a given, especially for men. But, considering that most Jews did not live in a Hebrew-speaking environment, a second language was always necessary, whether it was Aramaic, Persian, Greek, Arabic, Latin, or Chinese, in the ancient world, or French, Spanish, Portuguese, German, Russian, Italian, or English in the early modern or modern world. Most usually spoke a third language, which combined the two: Judeo-German (Yiddish), Judeo-Arabic, Judeo-Spanish (Ladino), Judeo-Persian, or Judeo-Italian. There probably was Judeo-Chinese, but we have not found written proof if it. If the Jewish family was middle class, it educated its children in more languages in order for them to have access to the intellectual sources of their period or to be able to easily communicate with business partners—often branches of the family—in other countries.

The key role played by the Jews of southern Italy and Spain in the Middle Ages was connected to their actions as translators, as the intellectual and scientific works of the ancient Greeks made their way into Arabic, and, from there, into Latin and often, on the way, into Hebrew as well. In the Ottoman Empire, the Turks disdained contacts with Europeans, and often used their multilingual Jews, especially the newly arrived Sephardim, as their representatives there.

For my class on the Middle East, my students read the autobiography of an Egyptian woman whose life began in the late 1800s and who describes the end of the harem system. One clue leading to her intellectual growth that the class must discover is her knowledge of French. That language opened the door to the ideas of the West.

Moses Mendelssohn translated the Bible into beautiful modern German, hoping to show the assimilated Jews of Germany the glory of Judaism and lead them back into the fold. Instead, he gave many traditional Jews a bridge into the German-speaking world and modernity.

It is only in America, as Jews reflect American culture, that most Jews have become monolingual, or at most, speakers of English and Hebrew. Translations of foreign literature and thought are almost simultaneous with the publication in the original language. But America is learning that there is a world out there that speaks Chinese, Arabic, Japanese, and Spanish, and money is again being poured into universities to educate students in all of them, plus others. So, as my daughter memorizes the new sounds, writing, and grammar of Chinese, and prepares to spend a second summer totally immersed in that language, she is part of a long chain of Jewish scholars of languages as well as in the forefront of American needs.

History

The Armies of Rome

September 16, 2005

I finally saw the movie *Cleopatra*, starring Elizabeth Taylor, Rex Harrison, and Richard Burton. It was shown on Channel 13 for four long hours, and, while some of the acting was excellent and some of it was not, what got my undivided attention were the battle scenes. The Roman legions were so well trained, like a well-oiled machine at times. For example, when Julius Caesar's forces were fighting Pompey's, the former called for a battle tactic called "The Turtle." About a hundred men formed a closed phalanx shaped like a rectangle, with their shields held overhead and at their sides. They marched in syncopated fashion, impervious to the arrows of their opponents as well as to the firebombs being thrown at them, as their shields approximated the protective cover of a turtle's shell. They marched straight into the ranks of the enemy, behind the fire-shooting catapults, and attacked from behind.

The fire and stone-throwing catapults are marvels of ancient machinery, as are the bireme (double rows of oarsmen) and trireme (triple rows of oarsmen) ships in the sea battles. The instantaneous contact with orders sent from the generals, usually behind the battlefronts, was made with a combination of mirrors, flags, and trumpets. Of course, what helped in the fighting was that each side wore uniforms, so that the two sides could distinguish each other.

This was the force that the Jewish army tried to defeat when they rose up in battle in 66 CE. The Jews had already seen Pompey's armies one hundred years earlier. They had also seen Julius Caesar's forces as well as Octavian's. How could they possibly have expected to defeat such a force? And yes, the revolt lasted for four long years, and Masada held out three years beyond that.

Yes, smaller armies can defeat larger ones, because the size, and even the capabilities, of an army are not the only factors contributing to success. New and unfamiliar tactics can be decisive—like the luring of the eastern Roman forces into the desert by the Arab armies. New weaponry can play a role—like the muskets and gunpowder used by the expanding Ottoman

Turks in the Balkans. Leadership qualities are of vital importance as well. But everyone agrees that a key factor is the belief in an idea. This was a major factor in the success of the American Revolution, in the expansion of the Arab armies in the seventh and eighth centuries, and, of course, in the 1948 Israeli War of Independence. Idealism, however, is not enough, but has to be combined with a number of the other factors mentioned above. After all, the idealism was there in the Jewish revolt against Rome, but unfortunately, it was not enough.

The Israeli army, like other armies, studies the battles of the past. Technology may be modern, but basic military tactics do not change much. In the 1948 war, for example, the Israelis used some Hasmonean tactics that were successful against the Syrian-Greeks. But they also were always aware of the sheer numbers of Arabs and were determined not to allow what happened in the battle against ancient Rome to ever happen again.

The second item that the movie *Cleopatra* clarified was the Roman use of the victory marches as public propaganda and entertainment. Cleopatra's entrance into Rome to pay homage to Julius Caesar was remarkable and, even if the movie exaggerated it, the historical records of Rome attest to its effectiveness. No wonder Titus insisted on marching the best-looking young men through Rome after conquering Judea, as well as constructing the arch named after him as eternal testimony to his accomplishment. And no wonder, that when the State of Israel was declared, some young Roman Jews climbed over the fence around the Arch of Titus and planted Israeli flags there. The symbolism was obvious: ancient Rome is dead— long live the Jewish state.

History

Setting the Calendar
October 14, 2005

During the month of *Tishrei*, we are almost as constantly aware of the calendar as during the month of *Nissan*. We take the accuracy of the Jewish calendar for granted. No one would dream of challenging the holiday dates set down year after year by the rabbis following a time-hallowed formula. And yet we have examples of just such challenges sprinkled throughout Jewish history.

In 922 CE, Aaron Ben Meir, head of the Jerusalem Academy, announced that Passover would fall on Sunday. The *Geonim* (heads) of the Babylonian academies, located in Baghdad, declared that it would fall on Tuesday. That, of course, meant different dates for Rosh Hashana, as well as all other holidays of 923/24. What ensued was not just a difference of *halakhic* opinion, but a conflict of leadership. This conflict dated back to the Talmudic period, but reached a new peak in the tenth century, reflecting the Islamic political split between the Sunni Abbasids, with their capital in Baghdad, and the Shi'i Fatimids, with their new capital in Cairo and in control of the land of Israel and Syria.

The main personality who became embroiled in this conflict was Saadya ben Joseph, who at that time had left his birthplace in Egypt and was travelling through Israel and Syria. Saadya, who already had a reputation as an outstanding scholar, was in Aleppo in 922, and was informed of the dispute. He sided with the interpretation of the Babylonian scholars and attempted to dissuade Ben Meir from implementing his calendar.

On the contrary, Ben Meir dug in his heels and demanded that Babylonian Jewry obey the decision from the land of Israel. He had his son declare from the Mount of Olives that Rosh Hashana would fall on Thursday and Passover on Sunday. An impending schism loomed.

Letters were dispatched by fast couriers riding along the protected mail routes. Back and forth the controversy raged. From a gloating Karaite source, we know that Rosh Hashana was observed that year on different days in the two centers. Saadya was requested by the Babylonian leaders to write a detailed account of the event. It is known as *Sefer ha-Zikkaron* and was read in public in Elul of 922. His *Sefer ha-Mo'adim* gives a more complete account of the dispute, in which, in the end, Babylonia was victorious, although the manner in which the schism was resolved is unclear.

Saadya arrived in Baghdad in 922, and, as his reputation spread, he eventually was appointed by the Exilarch David ben Zakkai as the Gaon of the Sura Academy. He then became the center of new power struggles, first with the Karaites, and then, second, with the Exilarch himself. Perhaps, in appointing him as the Gaon of Sura, the Exilarch figured that he could control an outsider, namely, an Egyptian Jew with no family connections in Baghdad. If so, he erred completely, for Saadya was his own man. He was a man whose legal decision were his own, not to be influenced by anyone, including an Exilarch.

We no longer had disputes over the calendar. But we certainly still have disputes of centers of power. In that respect, we Jews have not changed.

History

Dancing
March 2, 2007

I recently went to a flamenco performance at City Center. Flamenco music and dance — part of the national art of Spain — is an acquired taste, for there are people who love it and people who hate it. I hear echoes of the Jews of Spain in the music, but there is absolutely no echo of that kind of dancing in Sephardic communities.

Why is there no real "Jewish" dancing? There are a few references to dancing in the Bible. There is the well-known one of Miriam leading the women in song and dance paralleling the celebration of Moshe and the men after crossing the Sea of Reeds. There is the reference to Yiftach's daughter, who greeted his military success with song and dance. But it was not only women who danced, for King David expressed his joy at moving the Ark of the Covenant into Jerusalem by dancing, to the dismay of his aristocratic wife, Michal.

But there was no dancing as part of Temple ritual. Music, yes, using choirs of Levites as well as various musical instruments; but dance, no. Perhaps this was to make a strong line of demarcation between monotheism and the pagan cults, which incorporated dance into their ritual, according to most scholars.

The urge to express oneself through dance is human, but the way of expressing this is culturally determined. This is why folk dancing of Japan, Mexico, Zimbabwe, Rumania, and England all have similarities, but yet are quite different. Israeli dancing is not really "Israeli" but more a manifestation of the "ingathering of the exiles," for Israeli dance is Rumanian, Yemenite, Kurdish, and Russian.

Jews had no homeland for such a long time that whatever existed in the Biblical period was lost, or long ago merged into the dance forms of whatever Diaspora communities into which Jews were relocated.

There is another element of dance that should be mentioned as well. In addition to folk dancing of the ordinary populace, there was always court dancing, which was performed either by dance specialists as entertainment for an audience, or performed by the aristocracy themselves for their own entertainment. Jews were seldom part of this court setup, with the notable exceptions of certain periods of time in Spain and in Italy. We know of Jewish dance masters in the Italian Renaissance who taught the young aristocrats the latest styles of dancing. But this was the exception.

Dance became popular among Jews with the rise and spread of the Hasidic movement. It became acceptable to express joy in worship through dancing as well as singing. But the steps as well as much of the music is heavily influenced by the Eastern European cultures.

There is nothing wrong in this, as we consistently manifest our acculturation throughout our history, while reshaping things to our own specific needs. Men and women dance separately in many cultures, for example, and often the steps themselves as well as the body movements are geared to masculinity or femininity.

Flamenco combines guitar playing, singing, chanting, dancing, and staccato hand clapping, and often the use of castanets. The dancer performs with passion and fervor. Flamenco blends ancient Greek and Roman elements with Arab music brought from the heartland of Damascus and Baghdad. The four-stringed lute became the five-stringed Andalusian guitar. The Gypsies, arriving in Spain in the fifteenth century brought intensity and tragedy to these themes. By the time it developed into its definitive dance form, in the eighteenth and nineteenth centuries, Jews no longer lived in Spain. So it is only in the guitar music and song that Sephardim still maintain this connection to Andalusian culture.

History

Stereotyping

October 9, 2009

Recently, as my family was taking a leisurely Shabbat afternoon stroll in Fort Tryon Park, we overheard a woman conversing with a friend stridently saying, "And I don't want to wear a diamond, like all those Jews do!" We were in a state of shock at what we heard and debated whether to confront her or not. In the end we decided it was not worth the aggravation, but the comment kept niggling at me. Are we the only ones who purchase diamonds? If that were so, the industry would not last very long. Yet the stereotype of a diamond wearer is that of a Jew.

Conspicuous consumption on the part of Jews has cropped up throughout our history, and Jewish communities have responded to the fear of Gentile envy by passing sumptuary laws. Here are some examples:

"[N]o Jew . . . shall be so arrogant as to wear a fur-lined jacket . . . no woman shall openly wear any . . . belt if its silver weighs more than ten ounces." (Forli, Italy, 1418)

"No son of Israel of the age of 15 or more shall wear any cloak of gold-thread, olive-colored material or silk, or any cloak trimmed with gold." (Valladolid, Spain, 1432)

"One is permitted to wear only two rings on weekdays, four on the Sabbath and six on the holiday. Both men and women are absolutely forbidden to wear precious stones." (Cracow, Poland, 1615/16)

"Shoes . . . in red or blue leather, or in any other color except black and white, are forbidden to everyone." (Metz, France, 1690)

These excerpts deal with clothing. Other laws deal with how many guests one can invite to a celebration, and even what foods can be served. But that was in the premodern world, when the Jews were a visible minority fearing attack. Yet the negative stereotypes have survived into contemporary times. In my mind, one of the contributors to this is Shakespeare, through his creation of Shylock. No matter that teachers explain that this is a literary creation, furthering Shakespeare's plot, the powerful negative image is there.

The stereotypes are also leftovers from a long history of Christian antipathy to Jews, especially on the level of folk religion and superstition. In the Middle East, the stereotype of the Jews—until the creation of the State of Israel—was that of a coward or a weakling.

"Don't Jew me," a man once said to me while we were bargaining in a market in New Hampshire. I almost punched him out. "What did you say?" He looked at me blankly, for the expression was just that to him, an expression, and he had not realized just how offensive it was to a Jew. I hope that he never used it again.

Why can't people use "Jew" in a positive way? "How Jewish you are!"—meaning how charitable, as Jewish philanthropists build hospitals, museums, schools, clinics, and libraries. Or meaning how educated, creative, intelligent, compassionate. Or meaning family-oriented, child-centered, respectful of elders.

I should live so long.

History

The Game of Chess
December 1, 2011

I just got back from visiting the exhibit entitled "The Game of Kings: Medieval Ivory Chessmen from the Isle of Lewis," presented at the Cloisters, the Metropolitan Museum of Art's center for medieval art. It combines thirty-four pieces from the British Museum, which I saw years ago, with some of the Met's own chess pieces.

The kings sit on ornate carved thrones, with their long braids spilling down their backs, and their swords across their laps. The queens, also on carved thrones, have their hands cupping their cheeks. Each bishop is holding a book in one hand and wears a miter. The knights ride tiny horses, and the pawns are the most stylized of all, resembling checkers. Instead of rooks or castles, there are warders, who were fierce warriors, some of which have their teeth overlapping their shields.

When the game of chess, invented probably in India, made its way across ancient Persia to Europe via the conquering Arabs, the pieces were not exactly the same. They used ministers and elephants, which were replaced in Christian Europe by bishops and queens. The moves also changed slightly over the centuries.

Chess is a game that was quickly picked up by the Jews of the Middle East, as well as the Jews of Spain and Italy. The game crossed the Pyrenees into Provence and across the Alps into France, Germany, and England. Obviously, not all chess sets were as intricately carved as these are, but we know of their existence from a number of Jewish sources. Yehuda Halevi refers to the game in his *Kuzari*. Abraham Ibn Ezra may have known the game. Maimonides disapproved of chess, but only when it was played for money. Some condemned it, while others approved of it. Some Italian *ketubot* of the Renaissance include a chess set as one of the items being brought by the bride into the marriage. Another source, an Italian Jewish Responsum dealing with whether or not Jews can play tennis on Shabbat, mentions that it is not like chess.

We have etchings of Jews playing chess, and, with the invention of photography, we have charming shots taken in Eastern Europe of boys and men playing. Some scholars say that the game was originally played by Jewish women, before it was picked up by the men.

Chess is a challenging mental game, perfect for the leisure time of a people immersed in mental exercises. And if this was what a cultured Gentile would do, the cultured Jews would follow suit.

On a personal level, I clearly remember my cousin's stories about surviving World War II, first in Japan and then in Shanghai, with the Mir Yeshiva. They made chess pieces out of inedible bread, and whiled away the time, when not studying, planning out chess strategies. My cousin taught my older brother, who became good at the game, but he refused to teach me. No one beat my cousin. Except my father, that is. When the two of them played, it was really war, which is what chess is all about.

What makes chess so attractive to Jews is an interesting question. It may have started as a cultural issue, that educated wealthy Jews wanted to imitate their non-Jewish cultured neighbors and patrons, and from there it filtered down to middle-class Jews, and then even farther down the economic strata. This is part of the history of fashion and style. But there is something intrinsically intellectually attractive about the game that has led to so many Jewish chess champions on both the national and international scenes, starting in the nineteenth century and spanning the entire twentieth century. Chess remains a favorite game among Jews to while away the long winter Friday nights as well as the long summer *Shabatot*.

History

Tombstones

January 13, 2012

It is obligatory on Jews to bury the dead. In ancient Israel, we see that only important people were buried in sepulchers often hewn into caves. The family grave of the patriarchs and matriarchs in Hebron is a prime example of this.

We can presume that when the Israelites entered the land of Israel, led by Joshua, and began settling down, communal burial grounds were set up outside towns and cities. Families were responsible for burial of their dead, which was done as quickly as possible. If there was no family to do this, it was the community's obligation. Rules were also in place for burying those who were executed for crimes.

The question of markers for cemeteries is an interesting one. We know that Jacob set up a marker over the grave of Rachel, but this may have been an exceptional act, for the family was still in its nomadic stage. With the settling down of the tribes, markers for graves of ordinary people may have developed as a way of warning *Kohanim* to stay away from this place of ritual impurity.

By the end of the period of the Second Temple, we have a plethora of ornate monumental tombstones for the nobility both in Israel and in Diaspora communities. Scholars developed varying viewpoints over the importance of having tombstones, and, as usual, some were in favor of this—for example, Rabbi Isaac Luria—and some were against this—for example, Rabban Shimon ben Gamliel.

Over the centuries, the erection of tombstones became a universal Jewish custom. Ashkenazi Jews usually have upright stones; Middle Eastern and Sephardi Jews usually have horizontal stones. Some communities have a special order of service that they follow at the official "unveiling" of the tombstone. These communities also developed a variety of customs as to what is written on the tombstone, i.e., the epigraph. Some cover the stone with writing, while others use a variety of artistic motifs. The oldest artistic motifs show that the deceased was a *Kohen*, with two hands raised in the format of the priestly blessing. Others—in ancient

Roman catacombs and cemeteries—bear the motifs of the *shofar, menorah, lulav, etrog,* and oil lamps, marking them as Jewish.

Tombstones serve as wonderful primary sources for historians. Their carving provided a lucrative profession for some families. The elaborate carving of some mausoleums is remarkable. Recently, the leading journal of Hebrew studies in Italy, *Materia Hebraica,* edited by Prof. Maruo Perani, published an article on a tombstone discovered in the northwest of the island of Sardinia, attesting to a Jewish presence dating back to 19 CE, when the emperor Tiberius shipped off thousands of young Jewish men to that island. Prof. Perani has published scholarly articles on the Italian Jewish art of writing Hebrew epigraphs, which by the sixteenth century was a creative art form of leading rabbis and scholars, often expressing itself in intricate Hebrew poetry.

I am off to Israel to take care of the "unveiling" for my brother's tombstone. He died less than a year ago. Following my family's customs, his tombstone will be simple, and the service will as well. Psalm 119 will spell out his name, one or two other Psalms will be read, and—if a *minyan* shows up—Kaddish will be recited. We Litvaks don't really make a big deal about this. And that will be the end of my obligation toward my dead brother, aside from his *yahrzeit.*

Noah's Wife
October 27, 1995

One of the most dramatic accounts in the Bible is that of Noah, the flood, the ark, the animals, and the rainbow. From the time that we are children, we are inspired by this narrative, and we have all drawn pictures of the animals arriving at the ark "two by two."

We read of Noah and his wife, his three sons—Shem, Ham, and Yafet—and his three daughters-in-law closing the doors of the ark to the rest of humanity, which then drowned during the forty days of endless rainfall. Yet despite the all-important role of regeneration that these four women play, the text does not name them.

The Bible abounds with nameless women, most of them wives of identified men, for example, the daughter of Shu'a who is married to Judah. There is Manoach's wife (mother of Samson). There is also the nameless widow who is helped by the prophet Elisha when her borrowed vessels are filled with precious oil, as well as the wealthy Shunamite who provides Elisha with a private apartment and is rewarded with a son for her deed. Pharaoh's daughter who saves Moshe is nameless too.

The question of anonymity is one that the commentators wrestled with, and in the case of Noah's wife, they came up with a variety of opinions as to when Noah married: one opinion is that he married at a normal age but refused to have children so as not to see them perish in the flood. Another opinion is that he married at age 498, and only when ordered to do so by God. He had only three sons so that he might be spared the necessity of building the ark on an overlarge scale in case they were pious, and be spared the sorrow of their destruction should they turn out to be depraved. Whom did he marry? Na'amah the sister of Tubal-Cain or Na'amah without any lineage assigned to her. Most opinions make her as pious as her husband. But there is a Na'amah in the *midrashim* who is the mother of Ashmedai, the devil par excellence, and seducer of men in their dreams. Great care is taken not to confuse the two. A totally different opinion is that Noah's wife was Noamzara (or Amzara), the daughter of Bakiel, his father's brother.

The only other *midrash* dealing with Noah's wife is the one that lists her among the twenty-two "women of valor" of the Bible. Here she reverts to her anonymous self.

It is interesting that the commentators search for names for most of these nameless women. It is also interesting that they do not ask why certain women are named and certain women are not. In other words, is there some criterion that determines anonymity? We can understand that in the case of Eliezer performing as the representative of Abraham in choosing a wife for Isaac, he is not named. We can also understand that since the focus of the story of the birth of Moshe is on the child, the names of his parents are unimportant at that time and thus omitted.

It becomes more difficult to deal with namelessness when we deal with Samson's mother, who is much smarter than her husband Manoach and plays just as important a role in parenting him. So too with Noah's wife, for repopulating the world required both genders working in tandem. Perhaps that is why the commentators rushed in with a variety of possible names for her. Be that as it may, Na'amah is a name that is still used for Jewish women down to this day.

Biblical Women

Childlessness Then and Now

September 27, 1996

On Rosh Hashana we read of the childlessness of both Sara and Chana. Both women are desperate in their barrenness, so desperate that the first woman takes steps to have her husband take a secondary wife, so that she, Sara, can adopt the child she has. Chana, on the other hand, turns totally to her maker, spilling her heart out in that most beautiful, personal prayer.

Interestingly, in making the decision to have the patriarch take a secondary wife for reasons of procreation, the matriarch Sara and later Rachel do not consult their husbands. The text's silence seems to imply that decisions affecting procreation were within the many rights of the primary wife. In Sara's case, however, it seems that the adoption of Ishmael never took place. Perhaps she changed her mind as a result of her confrontation with Hagar. We can only surmise and muse on this. Rachel, on the other hand, does adopt her slave Bilha's sons Dan and Naftali. This is clearly implied by the act of Rachel in naming them. These sons are free and equal to Jacob's other sons of his primary wives.

Chana already has a co-wife, a second woman jealous of Chana's favored status. In asking what happened to suddenly cause Chana to have a crisis over her barrenness when she had been childless for many years, a leading modern scholar wrote that it was probably caused by Elkana's statement, "Am I not better than ten sons?" Family members rely on each other for moral support—children on parents, siblings on each other, spouses on each other. Over the years Elkana had been as hopeful as Chana that one day they would conceive a child together. But in making the above statement, Elkana seems to have given up this hope. With her husband no longer her prop, Chana turned totally to God to spill out her desperation and her longing.

The desire of an infertile woman to bear a child fills modern articles, essays, and other media. Our scientifically creative times have addressed this topic, and one answer has been *in vitro* fertilization with the freezing of embryos to be implanted wither in the mother or in a "surrogate." Without getting into the *halakhic* implications of this topic, the Supreme Court of Israel, in early September, made a landmark decision on reproductive rights. A fifteen-member panel of judges voted 11–4 that the right of the woman to be a mother outweighed objections to fatherhood made by the husband from whom the woman was separated.

In the United States there is no federal law regarding the fate of a frozen embryo, but the precedent is that until both parties agree, contested embryos remain in storage. All couple must sign such an agreement before any American facility will store them.

But Israel is a Jewish country and even though the Supreme Court is a secular institution, Jews are brought up on the Bible, and the narrative of our matriarchs become part and parcel of the Jewish psyche. This may be part of the unconscious and conscious reason on the part of the Supreme Court justices to decide in favor of the childless woman.

Biblical Women

A Husband's Obligations
November 1, 1991

Among the many lessons that can be learned about women from this week's Torah portion and *haftara* selection is the lesson of a husband's obligations to his wife. A husband is responsible to feed, clothe, and shelter his wife, but in the Torah selection we see immediately that the obligations are broader than just these three.

In the midst of his grief and sorrow, Abraham must rouse himself to find a burial place for his dead wife. As a foreigner in the land of Canaan, this was not an easy task, for the country was controlled by Canaanite city-states and strangers had no rights. He thus had to appear in front of a council of elders in Hebron and, in good Middle Eastern fashion, he negotiated for the cave that he wished.

The politeness of the negotiations is fascinating, for this is still the proper method for negotiating in this culture. The price was agreed on with Abraham refusing to haggle over something as important as this, the silver was weighed out in front of everyone, and the deed was written up and publicly presented to the new owner. The first piece of land owned by the ancestor of the Jewish people is a burial place bought by Abraham for his wife, for a husband's obligations include proper burial.

Proper burial is not an issue that could be taken for granted, for in many polygynous cultures some wives would be buried in the equivalent of paupers' graves. The scholars of old knew this and therefore made it a rabbinic injunction that this is an obligation on a Jewish husband. That is not to say that one should go overboard and spend a fortune fulfilling this obligation. On the contrary, democratic burial which dates back to the Mishnaic time—that is, plain shrouds, a plain coffin (if a coffin is used), and simplicity on all levels—includes burial of wives.

The only women we know of who received special honors in were—as with men—those recognized by the people as deserving of special honor because of how they led their lives. These women were honored by the attendance at the burial and the escorting of the body on the part of all the people who could do so.

The text also sheds some light on the complex obligations to a man's children, which differ depending on the status of the wife. Abraham "gave all that he had to Yitzhak" (Gen. 25:5), but to the sons of the concubines he gave gifts and sent them away. He not only protected the physical inheritance of his son by his primary wife, but also his spiritual inheritance.

Some women came into marriages with children from a previous marriage. Therefore, in addition to the complexities of polygyny, there appeared the need to determine a husband's obligations to this type of wife. The scholars wrestled with the issue and came to their conclusions, which are now part of Jewish law.

Surely one of the difficult decisions that had to be made was that of continuity of a monarchy. Abraham had only one son from a primary wife; David had many. It is interesting to note that his formal choice of Solomon is connected with a vow that he made to his wife, Bat-Sheva. A husband's obligation to his wife, in this case, was carried to the level of monarchic succession.

It was more important, however, for a husband to treat his wife properly while she lived, and thus the text turns from Abraham's purchase of a burial plot to the arrangement of the marriage between Yitzhak and Rivka.

Biblical Women

Toldot

November 9, 1990

The first ten verses of this week's Torah reading plunge us immediately into the realities of life in the Biblical period as well as the realities of this particular family. The first two verses describe Rivka's and Yitzchak's lineages, underlining once again their endogamous relationship, for the preferred marriage in those days was one of cousins. This type of marriage kept both the wealth and the children to be born within the extended family, as well as ensured the woman a continuation of her status.

The next verse tersely states the worst possible situation for a married woman in ancient times, namely, childlessness. But in contrast to Sara's continuous childlessness, despite many attempts to turn the situation around, Rivka's barrenness seems to be relatively easy to cure, as Yitzhak entreats God, and after twenty years God "let Himself be entreated."

The terseness of the verse does not alleviate the anguish this situation must have caused until the pregnancy was assured. But the pregnancy is an unusual one, and Rivka is upset enough by the amount of activity within her womb to try to find out its meaning. The poetic answer she gets helps set the tone for the relationships with her twin sons as well as with her husband, for the last phrase states: "And the elder shall serve the younger."

The fraternal twins are born, as different in physique as in character. The text does not quibble in describing the family situation, for despite all that we as parents know about the dangers of favoring one child over another, "Yitzhak loved Esau because he ate of his hunt and Rivka loved Ya'akov." The verse does not relate why she loved Ya'akov, but we may extrapolate that she could recognize his true character, and as the matriarch, was concerned about the continuity of the monotheistic heritage, just as much as her husband was.

We, the readers, are privy to the next story, of which Rivka and Yitzhak are ignorant, namely, the ease with which Esau trades his birthright to his brother for a portion of food. This corroborates Rivka's assessment of her two sons, and confirms that her actions to protect Ya'akov and to ensure his blessing are correct.

Why does Rivka have to resort to manipulation? Why can she not confront her husband the same way Sara confronted Abraham when it came to protecting their spiritual continuity? It appears that the relationship between the two couple is not the same. Sara and Abraham's marriage is one of equals, with each respecting the realm of the other. Rivka, on the other hand, realized early on the Yitzhak is "blinded" in more ways than one; he has poor vision physically, but also does not want to see the true character of his lusty, impetuous, and impious firstborn son, whose animal-like energy he seems to admire, perhaps because it is in stark contrast to his own character.

Be that is it may, Rivka is forced into action on hearing her husband say to Esau that the time has come to give the blessing of the firstborn son. This is not only a blessing of a larger share of property, so common among ancient Middle Easterners, but in this case, it also meant spiritual leadership. With the memory of the prophecy that "the elder shall serve the younger," Rivka sets to work on both her son and her husband to ensure the lineage of the Jewish people.

Biblical Women

A Thread of Clothing
November 29, 1991

A peculiar theme seems to thread its way through this week's Torah portion: articles of clothing. The first item of clothing is Joseph's coat of many colors, the garment that symbolizes his father's favoritism and, therefore, his brothers' envy. The only other reference in the Bible to such a multicolored garment is in connection with Tamar, daughter of King David. In both cases the robe signifies royalty and leadership, and, in both cases, the final use of the robe is disaster: in Joseph's case the bloodied garment is used to prove his death, and in Tamar's case the ripped garment is symbolic of her rape and dishonor.

The second article of clothing is a veil. As contrasted to the only other reference to the veil in the Torah, i.e., that used by Rivka on hearing that the man approaching the caravan was her betrothed, the veil in this Torah portion is used in a totally different manner. Here it is used by a temple prostitute, the kind that plied her trade at the crossroads. We presume it was used to conceal her identity. The word used numerous times in the text is *kedeisha*, meaning temple prostitute or a woman whose function in Canaanite society was related to fertility rituals.

Tamar, abandoned and status-less Canaanite daughter-in-law of Judah, resorts to a drastic action, an action which should be understood within the context of the desperation of the powerless. Tamar's fate rests totally within the hands of her father-in-law, who was obliged to marry her to his third son after the deaths of his first two sons. Judah has no intention of fulfilling his obligation to arrange for this levirate marriage and thus sends Tamar back to her father's house, ostensibly to send for her when his third son is ready for marriage.

Tamar is not single nor is she married. Only a desperate woman would do what she did to move her life out of the oblivion into which it had sunk. Judah, in the face-to-face confrontation with her, confesses his failing. More importantly, God approved of her action, for David was among Tamar's descendants.

The third article again belonged to Joseph, but this time it was the covering he left in fleeing Potiphar's wife. In this case the clothing is not symbolic of jealousy nor of desperation, but of thwarted lust. Potiphar's wife, spurned by her would-be lover, uses Joseph's abandoned garment as evidence to convict him of attempted rape. Yet his garment may also have served to put doubts into Potiphar's mind as to the veracity of his wife's accusation, or he would have had Joseph executed.

Clothing, at its most basic level, is purely functional. Yet in all societies the colors or the styles or the fabrics have served to differentiate between classes and genders. In the ancient world, a rich fabric could be worth a fortune. No wonder, then, that Esau's best clothing remained in the care of his mother and not his wives. Poor people, on the other hand, owned only one garment and, therefore, the garment (used as collateral) had to be returned to a poverty-stricken borrower to sleep in at night. In this Torah portion we see that we can even learn moral lessons from articles of clothing.

Biblical Women

Bilha and Zilpa

November 15, 1991

The Torah portion for this week gives us an in-depth view of Ya'akov's family life while living within the domain of his father-in-law, Lavan. For a change, let us focus not on the dominant figures but on two relatively minor ones in this panorama of human relationships, namely, on the two slave women, Bilha and Zilpa.

Among the wealthier people of the ancient Middle East, it was customary for a father to give a daughter who was about to be married a personal female slave. This was a valuable gift, and personal slaves could reach positions of great importance in a household as, for example, Eliezer, the slave of Abraham. Female slaves relieved their owners of some of the onerous burdens of housekeeping and childcare. Let us not forget that the burdens of housekeeping included the grinding of flour for bread, the carrying of water, the laundering of clothing, the spinning and weaving of cloth, and so on.

Zilpa and Bilha came into Ya'akov's household as personal slaves of Leah and Rachel. But when Rachel could not conceive a child, she followed Sara's example by giving her slave, Bilha, to her husband as a wife. She was not to become a primary wife, with all the rights and privileges of Leah and Rachel, but a secondary wife. This is manifested quite clearly, first by Rachel's announcement to Ya'akov that he must take Bilha, "the she may give birth on my knees (thighs) and I shall be built up through her." In other words, Bilha's child will be adopted by Rachel possibly through the physical act of kneeling before Bilha during the birth so that the infant would land on her lap as soon as it emerged into the world.

Did Ya'akov have any say in this matter? No, no more than Abraham had any say about Hagar. Primary wives, it seems, controlled this aspect of life. Did Bilha have any say? No, for she was Rachel's slave.

Another way that Rachel manifested her continued control over Bilha even after she slept with Ya'akov, thus becoming his wife, was in the naming of Bilha's two sons. It is Rachel who named Dan and Naftali, not their biological mother. Thus, despite bearing Ya'akov's sons, Bilha remained Rachel's slave just as Hagar remained Sara's slave.

The same thing happened with Leah's slave, Zilpa; the same reason was given to Ya'akov for the union, and Leah named both Gad and Asher instead of Zilpa, their biological mother.

Did secondary wives have any rights at all? Indirectly they did, but this depended on the patriarch of the extended family. The patriarch could choose not to treat his children equally, as has been related to us in an interesting legend, namely, that Bilha and Zilpa were Lavan's daughters borne to him by his concubines. Obviously he chose to keep them as slaves, for he presented these half-sisters to his daughters via his primary wife as presents on their marriages.

In stark contrast, we have Ya'akov, who decided that all of his children were to be treated equally, and the sons of the secondary wives could inherit an equal share of the property, thus ensuring the care of their mothers after the death of the patriarch. This did not ensure, however, that the children themselves would treat each other as equals.

Va-Yishlach

November 30, 1990

"Dina . . . went out to see the daughters of the land." What more normal thing for a newly arrived young woman with many brothers to do than to seek out other young women to befriend? Dina had no idea that Canaan was not Haran, a place with an open society where women could go out alone to shepherd the flocks and speak fearlessly to male strangers standing near the town well. Instead of friendship, she met with the most horrible thing that can happen to any woman: rape.

For the rest of the stormy passionate story concerning Dina, the woman herself plays a passive role. We don't even know where she is until twenty-six verses into the chapter. This passive role, however, does not diminish her importance in provoking a number of confrontations.

First, there is the confrontation of a powerful city-state society of Canaan, in the person of Shechem, with the less powerful landless nomadic society of Jacob and his family. During the marriage negotiations conducted by the patriarch, in good Middle Eastern fashion, we see that the most important aspect of the bridegroom's offer is the acceptance of a nomadic group into the city-state via intermarriage.

The only thing that the bride's family has to offer, in this case, is Dina and the passion of Shechem for her. We surmise that in any other instance a city-state would not make such an offer.

A deeper confrontation provoked by the rape of Dina is that of a Middle Eastern culture, which views rape not only as the shame of an individual but also as shame of her group—family, clan, tribe—and therefore condones group revenge, with a newly emerging culture of monotheistic Judaism, which held each individual responsible for his/her own deeds. In Middle Eastern culture it is the obligation of the raped woman's full brothers to seek revenge for their sister's humiliation, and therefore Shimon and Levi act as they do. As for their attack on all the men of the city, again, the brothers act according to the concept of group revenge. Add onto that, rape was unacceptable in Canaan as well, but the community did not punish Shechem for his vile deed, making them complicit as well. Such a cruel act of group murder and group responsibility is alien to us today, for over the centuries of Biblical history the concept of the blood feud was weaned out of our culture. Muhammad tried to remove the blood feud with the introduction of Islam, but it did not work for the Middle Easterners as it did for the Jews.

Dina is rescued from Shechem's house by her avenging brothers, but we know nothing of her thoughts, her reaction, or her desires. The text only hints at what happened to her, for in enumerating the Israelites' descent to Egypt to join Joseph, it is written under Shimon's lineage: "Shaul the son of a Canaanite woman" (Gen. 46:10). Samuel David Luzzatto, the Italian Bible commentator, explains that this woman was the daughter of Dina and Shechem, the Canaanite. So in between the terse lines of the text we can surmise that in her pregnant condition Dina went to the more powerful of her two rescuing brothers, Shimon, was taken under his wing, and she and her child became part of his extended family. How wise a law we have in Judaism that traces our identification as Jews via the mother's lineage, or Dina's child would not have been accepted as part of the Children of Israel.

Biblical Women

Tamar and Judah
December 17, 1999

In 1950, Japanese film director Akiro Kurosawa stunned the western world with his *Rashomon*, today one of the top film classics of all time. His eloquent masterpiece illuminates the subjectivity of truth, as four different narrators describe the same brutal act—a woman's rape and her husband's consequent death. The facts continue to elude us as each interprets the events to make himself appear in the best light, according to the values of premodern Japanese culture. The four narrators are the rapist-brigand, the woman, the dead husband (speaking through a medium), and a woodcutter who just happens to pass by. The brigand boasts of both the rape and the honorable sword duel between himself and the husband, the husband tells of a perfidious wife and his honorable *hara-kiri* (suicide), and the wife tells of her powerlessness and anguish at her husband's rejection of her, with the possibility of her stabbing her husband in an emotionally unstable state. It is the last narrator who is the most believable because he is not emotionally involved (although Kurosawa even throws some doubt on his narrative).

The actions of the upper-class wife, the ultimate example of powerlessness in premodern Japan, brought to mind two Biblical women who are also examples of powerlessness within their society, namely, Dina and Tamar. But in stark contrast to the Japanese story, Tamar's actions were geared toward a positive goal.

When a woman married in the ancient Middle East, she moved into her husband's extended family. The patriarch—usually her father-in-law—was in total control of all the members of the household and responsible for them. Thus, when Er, Tamar's husband, died childless, it was Judah's responsibility to arrange the *Yibum* or levirate marriage with Onan. When Onan also died, it was Judah's responsibility to set up a *Yibum* marriage with Shelah. However, not only did he not do so, but also he did something unusual: he sent her back to her biological family to await Shelah's reaching maturity when this marriage would talk place. "Out of sight, out of mind" describes Judah's lack of responsible action, for, as was

84

common then (as now in some cultures), a woman who had buried two husbands was feared.

Kurosawa would then have switched the camera to Tamar, sitting month after month, year after year awaiting an end to her lack of status, for she was neither a widow, free to marry, nor a wife. The Torah does this in words. "And Tamar was told, 'Your father-in-law is coming up to Timna for the sheep shearing.' So she took off her widow's garb, covered her face with a veil, and, wrapping herself up, sat down at the entrance to Enayim, which is on the road to Timna, for she saw that Shelah was grown up, yet she had not been given to him as a wife" (Gen. 38:13–14). The powerless daughter-in-law, who could not remind Judah of his responsibility because it was "not done" in that society, took the only action she could think of to end her lack of status. Notice that the text refers to Judah as her father-in-law, even though she is living in her father's home. This is a subtle reminder that he was the responsible party.

Rabbi Ralph Tawil (*Judaic Seminar* Vol.7, no. 12) focuses on the symbolic elements in the request of Tamar for a pledge from Judah until payment would be made: Judah's seal, cord, and staff: "These are the signs of commitment, responsibility and authority. Tamar took them from Yehuda, symbolizing that Yehuda lacked these traits."

The final confrontation between the two, again stresses the lesson that Judah had to learn. Upon being told that Tamar was pregnant, obviously through harlotry, Judah, never questioning nor investigating, simply declared her a dead woman. She, on the other hand, tactfully revealed that he was the father of her child. The shock of seeing his seal, cord, and staff obviously brought about the realization of his faults, and Judah confessed to all that it was his lack of family responsibility and commitment that had led to Tamar's actions.

The final scene focuses on Tamar giving birth to her twin sons, ensured a place in Judah's—and Israel's—extended family, and Jewish history.

Biblical Women

A Matriarchal Legacy
October 30, 2016

In this week's Torah portion the central dramatic event is Jacob's poetic blessing of his sons. Nowhere do we find any record of Rachel's blessing, nor that of Leah, Rivka, or Sara. We have reference in the text to the deaths of only two matriarchs, and with regard to Sara, the recounting of the event seems to be more a matter of the problem of burial rather than the simple statement of her death.

The statement of Rachel's death is a combination of the problem of burial as well as a reflection of Jacob's grief at the untimely passing of the woman he so deeply loved. But there is nothing written about the blessing or oral legacies of the four matriarchs.

Does that mean that they did not bless their children before they died or leave them a legacy? On the contrary. But the legacy they left was not to be summed up in a dramatic prose-poem; rather, it was built up on a daily level of teaching and example. If, by the time these women died, their children had not learned the lessons so meticulously taught, no dramatic deathbed blessing would change this. Their job already done; there was nothing more to add.

With a few notable exceptions, this was the case for Jewish women through the millennia. The most outstanding of these exceptions left a written legacy that confirms the above idea, for Gluckel of Hameln's memoirs were written about her life's experiences to reconfirm the moral teachings she exemplified throughout her long life.

Gluckel, born in Hamburg in 1646, lived through the Thirty Years' War, and witnessed, at a distance, the Cossack massacres of Poland and the insanity of the messianic fervor over Shabtai Zvi. Married at age fourteen to Haym Hameln, she proceeded to have over a dozen children before losing her "dear friend" and "beloved companion."

Widowed at age forty-four, with eight children still unmarried, Gluckel took on her husband's business with such energy that it thrived and provided dowries for most of her children. Yet, as she wrote in Book I, she could not sleep at night and so started writing her memoirs "in the hope of distracting my soul from the burdens laid on it." She hastily added that it would not be a book of morals—for such the Sages already wrote, and the Torah itself provided all the wisdom that we need for the journey through life.

Yet we immediately see Gluckel, the human being, for she continued in the next paragraph: "The kernel of the Torah is, Thou shalt love thy neighbor as thyself. But in our days we seldom find it so, and few are they who love their fellow man with all their heart—on the contrary, if a man can contrive to ruin his neighbor, nothing pleases him more."

Pious, astute, educated, and talented, Gluckel provides a goldmine of material for the historian, sociologist, scholar of Judaic Studies, philologist, and student of literature. In writing of her own life and experiences, she painted a portrait of a period in Jewish history. She completed her memoirs in 1719 and died five years later at the age of seventy-eight. Her memoirs confirm the role of Jewish women from the Biblical period down to her day of daily teaching and example as the legacy to her children.

Biblical Women

Siblings

January 9, 1996

This week's Torah portion contains a detailed description of the impending death of Jacob, his blessing, and his funeral. The Torah states: "And when Joseph's brothers saw that their father was dead, they said, 'It may be that Joseph will hate us and will take revenge on us for all the evil that we did to him'" (Gen. 50:15). In other words, they feared that without the presence of their father as a deterrent, Joseph would now get even. This leads to the final scene of the relationship between the siblings in which Joseph reassures them of his forgiveness.

The rivalry, jealousy, and hatred of the sons of Jacob fill many chapters in the Torah. No one emerges looking good, and the Torah, as usual, presents real people with their good traits as well as their bad ones. The hatred of the brothers toward the youthful Joseph could have easily led to his death, as did the hatred of an earlier sibling pair—Cain and Abel. Nor was Jacob's fear of Esau's capability of murdering him a figment of his imagination.

The relationships of siblings are very complex. Those who grow up in and retain loving relationships should count their blessings, for too many of us do not. "Sibling rivalry" is not the only basis for dislike (in following the trend of discounting many of Freud's theories), but there can also be major differences in personalities, interests, intelligence, and education. In the Jewish world, there can also be the issue of religious observance, e.g., memories of aggravation caused to parents by a child who rebelled against Judaism and openly flouted its precepts. My father never forgave one of his older brothers for smoking a cigarette in front of their father on Shabbat.

These feelings and actions are not limited to brothers. One of the most prestigious and powerful women in Jewish history, Dona Gracia (Mendes) Nasi, the Portuguese *Converso*, was almost handed over to the Inquisition by her sister. The documents only discuss the fights over the control of the money of their vast international business, but between the lines, one glimpses elements other than wealth in the dislike Brianda

Mendes harbored for Dona Gracia. Dona Brianda had a hand in accusing her sister of being a secret Jew, with the result that this legally enabled the Inquisition to wield its power against her, even in Italy. In this case, the accusation backfired, and Dona Gracia left Venice first for Ferrara and then for Istanbul before any action was taken. It was only thanks to the intervention of the French ambassador that Dona Brianda herself was able to escape from Venice, for if one sister was a secret Jew—reasoned the Inquisitors—why not the other?

Most of us do not live such dramatic lives as did Joseph and his brothers or Dona Gracia and her sister. It is easy, in theory, to say that we should make peace with our siblings as Joseph did—saying that all that happened was part of God's larger plan. It is easier, in reality, to follow Dona Gracia's actions of never speaking to her sister again.

Biblical Women

Midwifery
January 30, 1998

The Torah portion of Exodus contains in it references to the two main midwives of the ancient Hebrews and names them. Shifra and Pu'ah play an important role in Pharaoh's descent into open annihilation of the Hebrews. They are part of the middle stage of such a policy: indirect murder caused by overwork, hidden murder done in secret by midwives, and open murder of throwing male newborns into the Nile.

How could the midwives get away with such deeds? One of the clues given is the use of the word *avnayyim*, which literally means double stones; most translators use the term "birthing stool." In ancient times—and we have extensive examples of this recovered from ancient Egyptian tombs—birthing women sat on low stools. These stools enabled the woman to lean back, while pushing the infant out in a naturally comfortable position (as comfortable as any woman giving birth can be), unlike the flat beds imposed on women by male doctors once they took over birthing from the midwives. The midwife knelt below the birthing mother to catch the newborn or to aid its exit from the womb. With the mother concerned with the contractions and the pain, and in a position higher than that of the kneeling midwife, the midwife could easily wrap the umbilical cord around the newborn's neck and claim that the newborn had been strangled during birth. That was the secretive murder that Pharaoh had in mind.

Midwives had power in ancient times, down to the time that modern doctors replaced them. They had folk medicines—herbal, floral, and mineral—that had been handed down from one generation to the next, for midwifery was a family profession for Jewish women, similar to that of medicine for Jewish men. They knew what positions in the womb the infants should be in for an easy delivery; they knew how to turn infants around inside the mother if they were wrong-side down. They also were expert enough to recognize a bad situation: Rachel's midwife knew that the birthing mother would not survive.

Yet the commentators state that in Egypt, the Hebrew women really were robust and vigorous and gave birth easily. Prof. S. D. Goitein comments on the Jewish women of Cairo in the twelfth century being similar to their ancestors, for if Geniza records are full of reports about bad health and illness, there is little on the inconveniences of pregnancy and death in childbed. That does not mean that the risk of childbirth was not great, and there are wills in the Geniza of pregnant women made in anticipation of that possibility. Wills exist which provide for the child, male or female, who would survive the mother. In addition, other wills also give generously to charities. One will turned over the birthing mother's assets to her mother on condition that she brings up the newborn; the reality was that the widower would soon remarry, and the grandmother would be a better substitute than a stepmother.

Midwives also had power because at the time of pain and fear of death, many secrets would be told to unburden oneself before going to the next world. Midwives who kept these secrets were well rewarded and esteemed, as well as feared. They were treated with great respect in the world of women, and unusual for the times, some names that have come down to us from medieval Cairo translate as "Son of the Little (Female) Doctor," and "Son of the Midwife." The midwife might not have been rich, but she never went hungry, and the community coffers paid her fees when she aided poor women.

In the Gentile world in Europe, unfortunately, during the same period of time, such knowledgeable women were feared to the point of facing the accusation of witchcraft. Such fears existed in the Middle East as well, but they rarely if ever led to the wholesale burning of witches such as occurred north of the Mediterranean.

Pharaoh may have wanted to kill Shifra and Pu'ah, but he was not quite sure if they were lying or not. Besides, they were female, and how much trouble could weak females cause?

Biblical Women

Some Thoughts on Miriam
June 7, 1991

The stories of Tzippora and Miriam are interspersed in the Torah. Miriam's life is one of the few of which we catch glimpses of her youth, womanhood, old age, and death. Of Tzippora we have even less detailed information in the text itself. Legend steps in to supplement the sparsity of Torah information.

The incident related in Numbers 12:1–16 may be connected with an earlier incident related in Exodus 18, tying the lives of the two women together. When Moshe had set out for Egypt, he had originally intended to take Tzippora with him, but because of the strange event at the inn, he had sent her back to Yitro, her father. Sending a wife back to her father was one way of divorcing a woman in ancient times, providing that the patriarch accepted this as an act of divorce. In the case of Yitro, the text repeatedly states, verse by verse almost, that Yitro was Moshe's father-in-law. Yitro took Tzippora, "Moshe's wife, after he had sent her away," and brought her to Moshe's camp in the desert, stating to Moshe that he was returning Moshe's wife and two sons to him. It seems that this is totally Yitro's doing and that Moshe had not sent for them. Was this possible, and if so, why?

Then we come to the puzzling story of Miriam and Aaron who spoke again Moshe because he had married a Cushite woman. Did Miriam, traditionally seen as the instigator of the speaking against Moshe, do this because she was a Cushite woman, or could there be something else here and the emphasis on the "Cushite" is misplaced? Perhaps the emphasis should be placed on the word "married," and thus the two stories are intertwined.

Miriam (and Aaron) were both prophets and had had experiences with God. They continued to have normal marital relations with their spouses. They observed, however, that Moshe's relationship with his wife Tzippora was not as it should be, and so Miriam protected her sister-in-law, who had the right to normal marital relations, and stated "Did God speak only to Moshe? Did God not speak also with us?" This may not be the evil tongue in the traditionally accepted sense, but it still is speaking against Moshe. And God heard it, and acted for Moshe, who was the most modest of all men on earth. Then followed the calling of all three siblings in front of the tent, and the statement—which makes sense in this context—that God may speak to others, e.g., the seventy prophets had just prophesied in the camp, but God's relationship with Moshe was unique. His spirituality raised him above the level of any human being and so transformed him that he no longer lived the life of an ordinary mortal on earth. How dare anyone question this? So Miriam was afflicted with leprosy.

A question raised is why Aaron was not likewise stricken, after all, the evil tongue requires a listener who is just as guilty as the speaker. A couple of years ago, in discussing this in class, a student raised the possibility that perhaps it was because Aaron's role as high priest would have been in jeopardy had he been a leper, that he was spared the disease. It is an idea worth cogitating. Let us not forget, however, that as a brother, he suffered agony over Miriam's disease (and his own role) and begged Moshe to pray to God to save her. Both brothers in the end, acting as brothers, succeeded.

Biblical Women

Deborah the Judge
February 6, 1993

Deborah the judge, Deborah the prophet, Deborah the wife, Deborah the poet: all of these were the roles played by one of the most outstanding women of antiquity. The *midreshei aggada* surrounding her life and deeds are understandably numerous, for this was a woman who did not fit into the "norm" of womanhood, in the Biblical period nor in the historical period nor in the historical period of the writing of these *midrashim*. It is understandable, then, that some of these embroideries or explanations of the text are laudatory and that some are not.

What to do with the woman who steps out of the boundaries (read that also as restrictions) of her cultural role? How do you cope with a woman who, despite all the obstacles presented to her, still manages to become her own person and follow her own dreams? Do you clamp down on her and force her into the pre-shaped mold, or do you admire her achievements, or do you explain her deeds away by finding excuses? Different interpreters of Biblical text have chosen all three paths, sometimes in the same hermeneutical passage. The same holds true for historians dealing with exceptional Jewish historical figures who happened to be women.

We are in an intellectually exciting time. For the first time in Jewish history the majority of the observant Jewish women are receiving an in-depth education in Torah and Jewish texts. Their minds are being challenged—from the more traditional yet intellectually creative question of "What is Rashi's difficulty (with the verse)?" to the twenty-first century difficulties of birth control, abortion, euthanasia, environmentalism, and genetic testing. As these generations of scholarly young women mature, they will apply their brains not only to secular subjects but also to religious ones as well. Their ideas and scholarship will be exciting to contemplate for they will bring their special perspective to Jewish study.

They will read and reread the text of Deborah and study the *midreshei aggada*. Some will choose to agree with the latter, but others will not. This group may decide that textual analysis is more important than later interpretations, and will follow in time-honored steps of writing their own interpretations, more on the lines of Rambam, Ibn Ezra, and Sforno.

For this writer, Deborah needs no embroidering nor "explaining away." She was what the text states: judge, prophet, wife, and poet. God chose her for the first two roles. Period. And no matter how much some try to downplay her powers, at heart, the scholars knew that she was God's choice. Why else would they choose to put her lofty song of praise and triumph as the *haftara* of the even loftier song of praise and triumph of the only man who experienced God as he did, namely, Moshe? The Song of Deborah resonates with passion, love of God, and triumph, utilizing the purest of poetic expression and the highest of linguistic development. Down through the ages our hearts have been touched and uplifted by the seemingly simple phrases of *"Uri, uri Dvorah / uri, uri dabri shir"* (Awake, awake Deborah / awake, awake, utter a song!). What a leader! What a poet! What a woman!

Biblical Women

The Roles of Avishag
December 5, 1997

At first glance, the story of Avishag the Shunamite appears rather strange. Why should the text report on the fact the King David was old and could not get warm? Other outstanding personalities are described as old, either by using the word *zaqen* or *ba ba-yamim*. But only David is described as unable to get warm.

The solution to the lack of blood circulation was to search the land for a young woman to serve the king, to be a kind of home attendant. Part of her duties was to sleep in the king's bed to keep him warm, but the text hastens to add that this had no sexual connotation and that the verb "to sleep" was to be understood literally.

The question is posed again: Why give these details unless they indicated something deeper? The clue to this seems to be the continuation of the chapter, which moves on to the attempt on the part of David's handsome son Adoniyahu to take over the throne even before David's demise. Two clues are provided as to why Adoniyahu did this and why he did it just then. First, the text parenthetically states that David had never berated his son but, on the contrary, had spoiled and indulged him. Secondly, the rebellion took place just then because with the arrival of Avishag, it appears that David withdrew from active rule. He may have simply taken to his bed, relying more and more on his caregiver, as many older ailing people seem to do.

When Adoniyahu saw this, he recognized that this was his chance. He knew that David had designated Solomon, his younger half-brother, as heir apparent. What he counted on was that his political party—made up of priests, generals, and upper level sympathizers—would prevail. What he had not counted on was the action taken by his half-brother's mother, Bat-Sheva. All mothers are out to protect their sons, but all the more so in the palace where the rivalry between the various princes could easily lead to death. Bat-Sheva was the *Gevira* or "Great Lady," the woman with the greatest power in the palace. She was the mother of the "crown" prince or heir apparent, and thus had access to the king. If you read the text carefully, you will see that she is the only person who does not have to be announced to the king and is not stopped by his guards. Access to power is power. Thus Bat-Sheva, acting on the advice of Nathan the prophet, but using her own knowledge of King David as well, manipulates the king into finally taking the desired action: he orders his men to publicly anoint Solomon king and place him, officially, on the throne.

Adoniyahu suddenly finds himself without friends. He saves himself by grasping the horns of the altar in the Sanctuary, saying that he will stay there forever unless his half-brother forgives him and promises not to kill him. Solomon gives in—probably against his mother's wishes, for she knew that a living Adoniyahu would continue to be her son's biggest rival for the throne. But Solomon added a caveat: he would tolerate his half-brother's existence, but only as long as he did not step out of line. One false move, and he was a dead man.

At first Adoniyahu behaved. But in the end his choice was: better to die gloriously in an attempt to gain the throne than to live out a long, boring, powerless life as the king's older brother. The ploy was based on a woman, the same woman who had symbolized for him the withdrawal of David from active power, namely, Avishag. And the ploy was again defeated by a woman, the same woman who had acted to defeat his first attempt at the throne, Bat-Sheva the *Gevira*.

Biblical Women

Some Lessons from Ruth
May 17, 1991

It is interesting to note that for a holiday marking the giving of the Ten Commandments, during which we read in the synagogue the description of this most important event of our nationhood and religion as well as a description of the sacrifices for the Shavuot festival, the Sages made two decisions. The first decision was to choose *haftarot*, first from Ezekiel describing his mysterious vision of the divine throne-chariot, a vision which serves as the oldest layer of Kabbala, and second, from Habakkuk, describing in lush poetic language the future manifestation of God. Both prophetic selections are personal descriptions tied to the mysteries of God's activities.

The second decision made by the Sages was to choose to have the book of Ruth read on Shavuot. They could not have chosen anything more concrete and more replete with historical reality than this brief book. It stands in stark contrast with the Torah and *haftara* selections of this holiday, and therefore should give us pause to ponder on the thinking behind this choice.

It is true that Ruth describes the barley harvest and the wheat harvest, the two harvests which connect the festivals of Pesach and Shavuot, thereby connecting physical redemption with spiritual freedom. But that is too simplistic. Surely there must be something in the book of Ruth that so appealed to the Sages that they ruled in favor of its reading on this festival.

What we find in Ruth is a description of a real woman who personifies in her character and deeds the lessons which the Torah teaches us in the abstract. During the Biblical period, when a woman married, she became part of her husband's family, and she practiced her husband's religion. We surmise that this held true for Ruth as well, for when her mother-in-law, Naomi, attempted to send her back to her own family, she added, "and to your gods." But Ruth, now out of her own choice, responded that "your God shall be my God." She thus fulfilled the first of the Ten Commandments. Her Judaism was the pure form of the *Ger Tzedek*, the "just convert," who choses her religion out of love and belief in the truth of God.

Ruth epitomizes not only purity of belief but also *chesed*, or lovingkindness. She could have chosen to leave her mother-in-law, who freed her to do so. She could have married any of the young men of Israel, as Boaz remarked. Instead she chose to tie her fate to Naomi's and to tie her fate also to the redemption of the land, which, as a widow, Naomi could not inherit.

He who acted as *go'el* (redeemer) for Elimelech's land also had to marry Ruth, and her child would be Naomi's spiritual grandchild, ensuring the older woman a family. This was not obligatory for Ruth but, again, a matter of choice.

Ruth's choices teach us in concrete terms the true message of the Torah on this holiday, commemorating its appearance on earth: purity of belief and the connected proper personal behavior of *chesed*. Combine these two characteristics, and you have a real Jew.

Kohelet

October 20, 2000

The book of Ecclesiastes or Kohelet, traditionally identified with King Solomon, contains twelve chapters of maxims and wise observations of the purpose of life. Pessimistically, the author deals with the futility of life. Whether examining the values of wisdom or pleasure or wealth, Kohelet declares that they do not lead to happiness. How is one to gain happiness? Does one follow wisdom or pleasure? Life is monotonous, and there is nothing new under the sun.

The scholars have dealt with the interesting question of how old King Solomon was when he wrote Kohelet, with one school of thought stating that he was old, for only the old see the futility of life, adding that he wrote the Song of Songs as a young man, for only young men think in such imagery. Another school of thought states the opposite, that only young people—particularly teenagers—see the futility of life (and therefore there is such a high suicide rate among this age group), whereas an older man looking back on life would write in the imagery of Song of Songs. Notice that both groups agree that Proverbs could only be written by a middle-aged person.

Age plays a role in one's perception of the world, but so does gender. Solomon wrote: "I find woman more bitter than death; she is all traps, her hands are fetters and her heart is snares. He who is pleasing to God escapes her, and he who is displeasing is caught by her . . . One man in a thousand have I found but one woman among them I have not found" (7:26–28).

A polygynous society seemed to produce a misogynistic king who was bitter about women. Was this the product of having too many wives? Was this the product of a harem system where the king's wives vied for his attention, each concerned over the future of her son? Solomon certainly remembered the actions taken by his mother Bat-Sheva to protect him from the machinations of his half-brother Adoniyahu, who tried to take control of the government before their father David had died. If not for her, it certainly was possible that his half-brother would have killed Solomon to ensure that this rivalry would end.

Yet, a few chapters later, Solomon writes almost the opposite: "Enjoy life with the wife you love all the fleeting days of life that He has granted to you under the sun—all your fleeting days. For that alone is your compensation in life and in your toil which you exert under the sun" (9:9). Perhaps he wrote this in the abstract, dreaming of one particular beloved; or perhaps Solomon actually had one beloved wife, but for political reasons had to marry all his other wives, to keep internal peace and unity as well as peace along the borders of the land of Israel.

This wavering back and forth, and the general feeling of futility, almost caused Kohelet to be left out of the Bible, despite its impassioned survey of mortal pain and pleasure, its noble sadness, and its spiritual illumination. It is the conclusion that legitimized it: "The sum of the matter, when all has been considered: Fear God and observe His commandments! For that is Man's whole duty" (12:13).

Biblical Women

The Captive Woman
August 23, 1991

We find numerous instances in the Torah that show that part of God's plan in adopting Israel as God's people was to raise the Israelites above and beyond the people of the rest of the world. We are to remember God in the seemingly most mundane moments of our lives as well as in the most momentous.

The Torah selection this week includes a section that would seem to be "un-Jewish," and yet fits into this overview of God's plan for raising Israel above the ordinary level of mankind. The Israelites—as the modern Israelis—had to fight battles to defend their borders, and, in some instances, were led to conquer nearby enemies and retain control over their lands. In ancient times—as in modern—during the lust of blood and the heat of battle, men carried their primitive feelings from the killing of men to the raping of women, for rape, too, is an act of power and dominance.

The Torah stepped in and set the ground rules for proper behavior even in a scenario as lust-ridden as the taking of women in war. The warrior here is enjoined not to just take her, but to marry her after an interval of a month. She is not property, but a human being, who is forced to leave her people and her religion and deserves the respect of one month's grief for her past.

The woman, whose good looks attracted the Israelite warrior in the first place, is to cut her nails (Onkelos says that she should grow her nails) and her hair to make herself less attractive. But if the captor still wishes her, he may marry her after that month passes.

The Torah, knowledgeable in the psychology of such marriages, does not stop here, but adds: "and it shall be if you do not delight in her, you shall let her go where she will" (Deut. 21:14). A marriage made on the basis of lust may die when the lust dies. But the husband must then let her go. The text strongly states the law, for he must let her go absolutely free and may not sell her or enslave her because he shamed her by forcing her to marry him.

When one thinks about the level of societies throughout the ancient world and their treatment of women as chattel, the issue of the marriage with a captive of war stands out as unique in its humanitarian elements. In recognizing man's base instincts, the Torah channels them into a controlled marriage forcing the man to view this captive as a human being with feelings and rights. Perhaps in so doing, the Torah prevented many such marriages from taking place. Eventually it became a moot subject, for the Jewish people became captives themselves and not until this century did we form a Jewish army once more. But in the millennia of exile, Jews carried with them these humanitarian ideas of just treatment of the weakest of all, perhaps learned from this case of the captive woman.

Jewish Women in History

Jewish Women of Turkey
October 4, 1991

I am off to Istanbul for a few days to participate in a Turkish-Jewish conference. In researching my paper, I came across many references to two outstanding Jewish women who lived in the Ottoman Empire. I expected that. What I did not expect to find were the references to many ordinary middle-class women, who were part of the commercial world in which so many of the Jews participated.

The most famous woman connected with the Ottoman Empire was Dona Gracia Nasi, a *Converso* of Portuguese birth, who returned to her religion in Italy but sought her final refuge under the sheltering wings of the Turks. Her vast wealth and important international connections enabled her to help her fellow Jews both intellectually and politically. She is the prime example of the proper way a wealthy Jew should behave, not only supporting her fellow Jews through the sharing of her wealth but also putting herself on the line by speaking out to protect her co-religionists both at home and abroad. Dona Gracia was the opposite of the stereotype of the protected and passive Mediterranean Jewish woman.

Another famous Jewish woman of the Ottoman Empire was Esther Kiera (Handali), who rose to power in the mid-sixteenth century through the position of supplying jewelry to the women of the royal harem. The harem women were totally cut off from the outside world, and only through commercial intermediaries—who had to be women—could news and information be passed in both directions.

Esther became the confidant of Safiyeh, favorite wife of Sultan Mehmet III. Through her personal contacts, Esther could and did act to protect her fellow Jews when the occasion arose. At the same time, she was known for her generous support of Jewish scholars. But, unlike Dona Gracia, Esther Kiera interfered in internal Turkish affairs, and her wealth was partly the result of special exemptions from taxes. She, thus, lent herself to accusations of treason on the part of a number of Turkish enemies anxious, among other things, to break the influence of Sultan Mehmet's mother.

Esther Kiera and her eldest son were executed in 1600 in a most barbaric fashion, and the Jews were thus reminded that any rise in influence depended solely on the goodwill of the ruler, who could just as quickly turn the other way.

These two women of political influence were examples of Jewish activity in court in the sixteenth century, the century which saw the peak of Jewish influence in the Ottoman Empire.

What surprised me was to find references to Jewish women who were active in the commercial world of the empire as well. For example, there were women who were moneylenders—not your typical profession for Jews in sixteenth-century Turkey—and who were not widows. Generally speaking, widowhood seemed to have been a prerequisite for a woman's official entry into the world of business. Not so in Istanbul. They made loans at the usual rate of interest, and the loans were to English traders and to the British Levant Company, which is why we have records. We surmise that they were also active in lending to others as well.

The archives are waiting to be culled for information on Jewish women.

Kiddush HaShem

May 3, 1991

"And you shall not profane My holy name, and I will be sanctified among the children of Israel" (Lev. 22:32).

Sanctifying the name of God or *Kiddush HaShem*, in both its positive and negative forms, is learned from this verse, although the text itself refers to the priests who were the appointed guardians of the Sanctuary. Since all women are responsible for all of the negative commandments, this is incumbent on them as well. The highest form of *Kiddush HaShem* is martyrdom, and our history is replete with nameless women who died rather than transgress the three fundamental laws of idolatry, incest, and murder, the only three laws for which a Jew may die.

Once in a while the name of a woman martyr comes into focus, and if we are lucky—from the historical perspective—we can even glean some details about her from the source materials. One such woman is Dulcia, wife of Eleazar ben Judah of Worms, known as the Rokeah. The city of Worms suffered an attack in 1197, and Dulcia as well as her two daughters, Bellette and Hannah, were murdered. The Rokeah composed a dirge (the text of which is in A. M. Haberman's *Sefer Gezerot Ashkenaz ve-Tzarfat*) to his wife, which not only praises her but portrays, as well, a Jewish family of the time.

The dirge paints the portrait of a well-educated woman, so well-educated in Torah that she taught Jewish laws and rituals to the women of Worms, and so well-educated in secular subjects that she kept the account books for her family. She took care of traditional women's activities, such as caring for the house and children, as well as other women's activities, such as sharing in, or taking charge of, family economics. As the wife of the *rosh yeshiva*, she also cared for the needs of his students. Dulcia was pious and exhibited this by constantly attending synagogue, and by stitching parchments together in preparing for the writing of Torah scrolls. The Rokeah added that his wife also sewed dresses for brides and prepared dead women for burial. The dirge is a testimony to the love and high regard he had for his wife.

The dirge about Dulcia in an exceptional piece of historical data that we have from the period of the Crusades; most of our information is based on chronicles and memorial lists. The picture we can draw is dry and impersonal, for aside from the fact that we learn that families chose to die together—a heart rending lesson—we know almost nothing of specific individuals. It is for that reason that the dirge to Dulcia is all the more important. We cannot relate to mass martyrdom, but we can relate to an individual. That is one of the reasons why *The Diary of Anne Frank* is so moving and has made such an impression on the world.

Dulcia fulfilled both the negative and positive sides of *Kiddush HaShem*; she died in the name of God, but only after she had lived a life of exemplary Jewishness.

Jewish Women in History

Gluckel the Working Woman
March 20, 1992

On the last Sunday of February, the Orthodox Union ran a morning symposium on "The Orthodox Working Woman: A Historical and Practical Perspective." My contribution was to the historical part. Obviously, I cannot report on all that I said, for a thirty-minute talk is approximately fifteen typewritten pages.

I will therefore focus on one of the last examples I gave to show that Jewish women have always worked and will elaborate on some of the lessons to be learned from the primary source used, i.e., *The Memoirs of Gluckel of Hameln*. Gluckel lived from 1646 to 1724, and as a result of her insomnia brought on by her beloved husband's untimely death, filled those lonely night hours by writing her memoirs in order to educate her children. Gluckel could not possibly have foreseen how important a document she was leaving for historians, sociologists, and scholars of language and literature.

My search of Gluckel's memoirs this time was for material on her working life. Early in the book she wrote: "I was about twenty-five years old. My blessed husband worked manfully at his business, and, although I was still young, I, too, did my share. Not that I mean to boast, but my husband took advice from no one else, and did nothing without our talking it over together."

Gluckel, thus, had a working relationship with her husband and at an early stage of their marriage, while running a household and an ever-growing brood of children, was developing her knowledge and expertise in his field as a merchant. Her husband's respect for her talents is further underscored later on, when Chayim of Hameln was on his deathbed. One of the leading members of the community asked him if he had any last wishes, meaning that they were ready to deal with his affairs should he so request. Chayim's reply was: "None. My wife knows everything. She shall do as she has always done."

Gluckel thus received formal sanction to carry on the business. She was outstandingly successful in this. What price did she pay with regard to her family relations? It is hard to say. Certainly, her relations with most of her dozen children was positive, so they either did not suffer from her long disappearances to the major trade fairs that Gluckel attended or they were realistic enough to accept it as their way of life.

A word that comes to mind in reading Gluckel's recorded thoughts and reflections on her own behavior as well as that of her children is practicality. Gluckel and our other medieval ancestors of Europe, Spain, and the Middle East, were eminently practical people. They knew from experience that life for women could change overnight either through death, disease, divorce, or abandonment. No woman should be left unskilled, uneducated, and unable to care for herself and her family. This is the reality of today as well, and we should learn Gluckel's lessons well.

Jewish Women in History

The Lady Was a Spy
June 11, 1993

We read in this week's *haftara* about the men sent by Joshua to spy out the land in preparation for conquest by the Israelites. Via prophecy, Joshua knew that the safe haven for them would be in the house of Rahav, the woman of Jericho who hid them and enabled them to escape and bring their vital information back to Joshua.

In a later period we had a similar situation, but this time the woman was the spy. During World War I, a small group of Palestinian Jews set up a clandestine operation transmitting military information about the Ottoman Turks, who at the time controlled Palestine, to the British, who were then in Egypt and were on the side opposing the Turks. The driving force behind the operation was Aaron Aaronsohn, an agronomist of international reputation, who ran an experimental station in Atlit, a coastal village at the tip of the Carmel mountain range.

Aaronsohn himself had to reach the appropriate British officials in order to offer the services of his group as well as to convince the British of the vulnerability of Ottoman controlled Palestine. The organization, named NILI (from the initials of its Hebrew password *Netzach Yisrael Lo Yishaker*—the Eternal One of Israel will not lie), wanted the Turkish rule overthrown and replaced by a British protectorate. Aaronsohn, in an incredibly bold and almost spy-fictionesque manner, managed to reach the proper British authorities in 1916, and convinced them of both the need for NILI's information and the desirability to invade Palestine.

It was Aaron's sister, Sarah Aaronsohn, who directed NILI's effort, along with an associate, Joseph Lishansky. They collected extensive information on Ottoman Turkish military bases and army movements, which was transmitted to a British frigate off the Atlit coast every two weeks at nightfall.

When General Allenby assumed command of the Egyptian Expeditionary Force in the spring of 1917, he asked the NILI spies for particulars on Turkish defenses around Beersheba, the site of his first offensive into Palestine. Sarah and her associate fulfilled the assignment, and the dispatches included vital data on the weather, the location of water sources and malarial swamps, and the precise location of every known route into Beersheba from the Egyptian border. There is no question that this information enabled Allenby to attack to effectively.

Unfortunately, unlike the story of the spies and Joshua, the ending of the NILI espionage ring was a disaster. In September 1917, one of the NILI carrier pigeons was caught by the Turks. Then one of the NILI men was caught trying to reach Egypt. The Turkish police traced the spy network back to Atlit, and some of the ring was arrested. Sarah had been forewarned of the imminent arrests and had ordered NILI members to disperse while she remained at home in Zichron Ya'akov to avoid incriminating rumors. Thus she facilitated the escape of some of her group. Sarah Aaronsohn turned herself in to spare her father, who had been arrested, further beatings. She was tortured to divulge her information, but disclosed nothing. On the third (or fourth) day, she managed to grab a revolver from a drawer and shot herself. She died a few days later.

Although only a tiny group of Palestinian Jews knew of NILI, it was only the imminent conquest of Palestine by the British that saved the Jews there from a fate similar to that of the Armenians.

Jewish Women in History

The First Woman Publisher

June 25, 1993

In 1933, A. M. Haberman printed a twenty-eight-page booklet entitled "Jewish Women as Printers, Publishers, and Supporters of Writers" (in Hebrew). He listed fifty-two such women, starting chronologically with the beginning of Hebrew printing during the Renaissance, and ending in the early twentieth century. He even included seven Christian women who ran Hebrew publishing houses.

In leafing through the booklet, I came across some names that I recognized, but most names I had never seen before. Was there a common denominator for all these women? Most were either daughters of printers or married to printers. A large proportion of them only became printers at the onset of widowhood, and are known as "The widow so-and-so." In other words, the old apprenticeship system played a large role in educating these women in the art of printing. I can see this apprenticeship system at work in my own home as I watch my eleven-year-old and my eight-year-old daughters handset both Hebrew and English type as my printer-husband supervises their meticulous work.

Daughters of printers seemed to marry men whose craft either was printing or became printing, or they married scholars who may have needed the books that their wives were printing. Haberman does not spell these things out clearly.

Women printers and publishers were to be found in all the main centers of printing, from Istanbul to northern Italy, to Austria-Hungary, to Eastern Europe. One that caught my eye was Reyna, daughter of Dona Gracia Nasi and wife of Don Joseph Nasi, known too as the Duke of Naxos. The two overwhelmingly important (aunt and nephew) *Conversos* usually were the center of attention, and few pay heed to Reyna, whose possible marriage to an Iberian nobleman first provoked the flight of this family from Portugal to the Lowlands to Italy to the Ottoman Empire.

Upon the death of Don Joseph Nasi, according to Haberman, the sultan of Turkey took back all his wealth and left his widow only the value of her marriage contract, some 90,000 dinars. With this money she set up a Hebrew printing house in 1592 in her home in Belvedere, near Istanbul, to be directed by Joseph b. Isaac Ashkeloni. It operated for two years, then for unknown reasons, was moved to another place on the European side of the Bosphorus, where it functioned from 1597 to 1599.

It is unknown whether more books were printed and were lost over the centuries. It is unknown why she chose to focus all her attention on the printing of Hebrew books. Certainly, her mother served as a fine example as a patron of Hebrew printing, for Dona Gracia had donated large sums of money for this purpose. Don Joseph Nasi had also been a patron of Hebrew printing. But both of these individuals had many other things to occupy them. All we know of Reyna (other than the bare outline of her life) is connected to her publishing house, and it is interesting to contemplate that this may have been her true love all along. In her independent position as a wealthy widow, she was finally able to express this love of printing, and it is not difficult to imagine her standing alongside her chief printer discussing the layout of a page, the ornamentation of a title page, and the choice of what to print in the first place, breathing in the pungent odors of ink and oil, and glowing over the creative feeling that only the completed book, leather bound, gold-lettered, can bring. She earned her place in history as the first woman publisher.

Jewish Women in History

Ugav Rahel
September 4, 1993

The first time that I came across the name of Rahel Morpurgo was while reading Cecil Roth's "The History of the Jews of Italy." It was only one intriguing sentence: "The tradition of Italian poetry was maintained not only by Luzzatto but also by . . . Rachel Morpurgo of Trieste, heiress to the literary tradition of Deborah Ascarelli, and Sarah Coppio Sullam two centuries before, whose verses attained perhaps a higher poetical level than his own." That was all that Roth wrote. I put her name on my mental list of "women to be looked into," and gradually began to fill in more information.

Born into the famous Luzzatto family in 1790, in the city of Trieste, which was home to Italian and Austrian Jews, Rahel was obviously provided with a wide-ranging Hebrew and Jewish education. Her family was famous for its scholarship, and she studied Torah with commentaries, Hebrew, Aramaic, Talmud, as well as secular subjects at home. Home education via private tutors was typical for the wealthier Italian Jews at the time, and we have numerous examples of girls who received quality Jewish education in this way.

Like Samuel David Luzzatto, her famous cousin and friend, Rahel became interested in the revival of Hebrew poetry in Italy. The earliest poem that we have of her was composed when she was about eighteen. Her cousin forwarded her poems for publication by Mendel Stern in the periodical *Kochavei Yitzhak* in Vienna. Her poems became very popular, and Rahel became famous among the circle of Hebrew readers.

Most of her poems have strong religious and mystical feeling, and many describe autobiographical or family incidents, but many also deal with Jewish historic values and traditions. Her poems vary in form, length, rhythm, and merit, but all display remarkable ingenuity and a mastery of the Hebrew language.

At the age of twenty-nine, Rahel finally overcame her family's resistance to her marrying Jacob Morpurgo, a merchant of Austrian-Jewish descent. (Upper-class Italian Jews were very resistant to inter-communal marriages.) They had four children, and Rahel attended to her household duties while continuing to write and publish her poetry. She met and corresponded with many Jewish scholars throughout her long life, and even traveled to Palestine with the Montefiores, thus fulfilling a life-long dream. She died in 1871 at the age of eighty-one.

One hundred year after her birth, Prof. Vittorio (Hayim Isaac) Castiglioni of Trieste collected as many of Rahel Morpurgo's poems and letters as he could find, and published them in a volume entitled *Ugav Rahel* (translated as "Rachel's Harp" or "Rachel's Guitar"). This activity is blessed by the overly effusive Sabato Morais in his "Italian Hebrew Literature" (1926): "All honor to Victor Castiglioni of Trieste, and may the name of the Italian Jewess, whose brilliant talents and mental activity he so becomingly illustrated, be sweetly embalmed in the memory of the lovers of Judaism and its great literature."

Jewish Women in History

Stereotypes and Jewish Women
Part 1

October 15, 1993

I never thought that I would hear it, but I did. I was buying some small items for my children, and, as I was about to pay, I jokingly asked the storekeeper if he gave discounts. He responded: "Are you trying to Jew me down?" I stood there open-mouthed both at the expression and at the fact that it came from the mouth of a heavily accented Korean-American. Since there was no one behind me waiting to pay, I quickly explained to him the pejorative stereotype involved in the expression and how insulting it was. He understood and apologized profusely, promising to make sure that no one else would use it around him.

So, the negative stereotype of the Jew, now that it has entered into linguistic usage, is alive and well. There are other stereotypes of Jews that are just as destructive that are geared exclusively at Jewish women. The two outstanding ones that have entered into American daily language are "The Jewish Mother" and the "Jewish American Princess."

How did these stereotypes come about? Why are they specifically female? Why are they specifically Jewish? How much truth is there in these stereotypes? How widespread is the use of the terms? Who is responsible for perpetuating the terms?

In tracing the historical roots of the stereotypes, one has to step back into the world of American Jewish history. The images are not based on the first sizeable Jewish immigration, that of the German Jews, who arrived between 1820 and 1880. Although large in number compared to the groups that predated it, German Jews came nowhere near the numbers that began arriving in the wake of the 1881 pogroms in Eastern Europe. These pogroms, and the May Laws of 1882, triggered one of the most massive demographic changes in Jewish history, for by 1914, almost two million Jews had left Eastern Europe, most heading for the "Golden Land."

These Eastern European Jews included women, whether they came at the same time as their men, or a few years later. These women were strong, both physically and psychologically. They carried with them the characteristics of survival that had evolved over the centuries.

They were either economic contributors to the family or the main economic support, as their husbands sat in the yeshiva and studied. They bought from the peasants and then sold small farm goods in the town. Or they had a shop, which was, in fact, the size of a closet with a shutter covering the front when not in use, and the woman sat in front and reached in to find whatever goods the customer wanted. Or they had moveable stands brought to market by human power or pulled by a horse. Or they sewed piecework.

These women were also informal educators of Judaism, especially about the Jewish kitchen. The recipes were by-products of the intricate lore of *kashrut* and holiday customs and Shabbat laws. The storytelling that accompanied women's work also supplemented the girls' Jewish knowledge as the two or three generations worked together at the endless tasks of homemaking.

Of course, these women were also wives and mothers.

When all of these roles came over to America in the figure of the Jewish woman, we got our first literary stereotype, but it was a positive one, namely, the "Yiddishe Mama."

Stereotypes and Jewish Women
Part 2

October 29, 1993

The "Yiddishe Mama" was a positive stereotype. She seemed able to do everything: wash, clean, cook, bake, mind the children, sew piecework on her machine, give good advice to all. She created extra space in the cold water flat for a "boarder" in order to make some extra money. She did this by putting up curtains to partition off a corner of the living room. She sold goods from a pushcart, or soon became the "Mom" in a "Mom-and-Pop" establishment. She is depicted as all of this through the rosy-tinted glasses of memory as written in the short stories of a later generation.

Yet, by the time we get to the 1940s, this positive image begins to fade. The literature begins to depict this woman as a figure to deride. She is no longer shown at work, for the Jews are becoming Americanized and this included accepting American ideals, which included a non-working wife. So if the Jewish woman drops by her husband's business, she is quickly made to feel—in the short stories—that she should go home where she belongs. She has lost her economic role.

We soon see that she has lost her educational role, for America is the land of the free and mandatory public school. For the first time in Jewish history the children become the teachers of the parents and the older generation is told to shape up and not act like old-fashioned "greenhorns." The Jewish community and the *Kehilla* structure is not recreated in America, and most Jews thus move into the world of free, secular education.

The Jewish woman is left with the dual roles of wife and mother. Since her husband is up at daybreak and returns at night exhausted, the Jewish woman's energies, inherited from generations of aggressive survivalist women, is focused on the one role remaining open to her, i.e., her children. The full-blown stereotype thus emerges in the 1960s and 1970s as "The Jewish Mother" epitomized by Philip Roth in *Portnoy's Complaint*.

Portnoy's mother is the source of all of his problems. Her overbearing smothering has destroyed him. She manipulates the ultimate weapon to ensure that she is obeyed: guilt.

How accurate is the stereotype? All stereotypes have a basis in some truth. Jewish mothers do pressure their children to perform for them. A positive result of this is the ability of their children to withstand peer pressure, which, as we know, can be the source of many types of negative behavior patterns. As for manipulation through guilt, there have been entire treatises written on who does this and why. Suffice it to say that most scholars conclude that this is a weapon of the powerless, not the powerful.

Third-generation (American) male writers deride second-generation women and refuse to accept that their problems are partly their own fault. This, in a nutshell, is part of the origins of "The Jewish Mother" as a negative stereotype, which by now—through men like Woody Allen—has reached the broad audience of Gentile America.

A Modern Zealot
1997 [rejected by the press]

A recent topic of discussion at the summer camp where I spend the most of July is that of the zealot. The catalyst for this topic was Pinchas, grandson of Aaron, and Eliyahu the prophet. They were both "jealous of God" (as most translations read), and both killed the enemies of God with their own hands. Our later image of Eliyahu as an old man in a long robe, with a white beard, visiting the Jews, and doing wondrous deeds is the Eliyahu of legend, not the historical Eliyahu who with burning zealotry slashed Baal-worshippers to death.

The discussion dealt with what makes a zealot, and single-mindedness was one of the characteristics that most agreed on. Single-mindedness can lead to tunnel vision in the sense of not seeing anything on the periphery of the focus of your attention.

This led to a further discussion, in my classes on Zionism, as to whether zealotry could be applied to the *chalutzim*, the pioneers who went to Israel from 1882 to 1948. We discussed some of the outstanding people of the Second Aliya in particular, and I found material on one specific woman who is now finally receiving the attention that she deserves. I refer to Manya Shochat, a figure of extreme complexity. "She was incredibly tough and unbelievably charitable; sentimental and fearless; a fanatic Zionist and a fanatic socialist, a co-founder of *Ha-Shomer* (an armed organization of settlers whose motto was: 'In blood and fire Judea fell; in blood and fire she shall rise again?'), and at the same time a leading member of the left-wing anti-nationalist League for Arab-Jewish Understanding" (Amon Elon, *The Israelis: Founders and Sons*, 185). Manya Shochat was among the group of Zionists that believed firmly that by raising Arab standards of living, the Arabs would acquiesce to a Jewish state.

Before her arrival in Palestine in 1904, she had been involved in Russian revolutionary circles and was a gunrunner. At the age of twenty, she had shot a Czarist spy, dismembered his corpse, placed the pieces in a suitcase, and sent it off by railroad to the depths of Siberia to a nonexistent address. Her family, to get her out of Russia, sent her to Palestine to visit a fictitious sick brother. Although upset at the ruse, Manya was induced to remain in Palestine, where she began to play a prominent role in early Yishuv society. As the years passed, she became a central figure in Histadrut (Jewish Federation of Labor) and a leader of the Kibbutz movement. She was one of the Founding Mothers of the Yishuv.

Her zealous single-mindedness is portrayed in an almost apocryphal story that took place in 1948, when she was captured by the Arabs and taken to military headquarters. "There she stood, unknown to her captors, an old lady of sixty-nine, of small stature, dressed in a long black Russian style *sarafan* dress, a short-cut bob, with blazing eyes and chin thrust forward, facing a fierce looking Arab guerrilla in a time of total war" (Elon, 185). The Arab said he was going to kill her. "Kill me? But why?" she asked in innocence.

"We kill Jews" was the logical reply.

"You won't kill me," she retorted.

"Why not?" asked the surprised Arab.

"Because I haven't done anything to you." This was reasonable to her—unafraid, strong in her ignorance, this story echoes her entire generation. In the end the Arabs let Manya Shochet walk back to the Jewish lines, with the message: "Go and tell the Jews how strong we are, and that they are lost."

They were wrong. It is the enemies of the zealots who are lost.

Jewish Women in History

The Realities of Widowhood
July 19, 1996

In the Torah portion of *Matot*, the first legal issue dealt with is that of vows. In ancient times women living in their father's houses could have their vows annulled by the patriarch of the household if he so chose, and a married woman could have her vows annulled by her husband should he so choose. The only exceptions to the annulment of vows are those of the widow and the divorcee (Num. 30:10).

Early widowhood was a reality of life in ancient times, medieval times, and early modern times, until the advent of the miracles of modern medicine. Family and community usually worked to get the young and middle-aged widow a new husband, especially if there were young children involved. The poorer the widow, the more powerless the woman, and the Torah reminds us of this by repeating a number of times the injunction of protecting such a woman.

Most Jews in ancient times lived in extended families. This carried over into the lives of Middle Eastern Jews until modernization and Westernization brought new life styles and modern cities. Families shared a kind of compound facing a courtyard, with small apartments for each son and his wife and children. The patriarch and his wife, or the widowed matriarch, had the biggest and airiest rooms, with the least productive son and his family inhabiting the least attractive living quarters. Should a woman be widowed young, this extended family acted to find her a new husband either through their own contacts or through professional matchmakers.

In Europe, on the other hand, the families tended to be smaller, but the intensely intimate communities acted as a surrogate extended family, helping their members in times of trouble. When wasn't there a time of trouble? Death and danger lurked everywhere. Few women went out alone, and in some Middle Eastern communities women did not even do the produce marketing, leaving it to their men to go and pick out fruit, vegetables, rice, beans, and oil. If Jewish women did go out, in many places they veiled themselves like the Muslim women, for self-protection.

In medieval Europe, you never knew when a pogrom could break out. Your husband went out to trade or even to the local market to shop or sell and could end up being brought back dead because some local Gentile was on a drunken, anti-Jewish binge.

On the other hand, the widow with means was one of the only independent women in the Jewish community. Her property was her own, her business was run by her, she could go where she wanted when she wanted, and the Torah reaffirms this by pointing out that as a fully responsible person, her vows were her own as well. Therefore, it is understandable that if she already had children and could live without the intimate company of a man, she opted not to remarry.

Family and community pressured widows, and most gave in, but we have evidence that a group of them did not. Some of this group worked for the benefit of the Jewish people through their generous charity to schools, yeshivot, the copying of books and Torah scrolls, the printing of books, the establishment of soup kitchens, and helping poor brides. Their names were thus recorded in community records and were made available, eventually, to the historian to learn whatever could be learned about the realities of Jewish widowhood.

Jewish Women in History

Anna of Rome
November 5, 1999

One of the frustrating elements involved in teaching women's history is finding primary sources. Most of what we find only indirectly reflects on women's lives. But once in a while, there is a real gem of a primary source, one that fires the imagination.

It is known, for instance, that during the Renaissance, Italian Jewish women, like their men, were engaged in all sorts of trades and professions. In the Sforza archive collection in Milan, a letter to Catherine (1465–1509) was discovered, written by a woman who signed her name "Anna the Hebrew," dated 1508.

We know nothing of Anna, but we know much about Catherine Sforza, who as Lady of Forli (a city near Ancona, in central Italy) had convinced her anti-Jewish officials that it was economically beneficial to invite a rich Jew to come from Bologna and serve as a loan-banker for local citizens. She was known to have been a very beautiful woman, but by 1508 was forty-five years old and had been married since age fourteen, had borne eight children, and had buried three husbands. She had survived a lifetime of plotting and conspiracies. Yet she was vain enough to want to maintain her fair complexion.

Of Anna we only have this letter, the contents of which are mainly business. She describes how to put on the creams:

To begin with, I gave him (her messenger) a black salve which removes roughness of the face, and makes the flesh supple and smooth. Put this salve on at night, and allow it to remain on till the morning. Then wash yourself with pure river water; next bathe your face in the lotion that is called Acqua de Canicare; then put on a dab of this white cream; and then take less than a chickpea grain of this powder, dissolve it in the lotion called Acqua Dolce, and put it on your face, the thinner the better.

She then lists the prices of each salve and cream, the total of which was more than an average person earned in a year.

Her postscript is interesting within the context of Catherine's' life: "The black salve is bitter. If it should happen to go into the mouth you may be assured that it is nothing dangerous; the bitterness comes from the aloes in it." In other words she is reassuring Catherine, mistress of poisons, that the bitter taste was from the aloes and not from anything else.

Yet we can also read some things about Anna between the lines. For example, she addresses Catherine as "my most honored patroness." Anna did not search out Catherine, but it was the other way around. It is to be surmised, then, that within the small circles of royalty and aristocracy, cosmetics producers such as Anna the Hebrew were discussed along with designers of gowns, producers of rich fabrics, and creators of jewelry and art. Catherine had sent a messenger to Rome to buy the facial creams. Rome was the largest center of Jewish settlement in Italy at the time. He probably found her easily enough by going to the Jewish neighborhoods (the ghetto of Rome had not yet been created). Considering the prices that Anna charged, we can also surmise that she lived well, in one of the better Jewish neighborhoods.

Where had she learned her craft? That is an intriguing question. Perhaps this can be connected with one of the long-time Jewish professions in Italy, namely, the production of pharmaceuticals, the knowledge of which was passed from one generation to the next within the family. Women were included in this passing of knowledge, and most small pharmaceutical establishments were family businesses. Anna may have been creative enough as well as canny enough to realize that there was a market for cosmetics especially among the very wealthy. She also must have had a break in attracting her first wealthy client, who then spread the word. But alas, we know nothing more of her other than what our imaginations can create.

Women and Synagogue Worship
June 19, 2009

In a recent interview with Rabbi Jonathan Sachs by a reporter for the *Jewish Press* (June 5, 2009) on the topic of his new translation/edition of the *siddur*, one of the comments dealt with women and synagogue. The rabbi is quoted as saying, "Way back in history, women didn't come to shul. The Altneu Shul in Prague, for example, was built without a women's gallery." I would like to disagree with the honorable rabbi, and try to set the historical record straight.

Women have participated in synagogue worship since the beginning of the existence of synagogues. One of the best scholarly works on this topic is *Daughters of the King: Women and the Synagogue*, edited by Susan Grossman and Rivka Haut (Jewish Publication Society of America, Philadelphia, 1992). In it, Hannah Safrai has an excellent chapter on "Women and the Ancient Synagogue," Emily Taitz has a chapter on "Women's Voices, Women's Prayers: the European Synagogues of the Middle Ages," Shulamith Z. Berger has one on "Tehines: A Brief Survey of Women's Prayers," and I have one on "Women and Synagogue in Medieval Cairo."

These chapters give detailed research on women and synagogue worship. There were very few countries in the Diaspora in which women did not go to the synagogue at least once a week; they certainly went on the holidays. A superb primary source attesting to this in Germany is Gluckel of Hameln's *Memoirs*, 1691. She gives details of such attendance, pointing out women who went every day, as well as describing a terrifying moment when women almost got trampled in a rush to exit the synagogue building. She even describes how men would cross through the women's section to get to their own section.

There were also the educated *firzogerin* (*zogerkes*) of Eastern Europe who sat near the *mechitza* both to translate the service into Yiddish, as well as to inform the women what the men were up to.

As for the lack of a gallery in the Altneu Shul in Prague, not all synagogues were built with galleries. Women often prayed in the back or along the side of the men's section, separated by a *mechitza*. In some very poor communities in the Middle East, where many women were illiterate, the women sat outside the room in which the men prayed, answering amen at the proper moments. But they did attend synagogue and they worshiped in their own way.

The only group to discourage women from going to the synagogue was the newly formed Hasidic movement. In that case it was the development of the custom of men and boys going to spend Shabbat at the rebbe's *shul*, often in a distant town; the women and girls were left behind. But this was the exception to the rule, for the rule was for women to go to synagogue.

Women were always part of worship. The Torah describes their contributions to the beautifying of the Tabernacle, and the Prophets describe how women went to the Tabernacle and later to the Temple on the three pilgrimage festivals of Pesach, Shavuot and Sukkot, even though it was not required of them. Just reading the story of Chana attests to this.

So, while it is admirable that Rabbi Sachs has worked on an inspiring and melodious translations of the *siddur*, I would like to set the record straight about women and the synagogue.

Second Thoughts on Rahav
July 3, 2009

I must have been in high school when I read the commentaries that defined *zonah* in connection with Rahav of Jericho as "innkeeper." I laughed to myself, looking on this as one more example of scholarly apologetics. But then, years later, immersed in my studies on Middle Eastern history, I had second thoughts.

First of all, linguistically, there are numerous examples in the Bible of words that had multiple meanings. For example, *ainayim* can mean eyes, but it can also mean facets of a dressed stone, hewn to reflect light. Jastrow's classic Hebrew dictionary defines *zonah* as prostitute, but it also means *enabler* in the sense of food.

From the linguistic issue, we move on to the historical material of the period of Joshua. People lived in walled cities for protection, and these cities were economic hubs, the destination of local as well as national and international trade. Conquerors decimated walled cities, but that was only a temporary phase, as the people regrouped and rebuilt. Jericho was one such city. Who lived where in these ancient Canaanite cities depended on their importance. The poorest and those at the bottom rungs of society lived in hovels. The middle and upper classes inhabited the houses built into the walls. A middle-class person would own an inn which had access to its own rooftop; a lower-class prostitute would not.

Another clue that Rahav was not a prostitute is that she lived with her family—her parents and her siblings were on the list of people she gave to the Israelite spies in her request that they be saved from the destruction of the city. Prostitutes—except for a temple prostitute, known as a *kedeisha*, not as a *zonah*—were outside society, living in a special area.

Therefore it stands to reason that the two Israelite spies went to Rahav's house because it was a normal place for travelers to go on their way through Canaan, and the spies were certainly trying to act normally.

That brings us to the question of why she chose to help the spies. One response is that Rahav is representative of Middle Eastern cultural values, namely, that anyone who is your guest gains your protection.

This relationship is comprised of one person serving food and the second person eating it. This cultural value is still alive and well throughout the Middle East today. How and why this became a value is discussed in many anthropological studies.

A final note on Rahav: many commentators and legends tell us that she converted to Judaism. There is nothing in the text to verify this, but the fact that there was this kind of conjecture, raises the question of, "Could she have converted, and if so, why?" We can superimpose what we know of the Islamic conquest many centuries later, and how many people willingly converted and even helped the conquest move forward by serving as Fifth Columns for the Muslim army. Rahav, just like everyone else in Canaan, was not only aware of the Israelite army's approach, but was also probably aware of some of the teachings of the new religion. This was a result of interactions over the years with travelers who reported on what they had seen and learned. Monotheism itself may have been a difficult leap to take, but the ethics and morals of the new religion might have been attractive to a Canaanite woman who lived in a city where firstborn babies were killed and buried under the doorpost of a new couple to ensure luck and fertility. Down the road there were cities in which older children were sacrificed to gods. Poverty-stricken families sold sons and daughters into permanent slavery. The cruelty of Canaanite paganism was contrasted to Judaism, and, possibly for Rahav, helped her decide. And so she entered Jewish legend, not only as a convert, but also as a wife of Joshua, and an ancestor of leading personalities in Israel.

Holocaust Studies

The Holocaust Museum
February 3, 1992

We just returned from a trip to Washington, DC. We did the usual tourist trek: the Capitol, the Air and Space Museum, the various monuments, the White House. As Jews, we were all overwhelmed by the Holocaust Museum. Kaleidoscopic images flash through my mind and I try to sort them out as well as examine my reactions to them. The top floor—the most historical—is the easiest to deal with on an emotional level, but is overwhelming in terms of pure information. The display on book burning is powerful: the maps showing the spread of Nazi power are ingeniously done; the material on the destruction of the mentally and physically impaired is heart-wrenching.

On the floor below, one enters a more emotional realm—walking through a cattle car; an ingenious way of dealing with the killing buildings, undressing, "gas showers," crematoria—all in miniature, stark white forms (some find this too depersonalizing); a pile of shoes with a Yiddish poem describing them; actual ovens; and work camp buildings.

My children (ages ten and twelve) were becoming agitated and wanted to leave, so we quickly went past many of the displays. Yet they went through the children's exhibit on "Daniel's Story" twice, recording their own impressions after the second trip. For me, this proved the value of such a display, and it also proved that the Holocaust can be taught to children if done properly.

We were all affected in many ways by the museum, and part of this was because of the large numbers of Gentiles visiting it. We could see how affected they all were. We were also impressed that they felt that this was one of the "musts" on a trip to Washington.

My daughters chose to wear buttons reading "Remember the Children" on their jackets as we left. As we stood in line about an hour later in front of the Washington Memorial, we found ourselves in the company of dozens of young people carrying anti-abortion posters. They had come for the annual anti-abortion rally on the anniversary of the *Roe vs. Wade* decision. They looked at my girls' buttons and looked again. They couldn't decide which side we were on or whether we were on any side, and so, diplomatically, discussed other things with us. I had a good laugh privately.

It took my younger daughter many hours to return to her usual happy self. She will draw or paint her feelings when we come home and come to terms with them that way. My older daughter's method of dealing with her emotions is verbal: she asked hundreds of questions about what she had seen in the museum, including "How could they smile for the camera?" about the photographs of the ghettos. "Why did the Nazis photograph all those things?" "Why did they keep all those shoes?" "Why did they shave their heads?" "Why were there so few uprisings?" "How do the survivors deal with memories?" "Were the Nazis punished?

On the long car ride home, I could hear the two of them discussing their visit. They both put the visit to the White House at the top of the "fun" things (although they would have loved to have seen Socks—the Clintons' cat). After a silence, however, they both agreed that they would never forget the Holocaust Museum, ever.

Holocaust Studies

Fifty Years Later
April 28, 1995

As *Yom Ha-Sho'ah* approaches, combined with the round number fifty—fifty years since the end of World War II—special commemorations are being planned and held around the world. Many commemorations are military ones—the fall of Berlin, of Rome, of Iwo Jima; many are seen as Jewish ones—the liberation of Auschwitz, Birkenau, Dachau, San Sabba. Survivors of all sorts are traveling back in time, mentally as well as physically returning to sites of battle and trauma. They are paying tribute to those who died, and reconfirming their own existence and survival, which also attest to the failure of the enemy to achieve its goals of conquest and/or annihilation.

As a student of Jewish history, I always had difficulty with the major tragedies of the destruction of the Temples, the fall of Bar Kochba's army; the Crusaders rampaging through Europe; the relatively "minor" expulsions from England, France, parts of Germany; the massive expulsions from Iberia; the Chmielnicki massacres; the almost yearly pogroms and attacks on the ghettos/mellahs/Juderias. My difficulty lay partly with in the incomprehension of how, on turning to the next page of my history book, the following paragraph usually described the next place to which the Jews moved and rebuilt their lives. What I have witnessed as a post-Holocaust person is this historical phenomenon of rebuilding.

We all know survivors of the camps or the flights away from the Nazis or those who hid in the woods or with Gentile neighbors or in Catholic institutions. They live among us and, depending on their personalities, either share their experiences or never speak of them at all.

The first survivor of the death camps whom I met was my piano teacher. The first time that I saw her tattooed number is etched in my memory. In Poland she had been a concert pianist, but "Hitler destroyed my fingers in Auschwitz" was all she ever said about her experiences. So she did what she could to earn a living, and only at her yearly concerts did I catch a glimpse of the young artist all dressed up for the performance.

I know more than a dozen people who, as children, were hidden for months or years on farms, in haystacks, in monasteries, in the mountains. The one that made the biggest impression on me was the first "hidden child" I met. He was one of my father's students at Yeshiva University—tall, handsome, dark, brilliant, kind. I was in grade school and he was in college, and I had my first major "crush" on him. It took a while for his story to come out, how he, alone of his family, survived; how he had been in a Catholic institution and had become one of the star pupils there; how he had been "found" by a Jewish organization after the war and brought to America, and his rediscovery of his Judaism. My father loved him, and he became a Shabbat fixture in our home. Then he went off to medical school, and periodically he would write to my father. I would overhear my parents discussing him—in Yiddish so that I supposedly would not understand—and how they worried that he was unmarried and so far away from a strong Jewish community. I was secretly hoping he would wait for me to grow up. Then came the day that I walked in from school to find my father crying at this desk—a letter had arrived after months of silence, telling my father that he had given up: he had given up his attempts to be Jewish and "different"; he had moved toward merging with the larger group; he was marrying a Gentile woman; he would never forget my father but his spiritual and psychological pain was too great to bear. We never heard from him again. In some cases Hitler did succeed.

There are studies now being done on these "hidden children," and, while many may find the results objectively interesting, I become subjectively involved in each case. That is one of the reason why I personally do not deal with Holocaust studies, except where they fit into my larger topics of Jewish history.

What we have witnessed over the past fifty years is Jewish history at the end of its most calamitous stage and, possibly, at its most constructive stage. We are witnessing the re-rooting of the Jewish people. We are seeing, via the individual stories of each and every survivor—who has married and had children, who has set up a new career or profession or business, who has worked to educate or nurse or comfort his or her people, who has normalized his or her life—a reaffirmation of the Jewish people and a reconnection with the past, plus a forging of a new link in the long chain of Jewish history, thus linking the present to both the past and the future.

Holocaust Studies

The Annual Conference
January 11, 2002

Every third week of December, the Association for Jewish Studies holds its annual conference. Scholars, graduate students, and the interested public gather for three intensive days of lectures and discussions that start at 8:30 a.m. and continue through dinner and beyond. This year's conference was held in Washington, DC, and covered Judaic Studies from every possible discipline and angle. There were sessions on Jews in film, Jews in caricatures, Jewish history from every part of the world and every century. There were sessions in Bible, Hebrew literature, Ladino poetry, American Jews in small towns, assimilation, acculturation.

I heard papers on mysticism, on Hasidism, on rereading Talmudic passages, and on the frontiers of northern Spain. One session in its entirety was devoted to the realities of the wine business—both Jewish and Gentile—in the Rhineland during the Middle Ages. We heard about storage, viticulture, climate, soil, river traffic, as well as small Jewish communities, *yayin nesekh* (libations), loans, and sureties. One paper showed how the new charitable organizations founded at the turn of the twentieth century in Bialistok were centers of power rivalry. One paper addressed how medieval Jewish travelers from the West had their own agendas in describing in detail the Davidic line in the Middle East.

Then there is all of the socializing, job hunting, and networking, along with the attempts to brainstorm and come up with new ideas for next year. Of course, one of the problems of coming up with new ideas is that the one who proposed them gets stuck with the job of organizing the panel and even writing a paper for it.

This year's guest of honor at the banquet was Prof. Debora Lipstadt of Emory University, a specialist in Holocaust studies. She described in detail her five-year lawsuit with David Irving, the British Holocaust denier. She detailed the legal aspects of the lawsuit (he sued her for libel), the scholarly aspects, and the personal ones. We were riveted in our seats as she described her reactions to the man himself as a manifestation of evil, who twisted the historical record to make it seem as though Hitler never wanted the destruction of the Jews. The most difficult thing for Prof. Lipstadt was to follow her British lawyers' directive not to say a thing. Irving kept baiting her on both a professional and personal level, but, as exuberant and contentious as she is, Prof. Lipstadt actually managed to keep silent.

The lawyers had to go through a mountain of material in order to prove that not only had Irving warped history, but that he had a pro-Hitler agenda behind his denial of the Holocaust. It took five years of litigation and millions of dollars in fees, but Lipstadt won.

Part of the payoff for her has been the inundation of letters and e-mails from around the world, from Holocaust survivors in particular. They had felt that Irving had been making them go through suffering a second time. One of them called her the modern-day Deborah who had fought for the Jewish people and won, just like the Biblical Deborah.

Prof. Lipstadt left the podium to thunderous applause. Irving had picked on the wrong woman when he thought that she would fold. If anything, she said that the experience has made her even stronger in her determination to fight the David Irvings of the world.

Holocaust Studies

A Busy Week
May 26, 2006

During this past week, the Department of Judaic Studies was actively involved not only with college classes, but also with intellectual activities of a different sort. The family of Frances Haidt, who graduated from Brooklyn College in 1944, set up an annual lecture on the campus in her memory. She was born in 1923, the daughter of Russian-Jewish immigrants. She went through the New York City public school system, graduated from Hunter College High School, and then attended Brooklyn College, majoring in political science. She served in the US Department of State during World War II, and then went on to become of the first women to be hired as a securities analyst by a Wall Street investment bank. She was always interested in Judaic Studies, and despite her busy schedule, devoted her Sundays to teaching Hebrew school. Her family felt that a lecture series in the Department of Judaic Studies honored her love of the subject and her commitment to teaching.

Prof. Lawrence H. Schiffman, chair of NYU's Department of Hebrew and Judaic Studies, delivered the first lecture. His topic was "The Dead Sea Scrolls: Artifacts of Ancient and Modern Culture." The spin that was given on the topic of the Dead Sea Scrolls was that of how it fits into modern culture, and Prof. Schiffman masterfully led the listeners through the background of the history of the scrolls before turning to this point.

The scrolls originally went to the Christian scholars, who had their own agenda and ended up trying to "Christianize" them. The Israelis, meanwhile, led in particular by Yigael Yadin, were trying to connect the scrolls to the Jewish past while using them for the new State of Israel. Once Israel recovered all of the scrolls, there still was a delay in publishing them. It awaited a new generation of Christian scholars to realize that their importance lay in the information provided on early Judaism and that these were totally Jewish texts.

The second intellectual forum was held in the Museum of Jewish Heritage and was a roundtable discussion on the origins of Holocaust studies and how things have changed (if they did) over the decades. The first group, all from CUNY, were among the founders of Holocaust studies and included Prof. Randolph Braham, who specializes in Hungarian Jews; Prof. Henry Feingold, who specializes in American Jewry and the Holocaust, Prof. Yaffa Eliach, who specializes in literature, films and memoirs of the Holocaust; and Prof. Henry Friedlander, who specializes in euthanasia, the war trials, and the concentration camps. One of Prof. Friedlander's main points was that the topic had to be addressed using the same tools as any other serious history; conclusions had to be based on intellect and not on emotions.

From my perspective, what seems to be happening to the topic of the Holocaust is that it is being folded into all other course that deal with the twentieth century. It is taught as part of a course on modern Israel, modern America, twentieth-century world history, and modern literature. It will continue to stand alone probably only in departments of Judaic Studies, and, from time to time, there may be a special topics course of an aspect of the Holocaust. The only other change that most scholars agree on is that since the word "Holocaust" is being hijacked by other groups—similar to the word "ghetto"—most writers are using the Hebrew word *Shoah* for what happened specifically to the Jews.

Holocaust Studies

Kristallnacht Seventy Years Later
December 5, 2008

There were memorials held in many parts of the world marking the seventieth anniversary of the "Shattering of the Glass" or *Kristallnacht*, which according to historians, marked the beginning of what came to be known as the Holocaust. The president of Germany gave a speech in a large synagogue in Germany, in a recreated community. The Pope spoke about it. The government of Israel held a commemoration in Yad Vashem. Jewish communities everywhere invited speakers to address a variety of topics connected to the Holocaust.

My synagogue, Mt. Sinai Jewish Center, has been marking *Kristallnacht* for twenty-seven years. Washington Heights, as is well known, contains a sizable group of survivors from both Austria and Germany, as well as from other European countries, although the number is gradually shrinking through natural causes.

The program began with the chanting of a chapter from Psalms, moved to the lighting of six candles by six survivors, and then Rabbi Mordechai Schnaidman spoke briefly, putting the commemoration into the larger historical context.

The guest speaker was Prof. Robert M. Shapiro, associate professor of the Department of Judaic Studies at Brooklyn College. He addressed the topic of "Why Didn't the Press Shout?" based on the book that he edited by the same name. Obviously, Prof. Shapiro could not cover all aspects of this topic in forty-five minutes, so he focused on what he considered to be the main points. What made the lecture particularly interesting was his method of moving to sidebars, in which he told of specific incidents or described certain people.

He also did something that a good educator would do: he analyzed how to judge the importance of an article in the *New York Times* by where it appeared on the front page, and if it was not there, where in the paper it was buried. Sure enough, if an article on the Jews during the war appeared, it usually was buried. Not only that, but similar to when the Russian press was finally reporting on the horrors of the death camps toward the end of the war, the word "Jew" was usually not used.

Of course, there were many major factors involved in the lack of coverage in the press, one of which was that the Nazis concealed their actions. Another major one was that the Allies had one goal that superseded all others, and that was to win the war. They could not let the Axis know, for example, that through the Enigma Project they had broken the code used by the Axis; the same held true for the breaking of the Japanese code.

So, decisions had to be made on a priority level that ended up with the ethical dilemma of sacrificing some human beings for the larger war effort. And, as Prof. Shapiro reminded the audience, the United States in the 1940s was a country full of anti-Semitism as well as racism.

The government did not want to make it seem that the Allies were fighting specifically to aid the Jews. Add onto that the human element, namely, the incapability of many people to grasp the enormity of what the Nazis were doing. How does one find words to describe the indescribable?

The conclusion was that this was the greatest failure of journalism in the twentieth century. To put a more positive spin on the topic, Prof. Shapiro concluded that we should all note how things have changed, what with the news coverage of the lead up to the election including the question of how the candidates would deal with Israel, as well as the topic, "How did Jews vote?" forming part of the post-election analysis. Ironically too, decades after the Holocaust, it continues to be covered by the media, whether in the form of legal claims to art holdings, a possible lawsuit again the French railway for collaborating with the Nazis, or in the form of articles about poverty-stricken survivors.

The evening ended with the mournful and ever-touching cadences of the *El Maleh Rakhamim* as each participant moved into his or her private world of remembering.

Reviews

A Woman of Enterprise
December 11, 1992

When I agreed to review a book as a favor for a desperate friend, I had no idea what I was getting myself into. The book, *Flowers in the Blood*, by Gay Courter, is a novel set in late nineteenth-century India, whose protagonists are Indian Jews. The blurb reads, "Beautiful Dinah Sassoon, daughter of an affluent opium trader and pillar of Calcutta's tight-knit Jewish community, sees her privileged future destroyed when her mother is mysteriously murdered. This tragic event leaves Dinah dishonored and virtually unmarriageable . . . until Edwin Salem, offering unconditional love, sparks her indomitable spirit and passionate ambition." If this gets you interested, do read it. It is not to my taste, and, to paraphrase a saying, "Great literature, it isn't."

My concern is the Jewish elements in the book, their accuracy, and—as with all popular novels on a Jewish theme—the possible long-range effects of such a book. Most of the descriptions of the origins of the Jews of India—mainly the Bene Israel—who spoke Marathi, the Baghdadis who spoke Judeo-Arabic, and the Western Jews who only arrived after the sixteenth century—are accurate. So are the descriptions of their rituals, synagogues, foods, and education. These details will only interest a few of the readers, for most will focus on the plot and the main actors.

Dinah Sassoon is the center of all the action, and the novel purports to be her memoir. There is no question in my mind that Dinah is a loose imitation of that outstanding Baghdadi-Indian Jew, Flora Sassoon (1859–1936). Born in India, she married her cousin, Solomon Sassoon, who headed the family businesses in Bombay, Shanghai, and Hong Kong. Upon his death in 1894, she took over control of the business, retaining it even after moving to London in 1901.

Unlike the fictional Dinah, Flora Sassoon was a Hebrew scholar in her own right, and a strictly Orthodox Jew. Whenever she traveled, which was quite often, she always included a ritual slaughterer and a quorum of men in her entourage. Her Jewish erudition was such that in 1925, at age sixty-five, she delivered a learned discourse on the Talmud at Jews College in London. At seventy-two, she published an essay on Rashi in The Jewish Forum.

If I were of the Sassoon family, I would take great exception to the fictional character of Dinah, who is anything but learned in Jewish things and whose religiosity is questionable in many instances. The only similarities lie in their names and their business acumen. However, worse harm is not the choice of the family names, but the field of enterprise that is the center of the novel and whose title emphasizes this even more.

Flowers in the Blood refers to the opium trade, which is the core of the novel. Opium, derived from poppies, was a major crop of India at the turn of the nineteenth century, for most of it was exported to China. Yes, the wealthiest Jews of India were involved in the export-import trade (the Sassoons in particular), but this was in cotton, jute, and tobacco. The long-term damage that can be done by a book like this is the generalization that most uninformed people will make and remember: Jews ran the opium trade between India and China.

This reminds me of other damaging uninformed statements: Jewish doctors were the main castrators of slaves in the Middle Ages, thus providing harems with a constant supply of eunuchs; or one that is more familiar—Jews were behind the African slave trade.

I don't know how many people will read this novel, and maybe I am being a worrywart, but I get very uncomfortable when I read something that puts Jews into a field of endeavor that is morally wrong. So I hereby defend the Sassoon name in general and Flora Sassoon in particular, and protest their defamation in a sensationalist novel.

Jewish Legal Writings by Women
A Review

November 20, 1998

One positive aspect of an edited book made up of many articles written by diverse authors is that there is bound to be something for everyone. This volume, *Jewish Legal Writings by Women*, edited by Micah D. Halpern and Chana Safrai, contains seventeen articles, divided into the rubrics of the body, the soul, the community, and the individual. The unifying thread is that each of the seventeen women authors has "entered into a new realm of knowledge—the world of *Halakha*." Their approach to Jewish law is one of respect yet at the same time—on the whole—is analytical of the texts. This is the *halakhic* process. Since the editors made the crucial decision of allowing each author's voice to be heard in her own style and language, the texture of the volume is bumpy at times. Some of the writers are gifted with language and presentation; others are less so.

I will focus only on the articles which caught my attention. For example, Tirzah Meacham's "Marriage of Minor Girls in Jewish Law: A Legal and Historical Overview" is well written, and its conclusion puts the issue squarely into the contemporary domain. Chana Safrai's piece on "Beauty, Beautification, and Cosmetics: Social Control and Halakha in Talmudic Times" is most interesting. Dr. Safrai's ability to find fascinating women's topics and sources from the distant past are well-known to scholars of Jewish women's history. Here she lives up to her reputation.

The second section, is entitled "The Soul," in which the writers probe prayer and learning, two central foci of Jewish life. Aliza Berger's "Wrapped Attention: May Women Wear *Tefillin*?" is a long historical analysis of this issue. Aviva Cayam's "Fringe Benefits: Women and Tzitzit" leaves out the tracing of historical development, either taking it for granted that the reader already has this knowledge, or that it is not important to her thesis.

"The Female Voice of Kaddish" by Rochelle Millen is excellent. This is a topic on which I have lectured, and the author used every source available and used them well. I may choose to differ with some minor points that Dr. Millen makes, but the overall presentation is superior.

Section three on "The Community," explores the concerns of woman and society. "The Bat Mitzvah in Jewish Law and Contemporary Practice" by Erica S. Brown is right on target. There is no woman who will not relate to the article at some point. Not so was my reaction to Chana Henkin's "Women and the Issuing of Halakhic Rulings." What starts out as a first-rate analysis deteriorates at the end into apologetics and polemics. As for the article by Maidi Katz, "Secular Studies at the Volozhin Yeshiva," while personally interesting because my grandfather attended it and I was brought up on all these stories, I cannot figure out why it is in this book.

The final section in Hebrew deals with "The Individual" and includes the topics of the blessing *She-lo Asani Isha* and its impact on women today (by Gili Zivan), how to deal with senile parents (by Malka Puterkovski), and artificial insemination in single women (by Dvora Ross). All three have contemporary impact.

A small point, but a bothersome one: it is very unprofessional to describe the authors' marital status (and number of children). It is also unprofessional to call them by their first names. Also, the contributors are described as "devout" and "observant": who determines this and how? Since when are the words "Ashkenazi" and "Sephardi" not capitalized or even italicized?

But let us not get petty—even though my name was misspelled in a citation. The book in general is worth reading, and the articles should provoke thought and discussion. With this achieved, i.e., that *halakhic* analysis is no longer the unique realm of men, I hope that—as with other women's scholarship—this will now be mainstreamed, and there will be no need to point out the scholars' gender nor choose a title like *Jewish Legal Writings by Women*.

Reviews

Biblical Films
February 26, 1999

Many years ago, I went with my father to see the movie "The Ten Commandments." The experience has remained with me for two reasons: First, the epic movie was overwhelming in all of its color, sound, and high drama. Second, my father, the Bible scholar, kept mumbling to himself in Hebrew throughout the movie, irritating the people around us to the point that we ended up isolated in the huge movie theater. What he was doing was citing the Biblical and Midrashic sources for various parts of the movie. His excitement was over the detailed work put in by the advisers to Cecil B. DeMille. He also liked Yul Brynner's acting more than Charlton Heston's. I agreed with him, but then the "bad guy" roles are usually the juicier ones.

Last month I took my two teenaged daughters to see "Prince of Egypt." They were the oldest "children" in the movie theater, and the three of us enjoyed this animated feature of Moses and Ramses on a level that was exhilarating. Animated films, one should state immediately, are not just for children, and this animated film feature is definitely for grownups. The artistic creativity that can be achieved via this medium is mind-boggling, for example, the hieroglyphics come alive in telling the story of how Pharaoh killed the newborn Hebrew baby boys. Yocheved's flight to the Nile River with the baby is dramatically rendered, and the survival of the infant Moses in the basket in the river is so well done that I plan to use the video in my class.

The portrayal of the construction labor done by the slaves is magnificent and historically authentic as is the architecture, statuary, costumes, and jewelry. Yes, the advisers kept to most of the Biblical narrative, but there are some drastic changes, I guess for the story line and for "political correctness." Miriam and Tzippora thus play much larger roles than in the Biblical narrative or even that which the *midrash aggada* gives them. Aaron becomes a secondary character. But the most interesting twist is that the movie-makers decided to interpret the relationship of Moses and Ramses as one of brotherly love and rivalry, that they truly loved each other but each had to follow his own destiny. The burden placed on Ramses by his father of carrying on the Pharaonic tradition no matter what the cost, not to be the weak link in the chain of his lineage, places an interesting slant on his subsequent stubborn refusal to allow the Hebrew slaves to leave Egypt.

The discussion after the movie was long, detailed, and intense. My daughters are well grounded in Bible studies as well as in ancient Egyptian history. They noticed, for example, how much the Egyptian royal family looked like the statuary and tomb paintings. They did not like the corruption of the text in terms of the roles of Miriam and Tzippora, but they, too, were very affected by the heartbreaking scenes in which Yocheved gave up her baby. They identified many *midreshei aggada*, such as the one with the fish swimming in the split Sea of Reeds. They also asked questions about Yitro and Middle Eastern nomadic life. All in all, it was a most satisfying experience. Too bad my father could not participate in it.

Reviews

Intellectual Stimulation

April 5, 2002

There are weeks that go by without any professional, intellectual stimulation. I prepare my classes, grade my papers, and attend endless meetings. Then in one week, I am treated to three lectures/discussions that set all the brain cells off again and remind me why I am in my field.

The first was a "Report from the Front" on the Israeli/Palestinian issue. The reporter was Henry Siegman, senior fellow at the Council on Foreign Relations and director of the council's United States/Middle East Project. Prof. J. C. Hurewitz was chairing the session at Columbia University's Middle East Institute's monthly seminar. It was his deft setting up of pertinent questions and jabs that kept Henry Siegman on track and not wandering off into his, by now, notorious anti-Israel diatribes. I went into the seminar totally depressed, but emerged hopeful that the Saudi Initiative may actually lead to something good for Israel and that the spiraling violence may soon be over.

From there, I walked over to the Jewish Studies seminar, chaired by Prof. Michael Stanislawski. The young professor from Princeton, Olga Litwak, who presented her latest research and thinking with a small group of scholars was enthusiastic and thought provoking. She focused on three violent episodes in Ashkenazi Jewish history, and looked at the literature that emerged from the Crusades, the 1648 Ukrainian attacks, and the Kishinev Pogrom of 1903. This new slant on the events allowed for new interpretations, and I will have to rethink how I use the term pogrom in my classes from now on.

The big treat came at the end of the week with the investiture of Prof. Haym Soloveichik as the Merkin Family Professor of Jewish History and Literature at the Revel Graduate School of Yeshiva University. Prof. Soloveichik's lecture, entitled "Halakha, Taboo, and the Origin of Jewish Moneylending," was masterful. He walked the audience—at the Fifth Avenue Synagogue—through the Jewish settlements along the Rhine River, and the geography and economics of the Rhine Valley. The bottom line was that the economy of the entire area was based on wine production. He then led the audience through multiple *halakhic* texts of the eleventh to the thirteenth centuries dealing with *yayn nesekh* (libated wine), and rabbinic *stam yeynam* (wine which could have been libated), showing that although there is no mention of Jews trading in wine, it did not mean that they were not receiving wine as payment in kind for loans taken out by the vintners. He proved brilliantly that between the ninth and fourteenth or fifteenth centuries Jews were heavily into viticulture and that moneylending and trade were always bound together at that time. The moneylending, however, was not seen as that but as extending credit to the vintners. It wasn't until the sixteenth century that Jews were pushed out of this and moved down the economic and social scale to pawnbroking.

This lecture will eventually be published for all to be able to share in the scholarship, but the reader will miss experiencing the excitement of the hunt, of the close reading of the texts, and of the erudite asides.

Yes, it was quite a week.

Reviews

The Jews of Brooklyn
May 17, 2002

The Brandeis Series in American Jewish History, Culture, and Life has recently published *Jews of Brooklyn*, edited by Ilana Abramovitch and Sean Galvin. It is a collection of over fifty chapters written by a group of scholars, journalists, and self-appointed experts on the topic, and is full of photographs as well as memoirs and interviews.

It is only fitting that one of the chapters should be entitled "Radically Right: The *Jewish Press*." Written by Dr. Jay Eidelman, an historian at the Museum of Jewish Heritage in New York City, he traces the newspaper from its founding in 1960 to today, stressing that its "distinct Orthodox perspective helps readers clearly demarcate the line between themselves and the rest of the Jewish community." While half of the article is directed to the Meir Kahane connection, the rest of it is comprehensive and balanced.

There are enough chapters in the book for a reader to find at least one that he or she really likes (and, of course, really dislikes). I personally like the description of the street games, and you didn't have to grow up in Brooklyn to play them. Stick ball with sewer covers as bases, handball bounced against the apartment house with each sidewalk line as a boundary, and heavy metal skates attached to the bottom of the shoes with a metal key and a leather ankle strap buckled up as tight as possible and then roaring into the street were some of these games. Girls usually played hopscotch in a chalked-in space, jumped rope to a series of ditties, or bounced a ball with an orderly series of under or over, or combination of arm and leg motions.

Then there is an entire chapter on candy stores and egg creams. Again, you need not be from Brooklyn to identify with this description. The egg cream has no egg and no cream, and there is no consensus of opinion on who invented it or where. But all New Yorkers of a certain age can tell you about the milk, chocolate syrup and seltzer that are its ingredients. We all differ on how to prepare it and what the proportions are. And, like the bagel, pickles, and knishes, it seems to be a specifically Jewish concoction.

Yet somewhere, somehow, it came to be identified with New York City as a whole.

The book is divided into three main sections: Coming to Brooklyn, Living in Brooklyn (subdivided into Coming of Age in Brooklyn's Neighborhoods, Cultural Influences and Community Life, and Jewish Institutions and Interethnic Life), and Leaving Brooklyn/Returning to Brooklyn. These are chronological divisions. There is a major attempt to be all-inclusive, so there are chapters on all Jewish denominations, Middle Eastern as well as Ashkenazi Jews, men as well as women, music, criminals, Williamsburg, Crown Heights, Brownsville, every Hasidic group, Yiddish radio, Jewish education, and the up-and-coming neighborhoods of Brooklyn Heights and Park Slope. Some of the memoirs are hilarious, some are educational, and some are ridiculous. There is certainly something for everyone.

Reviews

The Story of Blood
July 12, 2002

June moves us into summertime programs on television, which usually means reruns, bad movies, and awful talk shows. PBS surprised us by airing an excellent new program creatively entitled "Red Gold," which is the story of blood.

The program first briefly discussed the ancient history of medicine, focusing mainly on Galen, the Roman doctor, whose 350 books form the basis of western medicine. The program then turned to Renaissance Italy, specifically to Andreas Vesalius (the father of modern medicine) and William Harvey who, while in Italy, discovered both that the heart is a mechanical pump and that blood circulates around the body.

But before moving directly along the path of medical history, the show made a side trip into examining the religious and symbolic significance of blood. Using Renaissance prints from illustrated Bibles as visual tools, the narrator informed the audience of the Jewish use of blood offerings in the Temple in Jerusalem. I waited anxiously for what was coming next, envisioning blood libels, the Damascus Affair, St. Simon of Trent. What they moved to was the koshering of meat, i.e., the removal of blood in keeping with the Torah. "Only do not eat the blood, for the blood is the life, and you shall not eat the life with the meat" (Deut. 12:23).

"Well done," I thought, and sat back to enjoy the next part which discussed blood-letting, which killed innumerable people, including George Washington. This blood-letting was usually done by a barber, hence the red and white traditional barber pole—red for blood, white for bandages. Village barbers and "doctors" did this, or used leeches, in the belief that this would help cure sick people, well into the twentieth century. My father told stories of this treatment in Eastern Europe, along with *bankes* or hot cupping, which merely drew the blood vessels closer to the surface of the skin, but did not involve puncturing the skin.

The rest of the program dealt with the development of modern techniques of blood transfusions, made possible in part by the discovery of the four blood types in 1901. It was during the two world wars of the last century that the technology was perfected, and the use of sodium nitrate to prevent clotting and cold storage, as well as the use of plasma, began. Community donations of blood as an act of patriotism and charity were also perfected.

A footnote was the Nazi manipulation of statistics to prove that only Aryans had Type A blood; Type B was the "infectious" type of Jews, gypsies, and Slavs. (I guess that my daughters and I are secret Aryans.) They thus could barely treat their own wounded and had almost no transfusion apparatus.

Another footnote was the racial politics here in the United States: blacks could not donate blood. The fuss over the fact that blacks could die for the country in their segregated units, but could not give blood, led to amending this law. Blacks could give blood to be used for other blacks. The double irony of all this is that Dr. Charles Drew, the man who not only developed the technology for plasma but worked out its packaging, storing and effective distribution overseas, was black.

Kudos to Channel 13 for creating an informative, provocative, and fascinating show on a topic that we tend to take for granted, that is, until we find ourselves in dire need of a blood transfusion.

Reviews

Protecting Women

April 2005 [rejected by the press]

When I was growing up, my part of Washington Heights was a mixed neighborhood of Jews and Irish Catholics. The girls my age went either to yeshiva or to Catholic school. The local priest and my father had a respectful relationship, and whenever fights erupted between the two groups involving either of my brothers or myself, the Irish police knew to call my father immediately.

Imagine a bunch of ten to twelve year olds playing ball, jumping rope or hopscotch, talking about whatever girls that age discuss. All these years later I can remember of couple of outstanding comments. "I'm going to marry a Jewish boy — my mum says they make the best husbands." By that time I knew that the interpretation of that naïve comment was: Jewish men bring home their paychecks, and don't get drunk every Friday night and beat up their wives. I could hear our next-door neighbor doing just that, and the wife showing up for Sunday church trying to cover up her black eye.

Boys were kept in line with the threat that serious misbehavior would lead not just to parental or priestly punishment, but being sent off to "Father Flanagan's Boys' Farm." In my imagination it was someplace upstate, run along the lines of a juvenile prison but with corporal punishment. I wasn't far off. But the girls were threatened with being sent back to Ireland to work in "The Sisters' Laundry." I thought this was just an Irish parental threat until I saw the movie "The Magdalene Sisters." What a shock! To think that there existed a system that shipped young women off to work the laundries as virtual slaves, forbidden from even talking to each other. For what reasons? For "shaming" the family. Of the three main protagonists, one had given birth to a child without being married, one had been raped by a cousin, and one had been flirting with boys. And so their families condemned them to that hell on earth, run by sadistic nuns. The Irish Catholic church was a partner in this injustice, and it seemed that everyone in Ireland accepted this as right. Let it be clear that this is Irish only. Italian Catholics never had any such facilities, nor did the Spanish nor the French, nor the Poles nor the Germans. So we seem to be dealing with Celtic culture.

This set off all of my Jewish sensibilities, and I thought through our historical approach to these sensitive issues. Flirtatiousness would never have provoked punishment of this sort; rather, it would have called for parental rebuke, or, more probably, a marriage arrangement. Rape, of course, was more serious, but the reality of anti-Jewish attacks and pogroms always included the possibility of rape. These women were dealt with as compassionately as possible in a time of group recovery. The women would never be blamed nor punished for "shaming" the group. Jews tried to protect their women by teaching them not to talk to their non-Jewish neighbors, and in the Middle East, in a further attempt to segregate women from non-Jewish men, the Jewish men did the food shopping in the marketplaces.

As for the third example in the movie, the birth of a child to a single mother, this too would have been dealt with within the community. Rape could end up in pregnancy, and the harsh reality of life at least ensured that the child would be brought up as a Jew, since the mother was Jewish. Dina, daughter of Jacob, and raped by Shechem, became pregnant according to the commentators, and ended up protected by her full brother Shimon. Marriages were arranged when young women reached puberty—at about fourteen—so that single mothers would have been a rarity until modern times.

So while life for Jews may have been difficult as a minority group all over the world, traditional life took over, and family and community dealt with the good and the bad. Jews never punished their young women for deeds that were beyond their control. As for the Irish Magdalene Sisters' laundries, the last one closed in 1996.

Reviews

"Dr. Ruth"

May 11, 2007

The Department of Judaic Studies at Brooklyn College sponsored the second Frances Haidt '44 Memorial Lecture on April 24. Our lecturer was Dr. Ruth Westheimer, and it was a great success. Her personality, warmth, intellect, and sense of humor are unbelievable. Her topic was "The Jewish Family," which she connected to her latest book, *Heavenly Sex: Sexuality in the Jewish Tradition*.

"Dr. Ruth" began by describing her personal story, highlighting her birth in Frankfort-an-Main, and her education in the Samson Raphael Hirsch School, which was interrupted by *Kristallnacht* and its aftermath. At the age of ten she was part of the *Kindertransport*, crossing the border into Switzerland where she spent the war years, never to see her parents again. From there it was on to Mandated Palestine where she joined a kibbutz, and then the *Hagana*, where she became a sniper. (She claims that she can still aim a rifle with great accuracy.) She continued with her education, and in 1956 came to the United States to visit her uncle. She remained to obtain her higher education degrees; she also married and started a family.

Dr. Westheimer ardently presented her thesis that the roots of Jewish identity are tied to early childhood education in a family structure. For that matter, she has expanded this into her study of Ethiopian Jews and the Druze in Israel; their identity is connected with family experiences. As a result, she feels that one of the reasons for the failure of the kibbutz system is its negation of the traditional family. While praising the kibbutz system's setting up of children's houses in part to liberate women, she said that the downside of this was its effect on the children themselves.

Once she set out her main theme, she moved on to generally describe a wide gamut of issues connected to Jewish marital life, from the *halakhic* to the couples in need of therapy. Her openness is well-known, as is her wonderfully outrageous sense of humor. The audience appreciated the German-accented lecture, but it was the fielding of questions from the audience that showed her talent as a speaker, as well as her practical nature. The timing of her punch lines was perfect.

Students from my class on "The Jewish Woman' attended, and I could hear them laughing as loudly as I was. When I introduced her, I said that she represents the achievements of the immigrant Jewish woman in this country. I also said that she represents the serendipitous-ness of life. She used to teach in Brooklyn College but was not reappointed because of departmental politics. She was devastated at the time. What she did as a result was move from being Dr. Westheimer, a mere college professor, to being "Dr. Ruth," one of the best known Jewish women in America.

Reviews

Visions of Israel

June 20, 2008

"Visions of Israel" aired on PBS the same week as the Israel Day Parade marched up Fifth Avenue in New York City. The parade was noisy and organized in its disorder, and inspiring in its own special way. Across the street, at 60th and Fifth Avenue was a small Palestinian demonstration, and on the sidewalks were "Jews for Jesus" representatives trying to hand out flyers. In other words, it was a real New York experience.

The television program had Itzhak Perlman as the narrator, speaking about "homecoming" and a "journey of the heart." The lines were often kitschy and sugary, but the visuals were outstanding. We were carried on a virtual flight from Tel Aviv to Haifa, back down to the Negev, and up north again. We "flew" with the wild birds—mostly cranes on the migratory path between Asia and Africa—and I would love to know the technique behind taking such shots. The history of Israel was related through visuals of archaeology, like the Roman ruins at Bet-She'an, Caesaria, and Massada.

I sat there feeling very happy about what I was seeing until I realized that the shots made the country look as though there were huge, unbuilt open spaces, especially in the north. I also noticed that the music, although well-chosen and obviously well performed, was either classical or Yiddish or "early Israeli" like "Hava Nagila." There was almost nothing up-to-date and nothing with Middle Eastern influence.

The other thing missing was Middle Eastern Jews, let alone Ethiopian and Indian Jews. Yes, not everything can be included, but Middle Eastern Jews were numerically so important and played such a large role in building up the country. There were, however, a couple of segments on the Arabs.

So it was a "feel good" presentation, interrupted by fundraising attempts. I would like to know just how much they made that night. "Visions of Israel" was followed by a half-hour documentary on American Jews who fought in the 1948 War of Independence. That was an excellent piece of work and gave the viewer a taste of the excitement and zest of these then-young people who either came directly from Europe to Palestine or from the United States to contribute to the war effort.

One of the interviewees was Dr. Ruth Westheimer, who, along with other stories, told what a "great shot" she was with a rifle. This was followed by the story of another interviewee who said that he was given only three hours of training with live ammunition in his rifle, and then he was on his own. But this same man also said that it was the most exciting time of his life.

The students in my summer course on Israel were given the assignment of watching this program so that we could discuss it in class. They are being taught how to analyze primary sources, and documentaries are contemporary primary sources. Most of what we analyze, however, is written material, like the Sykes-Picot Agreement of 1916 and the Churchill White Paper of 1922.

Then, out of the blue, two non-Jewish students in that class said: "If that is what Israel looks like, I want to go to see it." If this was one of the aims of "Visions of Israel," then it succeeded.

Reviews

Book Day
April 25, 2008

Yeshiva of Flatbush High School held a "Book Day" for their juniors and seniors on March 25. All of the students had to read *Now They Call Me Infidel: Why I Renounced Jihad for America, Israel, and the War on Terror* by Egyptian-born Nonie Darwish. The students all gathered in the auditorium to hear the author highlight her metamorphosis from a brainwashed child to a thinking adult. Then they broke up into workshops, each student attending four in all, during the rest of the school day.

There were fourteen guest presenters in those workshops (including David Firestone, deputy national editor of the *New York Times*; Sheila Kurtzer, wife of the former United States ambassador to both Egypt and Israel; Special Agent James T. Screen, who is the joint terrorism task force coordinator; Councilman David Weprin; and myself) as well as faculty presenters.

It is ironic that today's *New York Times* (April 1) has a front-page article on the anti-Jewish and anti-Israel propaganda that is being taught and preached in Gaza today in the schools and mosques. This is exactly what Nonie Darwish describes in her book, as she was growing up in Gaza. When she moved from there back to Cairo, after the Israelis assassinated her father, a high-ranking Egyptian military officer, she remembers the special treatment that her family received as the relatives of a martyr; she also remembers songs about *jihad* and revenge.

But she developed a skeptical approach even as a youngster and began to question her culture, especially the status of women. Her book contains a scathing attack on women's position in Middle Eastern life, and her harshest words are aimed at the use of the veil and the Egyptian practice of "female circumcision." She also hammers away at the poverty in Egypt and Gaza, and describes how she came to realize that this was the fault of the government and not the Israelis. She realized, too, that the Arab governments, in general, focused on anti-Israel and anti-American propaganda to deflect attention away from the major internal problems of each country.

It was 9/11 that turned her into an activist and an advocate for America. She had been living in California for a number of years and had rapidly and gratefully become Americanized. But after 9/11, when she realized that her Egyptian family and friends—all well-educated and middle class—believed that America deserved the attack, she decided, "enough was enough." She started a website, "Arabs for Israel," and to her amazement, it became very popular. She was then approached to write this book. She is now therefore considered by Muslims to be an *infidel*, which is punishable by death in conservative Islamic law.

I sat next to Nonie Darwish in the auditorium before she spoke, and I asked her if she travels with a bodyguard. She responded that she did not want to live that way. But she will not stop advocating understanding and education, for "Arab children don't need hatred or *jihad*—they need jobs and hope." Her bravery is inspiring.

Reviews

Minhagei Lita
September 25, 2009

A number of weeks ago, *The Jewish Press* ran a review of *Minhagei Lita: Customs of Lithuanian Jewry*, authored by Rabbi Menachem Mendel Poliakoff, a leading personality in the Baltimore Jewish community. Although born in the United States, he was sent to Lithuania to study in the Telshe Yeshiva. I had read an early manuscript of the book and was eager to obtain a copy of the final version. It was impossible to find anywhere, as it had sold out, so I resorted to calling the author, whose wife kindly sent me one of the last copies.

As stated in the preface, Rabbi Poliakoff's purpose in writing this work was first to "clarify for present and future generations the authentic customs of Lithuanian Jewry in prayer and in common practice." The second purpose was to "highlight the Torah true approach and values that form the underpinnings of *Minhagei Lita*" that can be applied to today's issues.

In reading this brief book, I could hear the anger at what is now being called authentic Lithuanian customs. In my head I could also hear my father's deep voice railing at the same things. He was of Slobodka Yeshiva background, which was very close to what Telshe Yeshiva stood for.

Part of the move away from authentic Lithuanian customs, he writes, is that most Lithuanian Jews were annihilated or displaced during World War II, so there was a lack of continuity of practice. Another cause for the deviations is the reliance on the Chafetz Chaim's *Mishnah Berurah*, in which there are a number of decisions that were contrary to prevailing custom. Even in Radin, where the Chafetz Chaim had his yeshiva, they did not follow all of the things favored by him.

The focus of the first part of the book is on prayer, and the next part deals with laws and customs. In discussing the issue of *glatt* kosher, so prevalent in the United States, Rabbi Poliakoff clearly states that because rabbis in Lita were great scholars and so would decide *halakhic* questions with leniency (for this was a quality of a great scholar), there was no *glatt* kosher meat. There was just kosher meat. *Glatt* kosher raises the price of meat beyond what is acceptable, making this trend *halakhically* illegal.

Other topics addressed are parading piety, *chillul ha-Shem*, *tzitzis*, *gartel*, *payos*, and clothing. Under *tzitzis* he clearly states that *minhag Lita* was to wear the *tallis katan* under the shirt with the fringes tucked in. I have numerous photographs of my grandfather (Volozhin Yeshiva) and my father as a yeshiva student with no fringes hanging out. His anger at the new so-called Litvish custom of *upsherren* is wonderful, as is his description of those who reject the use of the *eruv*. Just about every community in Lita had an *eruv*. That is how my grandmother brought the *cholent* home from the baker's oven to the table on Shabbat. The ostentatious rejection of this in the United States by the overly pious is violating *halakha* according to the rabbi. As for the *upsherren*, those who practice it have adopted a pagan custom and so "have become *frum* worshippers." There really is a reason why Litvaks have been labeled *farbrent* (fiery).

The final two topics are *aguna* and *yom tovo sheni*, difficult contemporary issues for which Rabbi Poliakoff offers possible solutions.

Read the book, if you can find it. It definitely sets the record straight. Whether or not people will listen to what Rabbi Poliakoff writes is a different matter. If people do choose to do these variations of custom, they should not ascribe them to *minhagei Lita*.

Reviews

Italy and the Holocaust: A Reappraisal
December 4, 2009

Scholars have to keep up with the latest research in their fields. Most of us rely on book reviews published in specialized journals, and then decide whether or not we should actually read the entire book, since our time is so limited and there is so much out there.

I recently read one such book, containing the field's latest ideas and scholarship, entitled *Jews in Italy under Fascist and Nazi Rule, 1922–1945*, edited by Joshua D. Zimmerman (Cambridge University Press, 2005). This is a collection of essays based on papers delivered at a conference held at Yeshiva University in 2002.

The book is divided into five parts: Italian Jewry from Liberalism to Fascism, Rise of Racial Persecution, Catastrophe—the German Occupation, The Vatican and the Holocaust, and Aftermath—Contemporary Italy and Holocaust Memory. All of the scholars and writers address the question of Italian participation in the Holocaust, and challenge the half-century historical tenet that Italy was relatively "good" to her Jews. The key word her is "relatively," for relative to what? Yes, compared to Nazi Germany, Italy does very, very well. However, scholars like Michele Sarfatti conclude that the Racial Laws of 1938, cutting Jews off from most jobs, ousting them from universities and schools, and even forbidding their names from being listed in telephone books, were Mussolini's doing, and not prompted by his alliance with Hitler of that same year.

Both Annalisa Capristo and Roberto Finzi point out, the first in her article on the exclusion of Jews from the Italian Academies, and the second in his article on their exclusion from the universities, that the reaction among Italian intellectuals was that of a deafening silence. No one openly protested.

New material was provided by the unwilling opening of new CIA-OSS documents by the Americans, and a reappraisal of the operations in the two regions of German-occupied northern Italy, 1943–45, reaffirms that there were many anti-Semitic Italian Fascists, especially in these regions, one of which held the only death camp in Italy (there were a number concentration camps).

The most impressive article was the one by Susan Zuccotti, entitled "Pius XII and the Rescue of Jews in Italy: Evidence of a Papal Directive." She takes on all of the scholars to date who defend the Pope's actions, and in twenty pages demolishes their statements. The bottom line for her is that the Pope never issued a rescue order, neither in writing nor orally. The former is easier to refute than the latter, but she takes the reader step by step in destroying the statements made. She concludes on a more diplomatic tone, that, "Clearly papal involvement in Jewish rescue is not a black-or-white issue, but one of painfully nuanced shades of gray. Pius XII was a conscientious, deeply spiritual man, perhaps somewhat out of touch with reality and perhaps unable to comprehend fully the horrors of his age . . . In a context that did not involve Jews, he also accepted certain risks." She admires courageous acts of rescue taken by members of the church but states clearly that they acted on their own, without papal directive.

As for the aftermath of the Holocaust in Italy, the writers note that there are almost no national monuments to the Holocaust, only private Jewish ones. They ponder this and surmise that this may have to do with the fact that so many Italians were members of the Fascist party before and during the war, and that the shame is still there. (This book was written in 2002, and I can attest to the fact that things have changed in one sense, and that is that Italian television has multiple programs on the Holocaust, both documentaries and popular movies.)

The book is well edited, most of the chapters are well written, and Prof. Zimmerman is to be commended on his work.

Part II

Jewish Law and Custom

The Modern Day *Aguna*
February 14, 1992

When I was a child, there was a woman in my neighborhood who was married yet did not have a husband. "Was her husband dead?" I asked, knowledgeable about widows.

"No, he was just gone."

"Did he divorce her?" I queried, knowledgeable also about divorcees.

"No, he just left."

"So she's not married," I asserted.

"Oh yes, she is," I was told. That was my introduction to the concept of the *aguna*, the "anchored" or "chained" woman.

In traditional Judaism, the *aguna* was a woman whose husband disappeared without a trace. Since there were no witnesses, no one could say for certain that the husband had died, and therefore the woman's fate was to await his return. The only two ways to end a marriage were via death or divorce. This woman's marriage was over in fact but not in law, and therefore she could not remarry.

Throughout the millennia of Jewish history, the women who were affected most by the status of *aguna* were those whose husbands disappeared when their ships foundered at sea, or when their caravans were destroyed by bandits, or when the upheavals of war overtook them. The legists bent over backward to try to free the *aguna* from her status, even accepting—in only this instance—the testimony from one witness alone instead of the mandatory two witnesses.

Here and there we find evidence of a different kind of *aguna*, that is, a woman whose husband moved to a different city or country, took another wife, and never bothered divorcing the wife he left behind. These deserted wives were protected by the Jewish community, and the correspondence indicates that the rabbis in the two cities involved usually managed to convince the deserter to divorce his first wife.

The key element in the second type of *aguna* is community pressure. Jews in the long timespan of the Middle Ages had to live in a Jewish community. The only alternative to this was conversion to Christianity or Islam. There was no neutral secular ground as exists today. You were what you professed, and so community pressure could work, even from a distance, for the tendency of the rabbis was to prevent a status of *aguna* from overtaking any women.

In the twentieth century, in the United States, the issue of *aguna* became not one of a lost or missing spouse, but a case of the recalcitrant husband. In New York State alone, there are hundreds of Orthodox women whose husbands refuse to cooperate in the execution of a *get* (a document written by a scribe that declares that it is a bill of divorce that serves to dissolve a specific marriage). The couple may be undergoing a civil divorce, but the husband—either because of reason of animosity or in order to extort financial or custodial concessions—refuses to grant the woman a *get*. Without this *get* the woman is in the position of the Biblical *aguna*, neither married nor divorced, but "anchored."

The irony is, that the man who is doing this, using his civil divorces, may remarry. He is not "anchored," for Biblical law allowed for polygynous marriages, and despite later rabbinic amendments forbidding polygyny, the bottom line is Biblical law, and the offspring of this second marriage would not be *mamzeriem* (the children of a forbidden union, i.e., adultery or incest). Should the woman, without a *get*, remarry and have children, her second marriage would be regarded as adultery, and therefore her offspring would be *mamzerim* with all of the awful laws concomitant to this status.

So, why doesn't the *aguna* just leave Orthodoxy, if this is how she is treated? Judaism—in traditional Jewish life—is a package deal. One does not pick and choose, discarding what does not appeal to an individual, and keeping that which does appeal. Therefore the *aguna* must do something to prevail on her recalcitrant husband to change his mind. The question is how to do this.

In the State of Israel, where the interconnections and separations of religious law and "Israeli" law are a web of intricacies, some women were able to bring their cases in front of a famous family court justice, who, after trying all other means to convince the husband to execute the *get*, sentenced him to sit in prison. "You have put your wife into a prison; let us see how your being in one appeals to you," she would say (my paraphrase and writer's license). In over ninety-five percent of the cases, the husbands, after cooling their heels for a number of weeks, granted the *get*.

We do not live in Israel, and Orthodox Jews tend to try to keep legal issues away from the civil courts. The *agunot* try community pressure first, and only as a last resort do they move to civil courts.

As a product of the 1960s and as a "bleeding heart liberal," to quote my students, I could never have imagined that I would become an advocate of using the civil court system. But after personal experience with friends and acquaintances, who found themselves trapped in the recalcitrant husband prison, and agonizing with them over the hesitance on the part of the community leaders to do anything, and realizing that we live in a generation of over-cautious rabbis, who, as a group, do not and will not join together to deal with this issue, I have joined the small but growing ranks of people looking to the civil courts for help.

The major problem connected with the American judicial decisions reached over the past century is the incorrect perception of the nature of the *get* and of its execution. The most in-depth study of this is Dr. J. David Bleich's article, "Jewish Divorce: Judicial Misconceptions and Possible Means of Civil Enforcement" (*Connecticut Law Review*, Winter 1984, Vol. 16, no. 2, 201–89). He urges, in his conclusion, that a proper understanding of the *get* as the rescission of a contract and not as a religious act will remove the constitutional cloud that hovers over this issue. He also urges, that even if the civil court will not execute a *get*, it should act as a court of equity, and by withholding a decree of civil divorce in the absence of a *get* will thus prevent a gross inequity to the woman.

If the Orthodox world will not act to help these women, then perhaps the American judicial system will.

Jewish Law and Custom

Love of Parents

April 29, 1994

The other day when I was outside enjoying the glorious April sunshine, overseeing my nine-year-old painting a picture of the spring flowers, we were disturbed by a sound we could not identify. It sounded like a cat in distress or a strange bird call. We finally identified that the source of the noise was a squirrel high up in an oak tree frantically chattering—crying. What had probably happened was that the animal had returned home to find that "home" was gone. The tree cutters had worked all morning removing an ancient tree that had rotted and was a danger to the nearby houses. But the tree had also probably housed the squirrel's babies, as this is nesting time.

My daughter, no lover of flower-eating, birdseed-stealing squirrels, almost cried saying, "Even a squirrel loves her babies." Adding, "Just like you love me," and almost as an afterthought while resuming her drawing, "and just like I love you." I too had a momentary pang of sympathy for the animal, but it was my daughter's factual statements regarding life as she viewed it that occupied my attention.

The Torah tells us to love God, to love your friend, to love the stranger, and in a way, to love your spouse. The Torah does not command us to love our parents. In discussing this topic, there are scholars who note that in commanding us to love our friend (neighbor) and the stranger (*ger*), the Torah is talking about deeds and not about sentiments or feelings. We are to love our neighbor—as Rabbi Akiva said—as ourselves, meaning that we are not to do to a neighbor what we would not like done to us. The negative formulation is the more practical one. As for the stranger, we are to "love" him because it is obligatory on us to remember that we too were once strangers in a foreign land.

When it comes to love of God, we enter into a complex process, for here it is not only through deed that we are to manifest it, but we are to work on our emotions as well—"with all your heart, with all your soul, with all your might." How this is to be achieved is a topic for the commentators, philosophers, and mystics.

Why not an obligation to love your parents, either in deeds or in emotions? Perhaps the Torah approach was that it was unnecessary. For the child, whose relationship with his or her parent was already one of love, such an injunction is extraneous. For the child, whose relationship was one that was very far from a loving one, it was an impossible commandment to fulfill. Suffice it for this child to honor, fear, and obey such a parent.

We cannot predict our relationships with our parents nor with our children. The same mother can have a loving warm relationship with one daughter and a tense one with another daughter—same mother, two children. A child, similarly, can have a loving connection with her father and a tense on with her mother—same child, two parents. People are individuals with distinct "chemistries."

How wise the Torah is to have foreseen the practicalities of life and thus not give us an unnecessary or impossible law.

Jewish Law and Custom

The Proselyte

June 5, 1998

For most societies, the definition of a "hero" is that of warrior. In fact, the definition is broader even in Greek culture, for it is "a person regarded as a model of noble qualities." Culture then determines what these noble qualities are.

In the Biblical world, the warrior hero was admired, even if he was a flawed hero. Samson, Gideon, Saul, and David are part of a much longer list of such men. But also admired are the non-warriors, such as Abraham, Isaac, and Jacob. Their noble qualities as well as those of their wives are regarded as models for Jews to emulate. A "heroic" figure belonging to this second group is Ruth, the model of *chesed*, of lovingkindness. Ruth is the prototype of the proselyte by conviction, or the *ger tzedek*, that term which had come into use by the end of the period of the Second Temple. (In the Bible *ger* meant stranger or alien.) In the Talmud and the *midrashim* the accepted attitude toward proselytes was usually positive, but there is evidence of opposition as well. On close examination, it seems that the deciding factors were usually contemporary conditions and the personal experiences of the scholars. After all, that was the period of early Christianity, and not all potential proselytes were totally convinced of their Judaism; it was also the time of war and revolts. Yet this was also the time that proselytes out of conviction were mentioned in the benediction for the righteous and the pious in the *Amida* prayer.

A tendency to increase the honor of the proselytes and glorify conversions may be found in the tradition which traces the origins of such great personalities as Rabbi Meir, Rabbi Akiva, Shmaiya, and Avtalyon, to proselytes. The name of Rabbi Akiva's father doesn't appear in the Talmud, but it is related elsewhere, that his name was Joseph and he was a *ger tzedek*.

In his Responsa, Maimonides addresses a *ger tzedek* who had not been treated well: "Toward father and mother we are commanded honor and reverence, toward the prophets to obey them, but toward proselytes we are commanded to have great love in our inmost hearts . . . God, in His glory, loves proselytes . . . A man who left his father and birthplace and the realm of his people . . . and recognized and knew that their (the Jews') religion is true and righteous . . . and entered beneath the wings of the Divine Presence . . . the Lord [calls you] . . . intelligent and understanding, wise and walking correctly, a pupil of Abraham our father."

The imagery is taken directly from the Scroll of Ruth, read on Shavuot as a reminder of many things including the commandment to love the *ger*. How sad it is to learn that some *geirei tzedek* are not treated this way in some of our communities. But then, why should our generation be different from that of Maimonides'? There are always individuals who seem to forget that this is a basic injunction of Judaism. Our generation is unique in that one community has chosen to officially not recognize any conversions whatsoever, not even the ones presided over by the most careful, observant rabbis here or in Israel. Perhaps someone should remind them of Maimonides' Responsum and of the Scroll of Ruth.

Jewish Law and Custom

Decisions

October 26, 2001

Traditional Jews live their lives in a world of constant legal and moral decision-making. Most of the decisions that have to be made are easy ones, like looking for a *hekhsher* on a packaged product. Others are more complicated, like what to do with a *succa* roof that collapses in strong winds on a Friday night. Can one eat and say the blessing "sitting in the *succa*" in such a collapsed form?

Sometimes the legal part is overwhelmed by the moral part. For example, when Rabbi Simcha Zelig Reguer, the *dayan* of Brest-Litovsk, was about to part from his mentor, Rabbi Chaim Soloveitchik, during World War I, he said that while the two lived together, he—the younger of the two—followed Rabbi Soloveitchik's decision not to put on *tefillin* during *chol ha-mo'ed* of Sukkot out of respect. But once they would be parted, Rabbi Reguer would follow his own legal interpretation and put on *tefillin*.

The moral part of our lives, such as respect for the position of rabbi of the synagogue, is what keeps the more educated and knowledgeable lay leaders from correcting a rabbi who errs in how to shake the *lulav* during *Hallel*, or who blatantly disregards the community's desires and custom to say Kohelet. Tensions between the rabbi and the community are as old as the Jewish community itself, and cut across Ashkenazi, Middle Eastern, and Sephardic boundaries.

One of the retired members of my department died just after Yom Kippur. At first I was offended that we were not informed, neither of his death nor of his funeral. Then I realized that had I been told on time, I would have had to go up to Connecticut to participate, as my custom is to go to a funeral if informed on time. So, there are decisions based on custom as well.

Professors have to deal with students who think that just because they worked hard on a paper or studying for an examination, this hard work deserves a high grade. The ethical elements of human relationships should determine that the professor explain the reasons for the low grade in as gentle a manner as possible, directing the student how to rework the paper while building up on the positive things that were accomplished. Sometimes, however, it takes great creativity to find something positive. This holds true, of course, for all educators, whether secular or religious, for honey really does work better than vinegar, and regard for a student's feelings should weigh heavily on the educator's actions.

Then there are the really difficult decisions of life and death that fall into the lap of the *beit din*. These are not everyday issues, but heart-wrenching decisions that only a lifetime of study can handle: Are the wives of the missing husbands of the World Trade Center disaster widows or *agunot*? When can a family sit *shiva*? Can they sit *shiva*? Can DNA be the basis for a final *halakhic* decision? Without the healing power of the ritual steps of mourning—the *shiva*, the *shloshim*, and the year of mourning for parents—life cannot really continue. The scholars know this and have been deciding case by case, searching through past decision for principles of law on which to base these agonizing decisions. What cannot be provided, of course, is a funeral for those who were incinerated into nothingness. Our hearts go out to all of the families of those lost, and while we intone the traditional *Ha-Makom yenahem et-chem* (May God comfort you), many of us switch the word around to say *yenakem* (avenge) as well.

Jewish Law and Custom

Endless Summer

September 6, 2002

This has been one of the worst New York City summers that I can remember. The endless muggy over ninety degree Fahrenheit days without at nighttime cooling off has left me limp, without energy to teach, think, or write, let alone tackle homebased projects. I don't even want to leave home to walk the few blocks to a movie house, let alone face the furnace of subway platforms.

Broiling summers always are accompanied by increased activity on the part of the Angel of Death. It is a known fact that more people die in a heat wave than in hurricanes, tornados, or floods. Air conditioning is a lifesaver, but it is often not enough. What did we do before air conditioning? We sat out on stoops, on fire escapes, on park benches, fanning ourselves and drinking iced tea or soda.

We went to small bungalows in the Rockaways to spend mindless days on the beach, bringing the sand into our living quarters no matter how hard we tried to keep it out. We went to the Catskills bungalow colonies to swim in small lakes or streams, and fight the mosquitos and boredom.

In Lithuania my father went swimming in the Bug River with all the other little boys to escape the heat (he had no memory of girls doing the same). In Renaissance Rome, the Jews fled the oppressive heat by moving to Ostia Antiqua along the sea. The flight from Paris is to the Normandy Coast.

The arrival of the month of Elul usually ushers in revived interest in classes on *tshuva* or on prayer; the oppressive heat this year has made minds lethargic and plodding. It is as though Elul has come in the wrong season.

I remember one incredibly hot Rosh Hashana in Jerusalem, right after my parents made *aliya* in the mid-1970s. The synagogue did not have air conditioning, and sweat was pouring out of everyone, especially the men wrapped in their woolen *tallitot*. After the first person fainted, the community, in an unspoken decision, speeded up the service so that we were out of there in record time. It was health before holiness. Then it was just a matter of negotiating the broiling street until reaching home.

It is not accidental that societies that have a tradition of hell picture it as a searingly hot place. Dante's *Inferno* is exactly that, an inferno, and the more wicked the person the more intense the heat for him or her. Immanuel of Rome, the Jewish writer of that period, in his *Makhberot Immanuel* describes a similar place of eternal punishment for the wicked.

I would like to believe that Abu Nidal, recently assassinated in Baghdad, has a place of honor there alongside all of the other enemies of the Jewish people. It is only fitting that he died on the week when we read "Remember what Amalek did to you," in the Torah.

As the month of Elul moves inexorably toward Tishrei, we should assess our deeds over the past year, take stock of our lives, and contemplate both the horrors of the year as well as the high points. We must work toward renewing our faith as well, as we struggle to see the Divine Will working behind the scenes all over the world. May this New Year be one of real and lasting peace.

Jewish Law and Custom

Local Custom
November 29, 2002

Ever since synagogues have come into existence and customs connected to praying and the synagogue service have multiplied, Jews in various parts of the world have had to deal with the recurring question of what to do when the congregation members have more than one custom. This happened each time there was a movement of Jews from country to country (or even city to city), as a result of religious persecution or the search for a better economic situation.

Invariably the local rabbis—whether in Cairo, as the medieval traders arrived from Kairouan; or in Rome, as the Sephardim arrived after 1492; or in Germany, when Polish Jews came westward in the nineteenth century—decided that local custom prevailed. The new arrivals therefore had to adapt themselves or form their own synagogue. We know that some did from the names given to them (often not their official names) as, for example, the Iraqi synagogue in medieval Cairo, the Portuguese synagogue in Livorno (Italy), and the Bukhari synagogue in Jerusalem.

In the United States, since two of the earliest synagogues—Shearith Israel (better known as the Spanish-Portuguese) in New York City and Touro Synagogue in Newport, Rhode Island—followed the Spanish rite, all Ashkenazi Jews who arrived later and joined them, followed the Spanish rite as well, down to today when most of the members of the two synagogues are neither of Spanish nor of Portuguese origin.

A different issue is what happens to synagogues that grow so large as to be almost unmanageable. Then the sameness of local custom subdivides into smaller, breakaway groups. For example, the Young Israel of Woodmere expanded and expanded to accommodate its rapidly increasing population. But some members solved the problem by focusing on what made them a sub-group—in this case that had grown up praying *nusakh Sfard*, the Hasidic custom, and therefore set up their own synagogue based on this new commonality.

Some large synagogues have new arrivals to the community requesting permission to set up a small *beit medrash* group, praying either in the basement or in the small chapel alongside the large sanctuary. It is up to the main group to give permission. Sometimes—as in Milan—the downstairs group can even outnumber the people praying in the main sanctuary.

The most difficult situations can arise when the synagogue group is small and from varied backgrounds. Then the basic cement of *minhag ha-makom*, local custom plays a powerful role in keeping peace in the synagogue. If this peace is shattered—either by an ineffective rabbi or a visiting *hazzan* who thinks that only *his* custom is valid, or by a combination of the two—it is very hard to get people back together again. History is replete with such examples.

The self-denigratory jokes connected with contentious Jews or multiplicity of places to pray contain a modicum of truth, and that is why Responsa from across the ages and across the Jewish world strongly adhered to the principal of "local custom prevails."

Jewish Law and Custom

Ramifications of *Kashrut* Laws
April 18, 2003

The laws of *kashrut*, as presented in Leviticus 11, can be viewed as a prototype for Jewish law and Jewish life in general. We are given the principles of the *kashrut* of four-legged mammals with specific examples of what is not allowed. Then we are given only the principles of the *kashrut* of fish. We are then given only specific examples for forbidden birds.

When the laws of *kashrut* fit into general philosophical approach that a basic element of Judaism is self-control, the laws, as presented, have led to the constant intellectual challenge of applicability. What happens, for example, when a new animal appears on the "radar screen" of traditional Jews? This happened when explorers moved southward through Africa and discovered the giraffe. Yes, it chews its cud and has wholly-divided hooves, but . . . Then, with the discovery of the New World came the discovery of the turkey, which, at that stage, was a wild bird, not the domesticated fowl of today. Australia has peculiar animals, as does Malaysia. These new animals tested the legal decisors, and we have records of their thinking.

The world of fish remained relatively unchallenged until the end of the nineteenth and early twentieth centuries. Then two issues arose challenging the minds of the scholars: What do you do with a fish (that until then was considered non-kosher) that biologists discovered had scales only in the water, but lost them when extracted from the sea? The second had to do with the discovery that some fish (until then considered non-kosher) had scales that could be seen with a microscope.

The constant intellectual challenge of the laws of *kashrut* expanded into packaged products as these were invented. Traditional Jews learned how to read labels, how to understand terms for *treif* products—e.g., glycerin—and for dairy products—e.g., whey. That was before *kashrut* labeling expanded throughout America, making life much easier for traditional Jews.

But laws of *kashrut*—as all other areas of Jewish life—also have an added layer of custom. As we move toward Passover, we should remember that rice is not forbidden on Passover in the Torah. South of the Mediterranean and across the Middle East, this is the basic food on the Passover table, not potatoes. This is becoming an issue again as more and more intercommunal marriages are taking place.

Returning to the challenge of applicability of the laws of *kashrut*, one should also keep in mind that historically, the local rabbis were faced with practical on-the-spot questions that required immediate decisions. For example, a woman came with a freshly killed chicken to a rabbi five hours before Shabbat (in a world without packaged chickens), saying that she could not find the gall while cleaning it—was it kosher? The easiest thing to say was "no," but Jewish law is seldom black and white, and the true scholar is the one who can move in the gray area, pulling out arguments allowing the woman to cook the chicken, or she and her family would go without meat on Shabbat.

That is the ultimate, intellectual *halakhic* challenge, which we are losing as our world becomes increasingly black and white.

Jewish Law and Custom

The Synagogue Service

October 17, 2003

In my class, "The Sephardic Experience," we are discussing, among other topics, the formation of the Jewish communities throughout the Middle East and Spain after the rise of Islam. One of the subtopics is the setting up of synagogues and their power structures. The writing down of the first "order" of prayer as the Responsum from Amram Gaon to the Jews of North Africa is not only important in its content, but also as an example of the centralization of religious power in the capital of the Abbasid Empire.

The early "order" of prayer, or *siddur*, would have kept people in the synagogue for about two hours. Add to that the reading of the Torah on Shabbat or holidays, and you have maybe another hour. The sermon or learned discourse would add twenty more minutes. This was true of what we can see of medieval and Renaissance Italy as well. So when did synagogue services turn into five- to six-hour marathons? And when did it become a matter of pride to state on Rosh Hashana, "Oh, we did not finish until 3:00 p.m."?

Tirkha de-tzibura (the burden on the populace) has always been an important concept in Judaism, and has always been a guideline for legal decisors. My grandfather always told his synagogue members not to wait for him to finish *Shmone-Esrei*, but to start the repetition without him, putting this concept into practical application. My father used to go up behind the *hazzan* who was warbling away in our synagogue in Washington Heights and stage whisper "Tirkha de-tzibura" to hurry him along.

True, most people do enjoy a *hazzan*. But, if the *hazzan* is only going to sing Rosh Hashana services from *Hineni ha-ani*, just before the *Musaf* service begins, then the earlier service should be said more quickly, or the services should begin much earlier. Surely, the majority of the people no longer appreciate the poetry of Elazar Ha-Kalir. Give me the religious poetry of the Spanish Jews any time, like Yehuda Ha-Levi, Solomon Ibn Gabirol, or Abraham Ibn Ezra. Poetry in the ancient Hebrew tradition had neither rhyme nor meter, but used parallelism for effect.

The new poetry of the Spanish Golden Age utilized Arab forms and themes which dramatically transformed religious as well as secular works. The intensive study of Hebrew and Bible—in part a reaction to Muslim study of Arabic and Qur'an—played a role in this transformation by enriching the poems with Biblical allusions. So did the inclusion of the poet's own religious feelings, reflecting the Psalms of David.

Anyone who says that Jewish tradition does not change does not really know Jewish history. The role of the *hazzan* today is not what his original role was. In the early stages of synagogue worship and well into the Middle Ages, the *hazzan* not only led the services, but he composed parts of the liturgy as well.

So, if prayer books could change over the centuries, as could the melodies, and the role of the *hazzan*, let alone the role of the rabbi, maybe it is time to rethink the length of our High Holiday services once more. Some groups already have—such as the Young Israel movement and the Ashkenazi Israeli neighborhood synagogues, both of which replaced the *hazzan* with a prayer leader. I personally like a *hazzan*, for a good one elevates the soul through his music and devotion.

Jewish Law and Custom

Social Justice
June 10, 2005

The Torah portion of *Be-har*, which covers the topics of the sabbatical year, the jubilee year, the poor, and slaves, is probably best analyzed from the perspective of social justice. We are not only reminded of the Creator of the earth, but, in returning the land to the original owners, we are enjoined to safeguard ourselves against having a split society, with the landless poor on one side and the rich landowners on the other. These laws set the groundwork for social justice and charity through the ages. Charity is directed first to your own poor, starting with your family, moving to your clan, and then your tribe. But right from the start the ethical and moral code of altruism included the non-Jew, for *ger ve-toshav* in Biblical Hebrew referred to non-Israelites.

Thus, the Torah, reinforced by the Prophets, provided the Jews with a kind of blueprint for charity which they carried into exile, and which became part and parcel of every Jewish community, no matter where it was, whether in Cairo, Meknes, Cordoba, Metz, Altona, Minsk, Baghdad, Bialystok, or Venice. What began to change came with modern times, as Jews moved out of their various ghettos and into post-French Revolution societies.

The Jewish community of the United States forms a prototype for the changes. At first, the charitable organizations formed were the self-help type such as the *landsmanschaften* (groups based on point of origin abroad), the Hebrew Burial Society, orphanages, and traditional synagogue charities. But in America, women also became involved in a variety of formal organizations too, geared to specific needs of girls and women, such as the National Council for Jewish Women, which, among many other things, met incoming ships at the docks to ensure that single women traveling alone were being met by family or legitimate people. Political Zionism was another modern element thrown into the charitable mix, not only manifesting itself through the ubiquitous blue and white *pushkas* for Keren Kayemet, but also in the formation of Hadassah, the international women's organization geared toward health care in the Palestine Mandate.

With the rise in economic status of the Jews in America as well as its secularization, charity gradually became philanthropy. The focus now became the setting up of hospitals, and cultural organizations such as concert halls and museums. The philanthropy and ideals of social justice for all harks back to the Bible, and manifested itself also in the 1950s and 1960s in Jewish activism in the civil rights movement.

The field of philanthropy is now being studied in many universities. Philanthropists have formed groups that hold seminars for younger donors on how to set up foundations and how to give wisely. Universities depend on their alumni to be generous, and Jews form an outstanding percentage among these donors. And we do give. There is nothing like growing up and watching your parents reach into their pockets or bags to put a coin into a beggar's hand to drive the point home. My father's repeated lesson was that anyone who opens his hand to you for money is desperate, and it is your obligation to put something into that outstretched hand.

So, what started off as divine dictum has become part and parcel of the Jewish psyche. We truly are a charitable and philanthropic people.

Jewish Law and Custom

In Memoriam

August 5, 2005

Observing a *yahrzeit* is a given for all observant—and not so observant—Jews. But how often do we contemplate the possible origins of this custom, and the customs surrounding the custom? Most scholars agree that the basic reason for observing a *yahrzeit* for a parent is the desire to honor one's father and mother. The Talmud refers to taking a vow to abstain from eating meat and wine on the day of the anniversary of a parent's death. In another brief comment, the Talmud refers to honoring a person through learning Torah. Hence, we have two of the most common practices for most Jews, although many have expanded the abstention from meat and wine into a total fast. In rationalizing this expansion, scholars claim that by fasting on the anniversary of the death of a parent, the children relive the pain of the loss.

What does one learn in "learning Torah"? The specific custom in my paternal family is learning Mishne. There is a key in some publications of the Mishne with all of the chapter headings listed alphabetically. Taking the name of the deceased, one learns one chapter per letter. My father's names add up to seven chapters; my mother's add up to three. Dozens of customs regarding what to learn exist.

But over the centuries and in different parts of the world, other customs arose too. The public chanting of the Mourner's Kaddish in the synagogue is one of the most popular. The reasoning behind this is obvious: if a child had to say Kaddish during the year after the death of a parent, it is only appropriate to recall this obligation on the anniversary of that parent's death. Note that the organizers of the synagogue service placed the Mourner's Kaddish both at the very beginning of the morning services and at the very end. This was probably an attempt to ensure the early convening of a quorum as well as maintaining the quorum until the end of services.

A final custom generally kept by all Jews is the lighting of a memorial light. Ashkenazi Jews use a candle; many Middle Eastern and Sephardi Jews use a floating wick, i.e., a wick on oil on water. The whole issue of light is a complex one, mixing the history of anti-Karaism, mysticism, and symbolism. Sometimes the original purpose of a custom has long been forgotten—like the anti-Karaism one—and a new definition takes on a life of its own.

Moroccan Jews visit the grave of the parent on the occasion of the *yahrzeit*; most Sephardic and Middle Eastern Jews do not. Hasidic Jews do not fast. They uniquely take the opposite position, that the soul of the deceased is ascending higher in the spiritual realm, and so it is a cause of celebration. Mitnagdim oppose this concept strenuously.

Almost all Jews also give charity to mark this event. This is a topic unto itself. Suffice it to say here that honoring one's parents this way is a very old custom unifying all of the various groups of Jews geographically and historically.

The best way, however, to honor one's parents is to live the life that they exemplified and taught us. That way a *yahrzeit* is almost unnecessary for us, since we remember them on a daily basis.

Jewish Law and Custom

Presentation
February 17, 2006

There are many people who judge their meal by the quantity on the plate before them, and, as long as the taste is acceptable, they are happy. There are others who are more judgmental about taste, but also demand quantity. The third type demands that more of their senses be satisfied, namely, taste, smell, and vision. In other words, the presentation of the food counts as much, if not more, than the quantity. My father belonged to the first group; my husband belongs to the third.

When kosher restaurants first opened in America, they catered mainly to the first approach. As years passed and competition grew, they moved into the second category. It is only lately, as the palates of kosher-observant Jews have become more sophisticated, that restaurants catering to them have opened as well. This holds true in Israel too, where at one time, you only could find "home-style" places, but now you can find restaurants as sophisticated as the Montifiore in *Mishkenot Sha-ananim* in Jerusalem.

Aesthetics have always been important to some Jews, but the poverty of Eastern Europe seemed to have taken its toll on this level. I am sure that there always were housewives who took the trouble to present food beautifully. We are enjoined to celebrate Shabbat and the holidays, to dress up, and to use finery for the table, if we had such finery. A tablecloth would be the most basic decoration for the table in almost all European households.

Always aware of what the larger Gentile community was doing, over time table decorations and cutlery, including napkins, forks, and crystal goblets, were copied by the Jews. The wealthier Jews were exposed to eating etiquette as well. It may be presumed that there were always some people who were more geared toward aesthetics than others, just as some were better cooks. Italy and France probably led the way in presentation of food, just as they led the way in other art forms.

Aesthetics were important to the Jews of antiquity. We don't know much about their eating habits, but we do know about their synagogue decoration. Anyone who has been to Bet-Alpha or Bet-She'an can attest to the wonderful mosaic floors that have been excavated. These decorations added to the spirituality of the sacred space.

There are many Jews who do not need decoration in the synagogue, and they can concentrate on their "inner spaces" while praying, oblivious to all else. There are other Jews who are satisfied with a synagogue that is clean and orderly. But a third group really finds aesthetic presentation a necessity in order to get into the right frame of mind for prayer. This is the group that, throughout the ages, insisted on beauty in the synagogue, whether it was the architecture or the ritual objects.

The Torah scroll in an Ashkenazi synagogue, with its rich velvet cover and silver decorations, is a given, but it is not enough, if the rest of the sacred space does not match it in elegance. Sometimes one doesn't realize what is missing from his or her synagogue until seeing it elsewhere. That is what happened to us in Jerusalem when we attended the Italian synagogue located on Rechov Hillel. It is not enormous, like the Great Synagogue or the nineteenth-century synagogues of Milan or Rome; it is also not small like so many of the overcrowded one-room neighborhood synagogues. All of the decorations were transported from Italy, and the interior architecture was copied from that of the original building. The ark is covered with phenomenal fabric, as is the inside; the backing of the Torah scroll is made of scarlet fabric. There is real pomp and ceremony here.

Jewish Law and Custom

Blessings
September 29, 2006

We make blessings on everything. Some we make daily, such as the blessing on eating bread. Others we may make once in a lifetime, like the blessing on being in the presence of royalty. I remember checking out the proper blessing before going to Queen Elizabeth's "walkabout" when I lived in London and how envious my father was over this.

Only traditional Jews get doubly excited over seeing a whale breaching, the expanse of the Sahara, or the vista of the Alps—excited over the experience and also over making the blessing over God's creativity. Thunder and lightning? It's a flashback to my childhood, reciting the two blessings with my father.

The connection of specific blessings with my mother took place after her death, when I began to light Shabbat candles and use the *miqve*. I thought of her and felt the link to the traditions of women.

We just put up our *mezuzot* in our new apartment, and each of us recited the blessing over a different room. I could picture the *mezuzah-*niches in the gates and outer doorjambs of the medieval Italian cities, as a last reminder of a piece of history, for those Jews had moved northward, leaving their old homes behind.

When I teach Judaic Studies 1001 and discuss the topic of blessings and that we bless just about everything, I wait for the wise guy who will say—"Even going to the bathroom?" "Oh yes," I reply, "Can you imagine your plumbing not working?" Silence. Then a quiet "wow," as I translate the blessing said after using the facilities.

We are now entering a new year, and the stress on newness is such that we all have the custom of eating new fruit. The problem is that we now have access to all kinds of fruit all year long—from Chile, Australia, Israel, China, let alone from the hothouses all over the United States. I had to grab away the fresh figs my husband was going to eat a few weeks ago to ensure that we could all use figs for our new fruit. The other fruit, for the second night, will be either pomegranates or star fruit. I go to fruit stores, especially upscale ones, espy something new, and make the storekeepers crazy by asking how it grows. "Waddaya mean, how it grows? It grows!" Does it grow on a vine like grapes, on a bush like blueberries, on the ground like pineapple, or on a tree like an avocado? In Chinatown I had to draw pictures to get my response, as we did not have a common language. "Crazy lady!" I can hear them thinking.

Yes, we Jews have to know really strange things about agriculture, botany, fish, cheese, and chemicals. The other day I explained to a Turkish grocer why I could not buy a certain product as it had milk in it. He read the ingredients carefully and said there was no milk listed. So he got an English lesson in whey and curds, and we talked about yoghurt (a Turkish staple), white cheese, and keeping kosher. He remembered with nostalgia the Jewish market in Istanbul with its special products.

So we will all eat foods dipped in honey to mark a sweet New Year, and we will bless God for granting us life and the ability to eat new fruits. And then we will move into pre-Yom Kippur mode of solemnity and repentance.

Jewish Law and Custom

A Moving Prayer
September 12, 2006

A pregnant woman was on her way to synagogue on the first day of Rosh Hashana when she felt the onset of labor pains. She told her six-year-old daughter to knock on a neighbor's door. The ambulance arrived quickly, the healthy baby was delivered, and the *brit* was scheduled.

A colleague of mine told me that on Rosh Hashana evening, an older man walked in to his synagogue, sat down, and died. He had not bought a seat, and no one recognized him. The police eventually found a receipt from Staples in his pocket, and they traced his identity via his charge card.

For me, the most moving prayer of the *machzor* read during the Days of Awe is *U'Netaneh Tokef*. It is one of the few examples of lofty prose-poetry written in Ashkenaz, for such poems were usually composed by Spanish Jews (such as Dunash Ibn Labrat or Yehuda Ha-Levi). Rabbi Amnon of Mayence is said to have composed it as he lay dying, later appearing to Rabbi Kalonymus ben Meshullam in a dream, teaching him this prayer.

The prayer describes the heavenly procedure on the Day of Judgment. No translation does justice to the purity of the Hebrew words and the precise imagery, which evokes the Bible. All people pass before the Judge of the world "like a flock of sheep," with each one passing individually for decision-making. By the time this was composed, there were very few Jews who were shepherds, but the stories of Jacob, Rachel, and David were engraved indelibly in the national imagination.

How perfect it is for the "People of the Book" to be inscribed in books, with one's destiny sealed on Yom Kippur. Then comes the list of what every human being fears—the ways one can die. Fire, water, war, animal attack, hunger, thirst, earthquake, plague, strangling, and stoning are enumerated. Each can be connected with current events, whether it is Hurricane Katrina, the war in Lebanon or explosions in Iraq, AIDS, shipwrecks, and stingray attacks.

It is interesting to note that the composer included peace of mind and peaceful settlement as a positive thing, as opposed to the tormented and the displaced. It is not easy to be uprooted and thus a refugee looking for safe haven, as has been a reality for Jews throughout history.

Economics always is part of our prayers, for aggravation over earning a living can ruin one's health physically, mentally and spiritually. "Who shall be lowered and who shall be raised" — the final poetic description — lends itself to multiple interpretations — economic, social and psychological.

We all hope that the stern decree, decided on by the Judge of the world, can be canceled on Yom Kippur through prayer, repentance, and charity. David repented in front of Nathan the prophet, and his sin was forgiven. Moshe prayed for Miriam, and her leprosy disappeared. As for charity, the Bible is replete with so many laws connected to this topic that Jews have become the epitome of philanthropy and generosity.

May we all be inscribed in the Book of Life.

Jewish Law and Custom

Tefillat Ha-Derech
June 8, 2007

We travel so much that many of us do not pay close attention any more to the words of *Tefillat Ha-Derech*, the Traveler's Prayer. It is only when something goes wrong that the true meaning of the prayer leaps into our minds. We request that we arrive at our destination in peace, using four different expressions, and that there should be no enemy attack along the way.

The composer of the prayer probably had in mind the long caravan trips across the Middle East, or the sea voyages across the Mediterranean or those hugging the coastlines of the Indian Ocean. Piracy was always a danger, as was illness and natural disasters. We usually do not think in those terms today. By the time we go through all the preliminaries of boarding a plane, including all the security searches, stuff our carry-on luggage wherever we can, and find our seat, we are so tired that we just mumble through the Traveler's Prayer once the plane is in the air.

That is, unless something goes wrong, like: "Ladies and Gentlemen, this is the captain. We are having some problems with the landing patterns at JFK International Airport due to weather conditions." Half an hour later, the same announcement is repeated, with the additional comment, "We may have to land in Syracuse." By this time everyone on the plane is silent. We are totally attuned to the banking motions, as we realize that we are circling again and again.

The captain keeps up his patter, trying to update us with the latest information, but after circling for over an hour and a half, he forgets that the intercom is on, and we hear: "Flight 34 to control. We have fifteen minutes left of fuel. Repeat, we have fifteen minutes left of fuel. Request immediate permission to land." After the initial dead silence, we can hear someone softly weeping, and various people praying in a variety of languages.

I had a window seat and had landed innumerable times at JFK. I did not recognize our landing path until we were almost on the ground. That was then it hit me—we had been directed to the takeoff runway. But land we did, to the cheers of everyone on board. We zoomed past jets that were already in pre-takeoff mode and ended up in the far end of what looked like an overgrown cement parking lot. No one minded that we had to sit there for almost an hour before a berth was found for our plane or that everyone with connecting flights missed their connections. Later we found out about the storm and that the sudden winds in New York City and the surrounding areas were of tornado force. My taxi driver filled me in on these details as we drove through the lashing rain.

So when we say *Tefillat Ha-Derech* on the return trip, we add the phrase that we "be safely returned to our homes." The author, living so very long ago, composed a prayer that resonates across time and place, as is true with so many of the prayers that we say that are connected to the human condition.

Jewish Law and Custom

A Special Relationship
August 14, 2009

Whenever I teach a class that included the rites of passage in Judaism, I end up spending more time on laws and customs connected to death than on any of the other topics. Non-Jews are very curious about what we do and why, and compare this to their own religious customs. Jewish students, even those with a yeshiva education, are often totally ignorant of the laws and customs, unless a grandparent had recently died. This is part of the general modern attitude of protecting the young from the disturbing realities of life.

One of the subtopics is the difference in the length of the mourning period for siblings, spouses, and children with that of the yearlong (minus one month) mourning period for parents. The practical aspect, historically, of the need to move on with life, especially if the living spouse is left with young children, overrides the emotional aspect of the relationship. Death was a constant possibility in a world without modern medicine, and women in childbirth were particularly vulnerable, as were very young children.

The longest mourning period is for parents, for you may have multiple siblings, spouses, and children, but you only have one mother and one father. That used to be the end of the discussion. But modern science, as well as the realities of modern life, brings about new questions. "My parents are divorced, and I was raised by my stepmother," says one student. "Does that mean that I do not mourn for the woman who raised me?" "My mother died when I was a baby, and I only know my stepmother, does that mean that I can't mourn for her?" Reshuffled marriages were a reality of the past, so these questions can be answered relatively easily.

New technology has allowed if *in vitro* fertilization and implanting the embryo into a woman who is a surrogate mother. She is the woman who carries the baby to term and gives birth. There is also the technology that allows for the removal of the nucleus of the ovum of a woman, to be replaced with that of a fertilized ovum of another woman. Again, the nonbiological mother carries the baby to term and gives birth. Who is the mother? Is she the birth mother or the biological mother? I heard a lecture on this topic by Rabbi J. David Bleich a number of years ago, and there are multiple *halakhic* ramifications to the issue of surrogacy.

Technology has certainly impacted our lives in incredible ways, but no technology can replace the bonds between mother and child. As a child, I thought that everyone had a relationship with her mother similar to mine. It wasn't until I was a young teenager that my innocence was shattered. I spent a Shabbat with a classmate and witnessed the excruciating verbal abuse by the mother, followed by the slaps across the face by the father, all in front of me, the guest. I sat there in paralyzed horror, and left for home right after Shabbat. Then I started really looking at my friends' relationships with their mothers and realized that I was one of the lucky ones.

That luck continued into adulthood. In a culture, which viewed as essential that women marry at a relatively young age, she stood by me as I refused to do so. In a culture that did not encourage women to study for a PhD, she stood by me as well. She even volunteered to travel through the Middle East with me when I won a travel grant and could find no one who would go with me. So, in her fifties, she found herself in southern Spain, Morocco, Lebanon, Iran, and finally Israel. Except for the time that I spent sick as a dog in, first, a Moroccan hospital, and then in a Spanish one, we had a wonderful time. It was forty years ago, and I can envision us standing in a park in Madrid looking up at the moon as the reports came in on the first moon landing.

Ten years later, my mother died in Jerusalem. My firstborn daughter is named after her, and I hope that the lessons I learned from my mother have been passed on to both of my daughters. The special relationship of mother-child is not a given; it has to be nurtured carefully.

Jewish Law and Custom

The *Eruv*

January 14, 2011

I grew up in neighborhoods without an *eruv*. Going to synagogue on Shabbat always involved the special house key, the wrist tying of linen or cotton handkerchiefs, and the checking of pockets to make sure they were empty.

The first time I remember carrying on Shabbat was in camp, and my father—as part of his duties—walked the perimeter to check if everything was in place. He often took me with him to serve as a second pair of eyes, and he entertained me by teaching me the laws of *eruv*, as well as telling me of his experiences with this in Eastern Europe. Daughters of rabbis learn *halakha* and *minhag* in practical ways such as this, as well as by simply observing what their fathers do at home and in synagogue. That is how I know, for example, how my father put on his *tefillin* and his *tallit*, and the melodies he used while praying. We have, in effect, a practical education. If we have a father like mine, who answered *halakhic* questions posed by his daughter by citing the legal reasons for doing something, then our practical education expands.

One of the nice things about living in Jerusalem was having an *eruv*. This was serious stuff, not just the small perimeter of a summer camp. This meant women could go to synagogue with young children, and not have to switch off child care duties with husbands, with one spouse going to an early *minyan* and another going to the regular one. Or, as often is the case, the woman simply does not go to the synagogue on Shabbat. As an ardent synagogue attendee, I find the latter situation deplorable.

Washington Heights has an *eruv*, which is diligently checked by members of the *eruv* committee of Mount Sinai Jewish Center every Friday afternoon. Rabbi Ezra Schwartz, the new rabbi of the synagogue, has given classes on the laws of *eruvin*. Yeshiva University has its own overlapping *eruv*. But there are always people who "don't recognize the *eruv*," and it is easy to pick them out, as the men are often wearing their *tallitot* under their coats. It's fine with me if people want to make this choice, but not if they then view themselves as "more religious" or "really Orthodox"—

whatever that means—in comparison to those who do wheel the baby carriage to synagogue.

What ticked me off recently was a comment made by someone that there was no use of an *eruv* in a place like Brest-Litovsk, in Jewish Lithuania, before World War II. Instead of losing my temper, I told the story my father had told me, of how, at least once a month, usually about two hours before Shabbat, a couple of *goyim* (his word) would rush up to his house, knocking loudly on the door: "Rabbi, Rabbi, come! Your fence is broken!" My grandfather would quickly go with them, check where he had already checked earlier that afternoon, and pay the *goyim* a few *groschen* to fix it. My father said he knew, and his father knew, these men had done the damage themselves in order to make a bit of money, but everyone played the game. The bottom line was that only with an *eruv* could the *cholent* be carried to the various homes from the baker's oven after synagogue was over for Shabbat lunch.

So don't tell me that there was no *eruv* in Brest-Litovsk. Why these false histories are being told is another story.

Jewish Law and Custom

My Brother's Death

February 25, 2011

On Shabbat afternoon, February 5, our doorbell rang. Two police officers were standing there. It is every parent's nightmare, but in this case it turned out that my nephew in Los Angeles had been frantically trying to reach me. He had just been informed that his father—my older brother—had died and he did not know what to do. He had called the local police to ask them to inform me.

My brother's death has turned into an international legal issue, as well as a *halakhic* one. He died alone, in a hotel on the island republic of Palau (I had to Google it as I had never heard of it). My nephew was listed as the person under "To be contacted in case of emergency or death," which is on every passport. The police of Palau took over, informed the American Embassy (Yes, there is one on an 18,000-person island republic), who contacted my nephew. Now come the complications: they would not release the body until a finalized police report was made and a death certificate issued. They are totally laid-back there, and the coroner probably comes to the island only once a week. Meanwhile the body was in the refrigerator of the local hospital, which would not release it until they were paid. No charge cards—only money orders, please.

To add to this is the complication of getting the body to Israel for burial. The *Chevra Kadisha* was notified. However, there are international laws as well as Israeli laws concerning unaccompanied bodies. Israel, worried about terror attacks, insists on having the name of a family member is Israel (or designee) meeting the plane. Only funeral homes can arrange for the flight. Everything has to be paid in advance. Who knew?

Then there is me: I called my rabbi right after Shabbat and asked if I was going to have to be an *onenet* for about a week, the condition of limbo of close relatives before the funeral takes place. He asked: Did your brother die in New York? Are you going to the funeral in Israel? No and no. So, as is written in Mo'ed Katan—*Hekhzir panav min ha-met*, I "turn my back" on the dead and focus on myself. I did *kri'a* and sat *shiva*. The irony was that I got up from my *shiva* before he was buried. I felt part of a long line of similar incidents that happened throughout Jewish history. Actually, some people who paid *shiva* calls entertained me with stories of deaths in Norway, even in Maine where the ground was frozen and no burial could take place for months. The rabbinically and *halakhically* knowledgeable people who came to the *shiva* were fascinated with the actuality of something they had studied theoretically. The lawyers were more fascinated by all the international legal implications.

My brother always wanted to be the center of attention. He managed to do this with his death, alone on an island on the edge of the Pacific Ocean, near the Philippines, north of Australia.

As I was writing this, the police report finally came through. The cause of death is listed as "probably myocardial infarction"—no autopsy was allowed, as he was a Jew. (Don't ask how many e-mails were sent making this clear to the authorities, along with forbidding embalming.) Now my nephew and cousins have to deal with the rest, and my brother's remains will make their way, soon we hope, to Bet Shemesh.

Jewish Law and Custom

The Glassmakers
May 20, 2012

One of the intellectually exciting and challenging things for a professor to do is to create a new course. This semester I am teaching "Making a Living: Jews, Business, and Professions from Antiquity up to the Modern Period." I have always included sidebars to my other classes touching on this topic, but now I have the chance to focus specifically on it.

Using chapters from the Bible, one can follow how the Hebrews started out as pastoralists, yet with the conquest of the land of Israel, most Israelites became farmers. Closely reading some chapters in Kings, one can find details of international trade, and what people at that time valued, such as precious metals—including copper and tin—dyes for textiles, textiles, wood, spices, olive oil, gemstones, grains, and slaves. Gemstones are also spelled out in the description of the twelve stones used by the High Priest on his breastplate. These stones included carnelian, jasper, amethyst, turquoise, lapis lazuli, and garnet. Spices were used for perfumes, incense, medicines, cosmetics, and preserving foods. At the time of King Solomon, what started out as a contract to import timber and qualified workers from Tyre (Phoenicia), ended up with the Israelites learning how to quarry the stone needed for the Temple, and to "dress" the stone into the desired shapes. Solomon also learned to build a merchant fleet, and to exact tolls on the north-south overland highways. Ezekiel 27 contains a detailed description of the trade of the Phoenicians along with the dirge of their demise.

Thus Israelites moved into new ways of earning a living, and those who grew wealthier—possibly from trade, possibly from crafts, and possibly from extending land ownership—spent it on better homes, better foods and more possessions. Along with this conspicuous consumption, as encouraged by the Torah, they also gave more to charity.

During the period of the Second Temple (536 BCE–70 CE), with the use of archaeological studies as well as by studying written texts, a specialized profession of the Jews comes to light: glassmaking. It did not start in Israel—probably in Sumer or Akkad—but was adopted quickly by the Jews and the countryside itself lent itself to this profession. The raw materials of ancient glassmaking, including silica, found, for example, in sand or quartz, are there, along with forests to provide the fuel needed for the furnaces. The Jews applied pyro-technology, including the use of glazes, and used bellows to control the fire. The centers of glassmaking were in the Galilee and the Judean hills, outside of towns and cities. The glassmaking used a core method at first; glassblowing came centuries later. Interestingly, the most desirable glass was not the colored kind but the clear products.

As Jews moved into large Diaspora communities, they brought the secrets of glassmaking with them. The Greeks in Alexandria disdained this kind of craft, as did the Romans in Rome and Aquileia, the Roman city in the northeast of Italy. They relegated glassmaking to inferior peoples, such as "Orientals," a general term which included Jews. There isn't even a word for "glass" in either Greek or Latin. But there certainly was a market for it. Glass beads were found all over the Mediterranean archaeological sites, and these beads even made it as far as China, following the Silk Route trade. When glassblowing was invented, glass became cheaper and would be used for tiny bottles to hold precious liquids, for containers of all sorts—the Romans used them to hold the ashes of their ancestors—for tableware, and for lamps.

The secrets of glassmaking remained a Jewish secret until the European Middle Ages in the West, and until the eve of modern times in the Middle East.

Italian Jews

A View from Naples

May 23, 1997

Looking out over the Bay of Naples, from halfway up the mountain, I can see the large curve of the port well protected from the sea. I can see the islands of Capri and Ischia in the distance, and on the shoreline I can clearly trace the distance between the two protective castles with their turrets and thick walls. I have already visited the castles and learned firsthand how easily they controlled entry to the port during the Renaissance period.

In my mind's eye, I can see the arrival of the Spanish Jews in 1492, because for an all-too-brief time the Kingdom of Naples offered protection to the refugees, before Spain took over southern Italy and exiled the Jews of the new provinces as well. Among the refugees were members of the Abrabanel family, headed by Don Samuel and his wife-cousin Bienvenida.

The Spanish viceroy, Pedro de Toledo, met these outstanding Spanish Jews and took advantage of Bienvenida's knowledge to use her to assist in the education of his daughter Leonora. One can walk down a main street in Naples which is lined with Renaissance palaces, still in use, albeit most not as palaces. Some of the buildings are used by the Istituto Universitario Orientale, where I have been lecturing students on women in the Bible. I can easily picture Dona Bienvenida arriving in a horse-drawn carriage from her home, bouncing along cobbled streets, emerging in her billowing skirts to quickly enter the gray stone or brightly painted palace (yellow and sienna red were the favorite colors), into rooms with gilded ceiling and wall moldings, lit by tapers in gilded candelabra, and lined with thick, flowered carpets, their walls decorated with paintings, statues, and colorful tiles, for which Naples was famous.

The friendship between the young Spanish noblewoman and her Spanish-Jewish teacher continued after the former's marriage to the Grand Duke of Tuscany. It was this tie that enabled the family to move north to Ferrara after the expulsion of the Jews from Naples in 1541, after almost ten years of disputing among the Neopolitans themselves. One can visit the "Parliament" chamber where they met to discuss the issue—in the main castle—but one cannot visit the old port from which the ships carrying the Jews northward embarked. That part has been built over, but it doesn't take too much imagination to picture the small wooden sailing vessels loading up, with the boxes and packages being brought out to the ships by smaller longboats. Finally, the passengers would be transported, tearful farewells have been completed. Once more the Abrabanel family and all other Spanish Jews were forced out—this time accompanied by all the Italian Jews, some of whom could trace themselves back to Roman times.

Ferrara is a lovely small inland city, but for Dona Bienvenida, used to the warmth and color and beauty of the port city of Naples, it must have been a difficult adjustment. No longer young, a widow at that point in her life, she focused both on rebuilding her home and on helping the larger Jewish community. I'm sure that from time to time she fondly remembered *Bella Napoli*.

Ghetto Jews

November 19, 1999

When, as a result of Pope Paul IV's bull of 1555, known as *Cum Nimis Absurdum* (after the opening words), the Jews of Italy were gradually forced behind the walls of the ghetto, the Jewish community was faced with a major question of internal organization. This was true of Jewish communities everywhere and throughout history, but ghetto-ization made internal organization even more important as there was limited space for ever growing numbers, fewer ways of earning a living, and rising numbers of the impoverished.

To prevent landlords from exploiting tenants as well as to prevent the tenants themselves from competing for the limited spaces, the rabbis used the law of *hazaka* or proprietary right. Tenancy right became absolute and could be inherited or used as part of a dowry.

In such close quarters, the Jews could enforce mandatory education for all children, boys and girls. This fulfilled the Jewish value of educating children, and it also kept children out of the labor market, providing more work for adults. To make sure that all children attended, schooling was free, the expenses covered by voluntary contributions. In Ferrara, instruction was mandatory until age sixteen at the communal free school. Elementary school teaching was mainly in the hands of "Dames' Schools" (conducted by women).

Besides education, almost every phase of life was cared for by the many pious confraternities (*hevrot*), which took care of the sick, the cemeteries, burial, birthing mothers, weddings for poor brides, and sometimes even Hannuka and Purim gifts of food and clothing to poor children.

The internal government of the ghetto was not democratic, but oligarchic. Each ghetto—especially the large ones such as in Rome, Venice, and Ferrara—had a General Congregation comprised of all the major contributors to communal taxation. (This effectively disenfranchised poor men, let alone all the women.) They elected a smaller responsible council from which three wardens (*massari*) were chosen by lot, to serve for three-month periods. These *massari* were the most powerful men in the ghetto, for they were ultimately responsible for raising the taxes to be paid to the government as well as to maintain the community. These taxes, for example, paid the salaries of the rabbi, the sexton, the ritual slaughterer, the secretary, the postman, and the gatekeeper.

Life became more harsh with the passage of time, and although intellectual life continued to flourish in the traditional rabbinic fields, as well as in literature and poetry, both Hebrew and Italian, and mystical thought—by the eighteenth century the majority of the Jews of Italy spent most of their time just trying to eke out a bare living. Men and women spent all their waking hours sewing and retailoring second-hand clothing, one of the few economic areas left open to them. Intellectual creativity became a luxury of the few wealthy families. Just as the ghetto walls seemed to become more narrow, so did the lives of the Jews within. Escape, for many, lay in either emigration or conversion. Liberation from the ghetto awaited nineteenth-century ideals and actions which culminated in a unified modern Italian state.

Jewish Symbols

October 1, 2004

In preparing for one of my classes on the Jews of Italy, I was searching for primary sources to show the students how historians learn from them and, in effect, how history is written. One of the more difficult periods is the classical period of ancient Rome. There are scattered Roman sources about Jews, such as works by Tacitus the historian and Juvenal the satirical writer. The search for Jewish sources is difficult, since each has its specific problems—for example, the works of Josephus Flavius and the Book of Maccabees.

So, I will supplement the written records with archaeological sources such as the catacombs with their carved inscriptions and images, as well as photographs of the ancient synagogues uncovered in Italy. The Romans remarked: "They (the Jews) bury the body rather than burn it" (Tacitus). This apparently astonished them. The Jews hollowed out underground crypts and burial chambers in soft volcanic rock. They not only incised or painted sepulchral inscriptions on or beside the burial site, but also made symbolic statements of Jewish identity as well. Since the words were often in Greek, and later in Latin, one cannot presume the Jewish identity by looking only for Hebrew lettering. That is why the symbols that are used take on added importance.

The most popular symbols include the seven-branched menorah, the lulav and etrog of the Sukkot festival, the cabinet or ark that hold the Torah scrolls, the shofar, flasks (for wine, perhaps), and disk-like objects that are probably matzot.

The frequency of use of these symbols shows their importance to the users, but one cannot read into these symbols any deep mystical or theological meaning, for the ancient Roman Jewish community was mainly an uneducated one, with a prevalence of craftspeople. But there was a commonality of belief, and the symbols chosen probably represented the same thing across the centuries: the menorah refers to the original one used in the Temple in Jerusalem and God's everlasting light; the Torah ark refers to the replacement of the Temple by the synagogue; the shofar—

associated with the High Holy Days—refers to a reaffirmation of belief and the Day of Judgment.

So these are symbols of connection to Judaism and to the Jewish people, and serve as signs of identity. The most important ancient synagogue, accidentally discovered in 1961 in Ostia, the ancient port of Rome, also contains these Jewish symbols. This is what probably clued the archeologists into the realization that the building was not just another ancient site. Upon closer examination, the layout showed it to be a synagogue, and the clay lamps found there with a menorah on each one confirmed it completely. The inscriptions confirm the fact even more, with the Torah ark set in the eastern wall so that the worshippers would all be facing Jerusalem.

The menorah, as we all know, symbolized the fall of Judea to Rome in 70 CE, as it was triumphantly carved into the Arch of Titus. But the Roman Jews used this to symbolize their identity, and this continues well after the fall of the Roman Empire. It is not accidental that the seven-branched menorah became the symbol of the newborn State of Israel.

As for the original menorah confiscated by Titus and paraded down the streets of ancient Rome, the search for it continues down to today. Does it still exist, was it buried under what became the Vatican buildings, or was it melted down by the northern invading "barbarians"?

Synagogue History
October 15, 2004

One of the most important laws passed by Julius Caesar that affected the Jews was the law exempting them from the regulation against private associations. This enabled synagogues to be founded and flourish. Synagogues served as community centers used for prayer, study, and social services such as distribution of charity. These synagogues were the stopping points for visiting scholars, who collected contributions for the academies in Israel after the destruction of the Second Temple. These visiting Palestinian scholars also helped organize and educate the Roman Jewish communities, and the mutual ties continued until the dissolution of the Patriarchate at about 400 CE.

The oldest synagogues also attracted pagans, and we read of converts as well as semi-converts who, for example, observed the Sabbath and were attracted by monotheistic ideas. More than one synagogue was to be found in larger centers. Rome itself had over a dozen different congregations. Some were organized on a district basis—namely, they were built where there were Jewish neighborhoods. Some were founded by worshippers who came from a particular place of origin, for example from Alexandria; some were founded by free slaves; some had their method of earning a living as their unifying bond, for example, the cobblers' synagogue of Rome.

The synagogues were organized, and used Greek titles. There was a council of elders, a supervisor of services, a sexton or *hazzan*, a secretary, a political representative, and there were honorific titles given to outstanding benefactors, both men and women. There was no rabbi.

But gradually, for a combination of reasons, the late Roman emperors began to pass a series of anti-Jewish laws. They could not revoke laws already passed, but they could move into the gray areas. Therefore, Jews could have synagogues but could not build new ones. The Romans understood the powerful attraction of these spiritual centers, and therefore attempted to limit them.

Once the Roman Empire fell, power moved into the hands of the bishop of Rome who, by the seventh century, took the title of Pope. At that point, the history of the Jews of Italy changed. Yet, almost ironically, the most powerful protector of the extant Jewish synagogues turned out to be Gregory the Great (590–604 CE). While fervently wanting all Jews to convert, he insisted on securing those rights that were theirs by law.

Gregory checked the abuse of the bishops who were confiscating synagogues by ordering inquiries, and if the law had been broken, either the synagogue or its value was to be returned to the Jews. This happened in Terracina, a seaport north of Naples, and in Palermo, the main city of Sicily.

As we follow the history of the synagogues of Italy through the Middle Ages into the Renaissance and the Ghetto period—there are many fascinating things to focus on. Synagogue architecture is one example, as is synagogue art and the varying customs they reflect.

We live in a country that prides itself on freedom of religion. One irony in our synagogue history is that in the United States, where we can pray as we wish and attend as we wish and build as we wish, we have a declining synagogue attendance, with the exception of the High Holy Days. A second irony is that when a group of Jews wants to set up a new synagogue because this group is drawn together by mutual interests (as was done in ancient Rome), it is not the governing authorities that put up obstacles, but fellow Jews, very often using the oldest weapon in the world, *lashon ha-ra*, slander.

The history of the American synagogues is being researched and written by scholars, and some of their conclusions are remarkable within the broad orbit of Jewish history.

Italian Jews

Completing a Course
January 7, 2005

In the final part of my course on the Jews of Italy, we actually reached the twentieth century, as described in my course outline. I say "actually," because I clearly remember both college and graduate courses that promised to cover the twentieth century, but the professors never got past World War I, if that far. But the buildup to the twentieth century is integral to the course, as I take the students out of the ghetto and through the full emancipation of the late nineteenth century.

The Jews of Italy began to see themselves as Italians who happened to be Jewish; otherwise, they were just like their neighbors who also viewed them this way. One of the reasons contributing to the low percentage of Jews killed in the Holocaust in Italy was the general attitude that Jews were citizens who happened to be Jewish. Their neighbors knew them, and many were willing to help them escape and even hide them. But this is a complex topic with many more factors involved.

We traced the Italianization of the Jews through Jewish artists such as Amadeo Modigliani, whose art is of his time and not particularly Jewish. We traced this also through literature, with students reporting on Natalia Ginsburg—the ultimate example of the assimilated Jew—and Giorgio Bassani (author of *The Garden of the Finio Continis*), whose writings reflect the acculturated Jew, and, of course, Primo Levi.

Primo Levi, an Italian Jew from Turin, was one of the thousands caught and sent to Auschwitz. He survived and considered it his duty to tell his story of survival in order to prove that Hitler had lost his "war against the Jews." Primo Levi wrote that it was rabid anti-Semitism that awakened his pride in his roots, but he was also Italian and chose to return home after the war.

Vittorio Segre, rejecting his assimilated parents' view on life, left Italy at the age of sixteen for Palestine just before the war. His writings represent a small group of Zionists who felt that a Jew's true home was in the Land of Israel.

World War II was the focus of a number of classes. The video *The Righteous Enemy* depicted how wherever the Italian armies went in Europe, ordinary soldiers as well as officers protected most Jews from deportation. These occupied areas were in southern France, Croatia, and Greece. The same thing happened in Libya and Tunisia. The average Italians flouted Mussolini's orders. The topics of both Mussolini's activities and those of Pope Pius XII were discussed at length, as well as the German occupation of northern Italy starting in September 1943. It was during German rule that the roundups and deportations of Jews took place.

Finally, we discussed contemporary Italy, the rising rate of intermarriage, and the arrival of the two newest Jewish groups that are succeeding in bringing stability to the communities of Rome and Milan in particular. I refer here to the Jews who arrived from Libya in the 1960s and settled in Rome, and to the Jews who arrived from Iran mainly after the fall of the Shah at the end of the 1970s and settled in Milan. I will be addressing these two groups and their impact on the Jews of Italy at a conference that will be held in January.

I don't get to teach this course very often, but when I do, I enjoy it immensely. I certainly hope that my students do as well.

Italian Journal
Part 1

February 1, 2008

I just spent the day in the city of Parma, at the Palatina Library. I held in my hands Hebrew manuscripts that date back to the Renaissance and earlier. Not only was I overwhelmed by the idea of physically touching Jewish history, I was also in awe over the first signature on the library slip of most of these manuscripts, namely, that of Solomon Schechter, who signed for these books in the late 1800s. No one had looked at these books in ten years, which is a shame because they are history.

Imagine what these books had survived—overuse, censorship, confiscation, time. Obviously, the paper used was of a very different quality than that used today. Some of the volumes were written or printed on parchment. The most worn-out sections of the *siddurim* and *machzorim* that I examined were the daily prayers, Shabbat prayers, and the Haggada (which in earlier times was often part of the general *siddur* or *machzor*). The least used parts were often in pristine condition. Some of the handwriting of the scribes was not very clear; other times the handwriting was wonderful.

To reach the rare book and manuscript section of the Palatina Library, one has to go through tight security and cross the main reading room. The building itself is from the Renaissance, and one has to climb majestic staircases—good exercise for the heart. The main reading room is at least three stories in height, and one's eye is led up, and further up, to row after row of bookshelves. The ceiling is ornate in its decoration and such beauty can easily distract the reader. The inner sanctum is much, much smaller.

The librarians follow a very old system. The reader fills out a form listing the call number of the manuscript. The reader also signs two books: one on receiving the manuscript and the second on returning it. The form is divided into three pieces—one for the manuscript itself, one to be exactly placed on the shelf in the stacks, and one kept by the librarian. This way there can be few mistakes in re-shelving and keeping track of it. The Ottoman Turks used a similar system.

Parma itself is a charming small city. There was once a small thriving Jewish community in Parma, but that was centuries ago. The Hebraica collection there, however, is much larger than the one housed in the Ambrosiana Library in Milan. The Ambrosiana dates back to 1609 and houses 30,000 volumes and 15,000 manuscripts, of which only 196 are in Hebrew. Most were acquired in the seventeenth century, as the founder of the Ambrosiana, Cardinal Federico Borromeo, was an avid scholar of Hebrew. Some were donated by people like Dr. Moshe Lattes.

The reading room is a converted, covered courtyard in a centuries old building, rising at least three stories high, with multiple statues set up around the huge room to distract the reader from his work. Here the wearing of white gloves is mandatory to protect the manuscripts from dirt and oils. Unlike the Palatina, which is state-owned and hires mostly women librarians, the Ambrosiana is private, Catholic, and run by men.

I had a chance to go through a fourteenth-century *machzor* and a Bible dating back to 1236. The Bible is divided into three parts and is illustrated. The beginning of each of the five books of the Torah (which has an Onkelos translation alongside the Hebrew) has gold-red-blue decorations, often of fantastic birds and animals. They are available in reproductions, but nothing matches seeing the real page yourself.

Now it's on to Florence, Rome, Venice, and Bologna in search of further manuscripts and early printed books.

Italian Journal
Part 2

February 15, 2008

The quest for information for my project took me from Milan to Florence, Rome, and Venice. After visiting the two overwhelming libraries of Parma and Milan, I took the other libraries in stride. The Vatican Collection is closed to the public for three years, so that visit was out, but the Hebraica Collections are on microfilm in—of all places—St. Louis, Missouri. That will require a separate visit.

Meanwhile, I enjoyed walking the streets of the three cities, trying to ignore the broken cobblestones of Florence and uneven sidewalks of Rome. The Jewish community of Florence is stable, and there is a kosher restaurant near the glorious nineteenth-century synagogue. There is also a not-so-subtle war between the Italian Jews and Chabad, which is going on in Venice and Milan as well.

The Venetian community is also a stable one, and praying in the beautifully decorated Sephardic synagogue was inspiring. The rabbi—Rav Ricchetti—is a personality, and his sermons are the traditional kind. Too bad many people there did not understand his erudition, for he spoke in Italian. There are young Italian Jews there too, but the community is too small to support a Hebrew day school or a yeshiva. Only Rome has those numbers, and I saw the students emerging from the newly acquired building behind the main synagogue in the ghetto. The school goes from kindergarten through high school and is the key to continuity of the Roman *kehilla*.

For the smaller communities, it is public school and private tutoring for Jewish subjects, a system that has been working in Italy for centuries. I met a number of young people who have been educated this way, and they are knowledgeable and Zionistic, yet proudly Italian. One young Venetian Jew was so homesick for Venice while he was studying in London that he simply had to go home. I understand that this is a personality quirk of many Venetians, Jews included.

You walk the streets of Venice, ride the *vaporettos*, trying to absorb all of that architectural beauty. Venice is like a fairy city with no cars, hundreds of bridges, piazzas, and under-the-building-passages. You easily get lost, as the signs leave much to be desired. You ask directions and are told something like, "Walk two bridges straight, take a *sottoportego* on the left, then the first *calle* on the right." Oh yes, like it really works. So when you get to the water, again, with no bridge or alley, you turn around and try again. The best promenade that I had was with a young Venetian professor of Judaic Studies who took us to see some of his favorite places. It was the only time that I could just relax and look, instead of worrying about getting lost.

Were the Jews influenced by the beauty that surrounded them over the centuries? Of course they were. That is why the synagogues are so beautiful, as are the ritual objects on display in the small museums. The Roman Jewish museum has been fixed up and expanded. I like the Torah "dresses" made of fabulous fabrics even more than the ark covers. And the lace decorations on the *tallitot* were marvelous.

I have two more days in Milan to finish my work, and then it's back to New York and reality. It has been a most productive trip.

Searching for Signs

November 6, 2009

I am on sabbatical this semester. Professors need sabbaticals to enable us to concentrate on research and writing, which also lets us recharge our batteries, so to speak. My project is a big one, and part of it includes searching for the remnants of the Jews of Sardinia, the island to the west of Italy. Much research has gone into the Jewish presence of the Roman period, when thousands of young Jewish men were exiled to the island by the Emperor Tiberius to work in the salt mines and to protect the Romans from Sardinian brigands.

My interest is in the next wave of Jews, arriving probably as early as the 1200s or 1300s from various provinces of Spain or southern France. They came as merchants, and, depending on who was ruling which section, they settled in small numbers in port cities such as Cagliari, the capital in the south, and Alghero, in the northwest. Jewish artisans began to arrive as well, specializing in dyeing and working with leather. By the 1400s the island was almost completely under the control of Aragon and Catalan, two of the main kingdoms of Spain before the country was unified. As a result, when the Jews were expelled from Spain in 1492, the expulsion extended to all Spanish provinces including Sardinia.

What happened to the Jews? Scholars have focused on the large cities of Alghero, Sassari, and Cagliari. They trace movement to the Italian mainland and the Kingdom of Naples. Some converted to Christianity, and the names can sometimes be traced through church records.

But some of the Sardinian Jews followed a Sardinian path, i.e., they moved away from the coast up the mountains to safety. Sardinia is not defined by its cities, but by its mountainous interior. Its people are as old as the Jews, and no one has yet been able to definitively determine where those first people came from nor how they built the *nuraghi*, those ancient circular stone towers, three to four stories high, with no cement. Any time there was an invasion, be it the ancient Phoenicians, the medieval Arabs, or the later medieval Spaniards, the Sardinians withdrew to their mountains and resisted change.

So I was determined to search for remnants of these Jews, as they became *Conversos* to "wait out" the Catholic pressure, especially of the Inquisition, in some mountain towns. I felt like a detective. Some interviews with people have led me on a wild goose chase. For example, one town is known as "the town of the Jews." It turns out that the reference is really to a pejorative stereotype, interesting in itself, for the townspeople are known for being stingy!

But then I lucked out and found a *carrela de sos Ebreos*—street of the Jews, in a small town in the central mountains where tradition has it that until the end of the twentieth century there were still some families practicing rituals that can definitely be traced to *Converso* practices, like lighting candles Friday night in a secret cabinet, blessing the bread and sprinkling it with salt, cleaning the house before Passover, and going to church only once a year and entering last via a side door, then leaving first through the same door.

It is very exciting on the one hand and terribly sad on the other. While lighting Shabbat candles this past Friday evening, I felt the ghosts of the past looking over my shoulder in contentment. *Written in Sardinia, October 21, 2009.*

Megillat Antiochus
December 3, 2010

On the Shabbat of Hannuka, Italian Jews read Megillat Antiochus. In the *siddur* of Rabbi Shmuel David Luzatto (SHADAL) it takes up about five pages. It is written in clear Hebrew, with echoes of Megillat Esther, and seems to be a summary of Maccabees of the Apocrypha, focusing first on Yochanan Ben Matityahu and his victory over Nikanor, Antiochus's general. The revenge of the king on the Jews includes the story of the nameless woman who circumcised her son in defiance of Antiochus, leaping off the wall of Jerusalem with her baby. It also includes the deaths of 1,000 Jews who refused to desecrate Shabbat. Then the text turns to the five sons of Matityahu and their successful uprising, detailing the deaths of both Judah Maccabee and Elazar, the reconquest of Jerusalem, and the miracle of the pure oil burning for eight days, setting the stage for the declaration of the eight-day holiday of Hannuka.

Yet, that is not all the Italian Jews read on Shabbat Hannuka. There is also a *Yotzer* for that day. This type of religious poem is a kind of *piyyut*, in keeping with Jewish poetic tradition going back to the Bible. The poet invokes a variety of Hannuka stories, unifying them in three-lined rhymes. Thus there are the tales of the heroic mothers circumcising their sons, the (nameless) mother and her seven sons, the daughter of Yochanan the Hasmonean (see below), the revolt of Judah Maccabee and finally the ultimate heroic figure of Hannuka for the poet—Judith.

> *The tyrant then added another horror*
> *When the bride was to enter the house of her husband*
> *She was first to sleep with the governor;*
> *This was the last straw*
> *It lasted forty moons and four months*
> *Until Judah, the holy priests rebelled.*
> *When the glass was full, God gave charm*
> *To the soon to be married daughter*
>   *Of Yochanan the Hasmonean*

Who gathered the people for the wedding feast.
The bride stripped off all of her clothing
And lifted a wineglass to the company
Who lowered their eyes so as not to look at her.
Her brother was in great rage against her
That the honored guests had seen this.
"How could you stand naked before them
                              like a prostitute?"
To whom the beautiful young woman replied:
"How dare you rebuke me so hypocritically
When you allow me to lie naked with
                    an uncircumcised heathen?"
Then the spirit of God possessed Judah
And his heart was full of strength and courage.
He prayed and was possessed by an ardent zeal.

How these customs arose among Italian Jews is part of scholarly speculation. It is presumed that when the first Jews came to settle in ancient Rome most came from Greek-speaking Alexandria, and they brought with them the Septuagint, the Greek translation of the Bible, which included the Apocrypha or "External Books." Maccabees and Judith are part of this collection. The earliest extant prayer books, following Roman custom, include both the *Yotzer* of Hannuka and, in many, Megillat Antiochus. Therefore, this must have been part of a long tradition. But the Judith of the *Yotzer* is not the very powerful Apocryphal figure, but a more toned-down *midrash* variant. Why this happened is also part of scholarly speculation.

A further custom of Italian Jews connected to Judith and Hannuka is the eating of salty cheese dishes, commemorating her act of feeding cheese to the Greek general to make him thirsty so that he would drink too much wine, thus enabling her to behead him. Renaissance art also produced *hannukyot* with heroic Judith figures holding a sword high in the air to symbolize Jewish victory.

(The translation of the *Yotzer* is mine.)

Opinion

Elul: A Lesson in Tolerance
September 7, 1991

My grandmother, who lived in Brest-Litovsk, used to go to the cemetery every Elul. My grandfather never went, and taught his children by example that attachment to the cemetery was wrong and could even be destructive. My grandfather proved to be right, if we look at how many Jews could not bring themselves to flee disasters that they knew were coming because of their attachment to the dead.

Jews were taught, right from the beginning of our nationhood, not to be attached to the dead. God hid Moshe's last resting place from us lest some kind of tomb pilgrimage with all its concomitant superstitions and false visions arise from knowledge of the location of Moshe's grave.

Lithuanian Jews in particular, with their rationalist approach to Judaism, followed this attitude toward non-attachment to cemeteries. Instead, when a *yahrzeit* arrived, they sat and studied things like chapters of *mishnayot* which began with letters that spell the name of the deceased, a custom still followed by my family.

If this was the attitude, why did my grandfather not prevail on my grandmother not to visit the cemetery? It took another woman to give me a plausible explanation. My mother, a woman blessed with incredible insight into her fellow-beings, said that perhaps her mother-in-law went to the cemetery for purely personal reasons. Life was very harsh in Brest-Litovsk in the inter-war years, and my grandmother also suffered from the aftereffects of a stroke. She had also buried who-knows-how-many infants in that cemetery. A trip out there was an acceptable way to cry and give vent to all her anguish, something she could not and would not do at home. After her catharsis of weeping, she could return home to carry on her life as best she could.

My grandfather probably understood this and therefore did not stand in her way by stating his long-held beliefs to his wife. *Shlom bayit* is one of the underpinnings of all marriages, and being dogmatic about things peripheral to Judaism's core can sometimes cause more harm than good.

The roles have switched in my generation. I do not go to the cemetery, not for *yahrzeits* and not in Elul. My younger brother does. He cries there, has private conversations, meditates, and finds his personal catharsis by going to our parents' graves. The conclusion I draw from this is that gender has nothing to do with who needs to visit the cemetery and who does not. I remember my parents and follow their teachings every day of my life; therefore, I have no need for cemeteries to connect me with the past, nor with the future, but I make no value judgments on other people's needs nor, of course, on other people's customs. *Shlom bayit* should not only be a major principle for domestic peace, but also for the entire "house" of Israel.

Opinion

A Legacy
October 18, 1991

The month of Cheshvan is called *mar* or "bitter" because, according to tradition, it contains no holidays. In my father's family, this month is truly bitter for on *rosh hodesh* the Nazis broke their pact with Stalin and invaded eastern Poland, moving in the direction of Moscow. Three days later, they reached Brest-Litovsk and proceeded with their unspeakable deeds, executing every Jew in the city. My grandfather was commanded to put on his *tallit* and was, as head of the community, shot first, before the eyes of his horrified and terrified *Kehilla*, which he had refused to abandon although a visa to the US had been obtained for him.

From the time I was very young, I understood that *mar Cheshvan* was a time for tears, as I heard my father studying *Mishnayot* aloud in the traditional mournful sing-song of the Litvaks. He did not believe in sparing the feelings of young children, but told us—as he learned the details from the few survivors of his city—what he knew. I knew the anger and frustration of young free Americans in trying to understand why the Nazis hated us and why we didn't fight back. I also gradually knew the resolve of continuity, but there, the frustration was different. How could I, a granddaughter, continue the family tradition, when rabbinic leadership was closed to me?

Great scholars and leaders generally have children, but there is no guarantee that these children will be male, nor that if there are male children, these will be the ones to inherit the intellectual ability or other talents of the father. In the patriarchal setup of Judaism this can cause frustration both on the parental side and the offspring side. Many daughters of rabbinic families have unquestioningly aspired to marry scholars, and through their sons, provide rabbinic continuity. Other daughters have fought this approach, and although agreeing that biological continuity was important, set out to be as educated as possible within the spheres of Jewish study left open to them.

Today, while still excluded from the all-male rabbinical arena, Orthodox women can and do develop their intellectual gifts, if so motivated.

They can and do become leaders and molders of minds as teachers, professors, public lecturers, writers, scholars—of Judaic Studies, which is an all-encompassing term. This is in addition to, and alongside the roles of wife/mother.

I personally feel saddened when I see a daughter of an outstanding rabbinic family using her intellectual talents to further the fields of computer science, economics, chemistry, etc., when I know that had she been male, there would have been no question that her talents would have been geared to Jewish fields. On the other hand, as daughters of rabbis, they have a wider arena of choice, and perhaps the sons resent their lack of choice in rabbinic continuity. Many sons of rabbis not only do not continue their father's role, but often move out of active Judaism altogether.

Why not take the easy way out? Ask the children of rabbis to find out about subtle and not-so-subtle lessons in communal responsibility, in the value of teaching, and, most of all, in the obligation to the Jewish people. Today's rabbinic daughters are caught up in this as well, and we have some fine examples of their contributions in all areas excluding the area of rabbi. The Jewish people are the benefactors of this modern phenomenon.

Opinion

"Jewish" Food

February 7, 1992

There are very few children who do not pass through a phase wherein they are sure that they were adopted. In my case, this feeling was based on two pieces of evidence. The first was that I could not stand "Jewish" food. Everyone raved about *kugels, tzimmis,* gefilte fish, chopped liver, sweet wine, and most of all, that epicure's delight, *cholent*. If this was culinary delight, why did I feel sick after every *Kiddush*, and after every Jewish party? The only answer I could think of was that my genes were not Jewish and so I could not digest these foods.

As the years passed, I realized that my mother had the same problem. Yes, she was an excellent cook, but, no, neither of us could digest "Jewish" food. Was she, too, adopted? Then I reached the age of being invited to dinner parties. What did I discover? Not all Jews ate "Jewish" food, but each ethnic group ate ethnic food that was kosher. What I had been exposed to all my young life was Eastern European food, more specifically, Polish-Lithuanian food. "Kosher" wine was, in fact, Concord super sweet grape wine, and there was an infinite variety of other wines including dry wine, all of which were kosher.

At school, in home economics classes, I discovered American food, including the fact that beef could be eaten rare instead of "Jewish," i.e., overcooked to the point of the inedible.

I've always maintained an interest in Jewish ethnic foods, for this has traditionally been the realm of the woman of the house. Since Jews were poor, generally, throughout history and in almost all geographic areas, foods had to be invented that were filling, healthy, inexpensive, and expansive. The last necessity was due to the fact that Jews are among the most hospitable in the world and therefore unexpected guests were common.

Thus, fish was chopped and padded with inexpensive fillers; meat could be treated the same way, or it could be the flavoring in a stew made up of inexpensive potatoes and/or beans. The women of Italy played with pasta recipes and with chopped-up vegetables that were the base of a chopped meat sauce. Middle Eastern women did the same thing with rice and couscous dishes. The differences lay in what was most easily available as well as what was in season.

Jewish holidays brought a massive flurry of activity in the kitchen. Imagine life without a refrigerator and where everything had to be prepared from even before "scratch," i.e., grinding the grain into flour, collecting the eggs from the hens, butchering the meat, plucking the chickens, drying the grapes for raisins. Holidays brought women's culinary creativity to a peak, and, carefully abiding by the strict laws of *kashrut*, Jewish women through the millennia have brought the glow of each Sabbath and holiday to the table. Hopefully, they were appreciated.

No wonder that even as many Jews of today move away from traditional Jewish life, their fondest memories of their youth seem to be almost totally connected to the traditional foods eaten on special occasions. These "gastronomical" Jews are proof of the lasting power of Jewish women's activities. Some of these wanderers end up in my classes, in later years, searching for some meaning for these memories. It is up to people like me to recharge these memories with something stronger than just an aroma of Judaism.

Opinion

The Cost of Being Jewish
October 31, 1992

In medieval times, Jewish communities generally imposed a tax on themselves, the details of which differed from community to community and from country to country. Thus a Jewish family in Mainz, Istanbul, Fez, and Venice paid money which was assessed by fellow Jews, and went toward normal community needs, such as synagogue upkeep, soup kitchens, and marrying off poor brides. Schools such as we know them today did not necessarily exist, but we have material to show that—in thirteenth-century Cairo, for example—community funds were used to educate orphan girls to read and write. The teachers taught more as tutors, rather than in a formal structure, although in late medieval Rome we know of Hebrew day schools for boys as well as for girls.

One of the results of the crisis of modernization was the weakening and then the disappearance of the Jewish communal structure. Certainly, the trip across the Atlantic to America saw its almost complete demise. Very few Jews tried to rebuild the communal structure of their old home, with some notable exceptions in the German and Syrian groups.

The availability of free public schooling combined with the separation of church and state enabled many Jewish immigrants to educate their children without fear of Gentile missionizing. They figured that in this new country the parents and the synagogue were enough to ensure their children's Jewishness. If any child did receive some Hebrew training, it was inevitably the male child, for girls "did not need" Hebrew education as they would "only" be responsible for a kosher kitchen and running a Jewish home.

Small groups of traditional Jews did begin to establish *yeshivot ketanot*, and the question of who should pay for this education reared its head quite early. Some school administrators decided that the school was like any other business, and only parents who paid would have their children educated.

We have a story in our family of how, some fifty years ago, a relative could not pay for his son's tuition in a well-known *yeshiva ketana*, and the boy was sent home from school as a result. Desperately reaching out to others, the father bitterly swallowed his pride and a compromise was reached; the boy went back to school. He is now a rabbi in the New York area. Imagine what could have happened to him—and to the community— had others not intervened. But for this one success story, how many others do each of us know, of children who were thrown out of or never even accepted to a *yeshiva ketana* because the parents could not afford to pay the tuition on the spot?

Who should pay for our children's Jewish education? Should these schools be run as "for-profit-only" enterprises? Is this what America has taught us? How can we get the entire Jewish community to recognize that investing in the Jewish schools which educate boys and girls is our insurance for Jewish continuity? How can we convince people who do have money to donate for plaques on doors, or plaques dedicating rooms, or plaques on an *aron kodesh*, or huge plaques in memory of the departed, that their money would be more productive in scholarship funds or in lower tuition attained through endowments? Step number one may be to raise the issue and underscore the fact that it is reaching crisis proportions.

Opinion

Intertwining Links
April 30, 1993

Anyone who had even the slightest contact with *HaRav* Dr. J. B. Soloveitchik, spent the days following the news of his death reliving their experiences. I am no different. I could see myself as a child being brought to his rooms at Yeshiva University by my father, each time being scared, each time being put at ease by the Rav. I was scared, I realize in retrospect, because there were very few people of whom my father spoke with such respect. I was also scared because the initial impact of meeting the Rav was the feeling of those powerful eyes seeing right into me. What was the topic of discussion? What I was learning in school, of course, secular as well as religious. This ritual was repeated year after year until I finally rebelled and refused to go unless I would not be tested.

The only time I spent alone with the Rav occurred the year that my mother died. I was in Boston for a conference and went to *daven* in the Maimonides *minyan* during the week, according to the obligations of a child during the year of mourning. When I went up to the Rav after the services to say hello and to thank him for his support (see my article "Kaddish from the 'Wrong' Side of the *Mechitza*" in *On Being a Jewish Feminist*, ed. by Susannah Heschel), he asked me to come visit him on Shabbat afternoon.

Taking a deep breath, I approached the house at about teatime. The Rav came into the room where I had been seated, and asked me if I was still pursuing my Jewish studies. It was as though his testing of me as a teenager had merely had a brief interruption instead of about a twenty-year break. When I told him what I had been doing, he nodded his head approvingly, saying that there was more than one way to contribute to the continuity of Judaism.

He spoke briefly of the hundred years of interconnections between our two families, checking to see if I knew all the relevant facts. With a sigh, he then asked how my father was dealing with the death of his beloved wife. When I described my father's difficulties, the Rav sadly nodded his head understandingly. Then he asked me something which at the time I thought strange: Did I remember his mother? Of course I remembered his mother.

Every Shabbat, in Washington Heights, I went with my mother to visit his mother, the *Rebbetzin*. In my life, there was no other *Rebbetzin*. She got smaller as I grew taller, but her persona never shrunk, not did her erudition. We discussed the weekly portion, what I was learning in Hebrew literature classes, and what I was reading in general. These conversations were usually cut short by the arrival of the "ladies" of the neighborhood when the topics turned to things of no interest to me.

The Rav said that his mother had had a great influence on his life, and that it made him feel good to know that there was a person of the next generation who could tell of her personal acquaintance with his mother to the generation after that. This personal link between the past and the future was the story of the continuity of the Jewish people. I am the next generation, the American generation, having had no experience with the European chapter other than reading books and listening to what the European generation had to say. My role, according to the Rav, was not just to study Jewish history and to teach it, and to inspire my students, but also to be the living link between the two generations. He could tell me personal stories of my grandfather, my father could tell personal stories of the Rav's grandfather, and I could tell stories of his mother, thus forging our intertwining links.

This principle applies to my minor contacts with the Rav—minor to him, major to me. For a man who defies description and whose incredible influence on American Jewish history has yet to be analyzed, this brief account of his kindness to an *avela* (mourner) and of his gentleness with children, can serve to illuminate a facet of the Rav's personality that is generally not depicted. He was not only a giant; he was a nice man. May his memory be a blessing.

Opinion

A Personal Chana

August 6, 1993

Most of us have a Chana or two in our family. It is one of the more popular Biblical names, possibly because the Biblical Chana is a woman with whom many of us can identify. She is not a heroic figure like Deborah, nor a larger-than-life figure like Miriam. She is a woman who wanted only one thing out of life: motherhood. When she finally attained that status she rose above the ordinary and became a religious poet *par excellence* composing a paean of praise to God, a poem on which the *Shmone Esrei* was designed. Perhaps this poetry was always within her, perhaps she composed poetry before this—we shall never know. The only thing we have in the text is the one poem.

The other Chana of great renown is of the Greek period, and is a totally different figure. This woman is nameless in the text of Maccabees and is only named Chana in the Talmud. She is the Jewish figure of tragedy, for hers is the story of the loss of seven sons. Her faith in God is firm, for she knows that idolatry must be shunned even at the expense of death.

Both Chanas are the objects of artistic expression in the Renaissance and in most illuminated manuscripts that have survived down to today. The paintings or etchings reflect the styles of the artists' times, but the message of religious joy or human tragedy is clear in each work of art.

There have been other Chanas—or the translation of the name—in all periods of Jewish history. Some of the more outstanding ones are Dona Gracia Nasi, Gracia being the Spanish translation. There is Grace Aguilar, the British defender of Judaism in the nineteenth century. Chana Senesz died heroically during World War II after parachuting behind enemy lines to try to help the Jews there. Anna Rovina was the famous star of the new Habima theater in Israel, remembered for her role as Leah in *The Dybbuk*.

I have two personal Chanas who are very close to me. My mother's name was officially Chana in Hebrew, Chan-tche in Yiddish, Anne in English. People have asked me why I mention my father here and there but rarely mention my mother. Perhaps it is because my feelings for my mother defy description. We were mother-daughter, but we were also best friends.

She made me humble, for with all of my knowledge and knowledgeable friends and colleagues, she—with her high school degree—was probably one of the most intelligent and wise people I have met. She could judge people instantly, but wisely kept her opinions to herself. She was never wrong, a fact that used to drive me wild as I was growing up.

She stood alongside my father as a fortress protecting me and yet allowing me to find my own way in life. She urged me to continue my education, to be independent, to travel the world; her implicit trust in me helped keep me on the right path. Her untimely death almost destroyed me, but I could hear her urging me back to life, to productivity, to happiness. She has been gone fourteen years, and I still miss her profoundly. A compensation for her loss is the second Chana—my daughter who is named after my mother. So far she is living up to her namesake.

Opinion
_____

In Defense of Vashti
1992 [rejected by the press]

When I was a child, I never wanted to masquerade as Queen Esther on Purim. Instead, I insisted on dressing up as Queen Vashti, and I decorated my face with pimples or my hair with horns, depending on which legend appealed to me more that year. When asked why I chose to be Vashti instead of Esther, I had difficulty articulating what was a gut reaction: something about Esther disturbed me and something about Vashti impressed me.

As I grew older, became more educated and more analytical, my attitude toward the two women did not change; in fact, it deepened. My questions about Esther became more distressing as did my questions about the commentators who, it seemed to me, were whitewashing her behavior. The bottom line for me was her passivity in her uncle's ordering her to participate in the "beauty contest" when it meant sleeping with and/or marrying a Gentile. One could get into details left out of the text—but conveniently supplied by the commentators like keeping Shabbat and *kashrut*. Just the fact that they saw fit to comment on these issues shows that the topics made them uncomfortable.

I find Esther, as a person, a tragic figure. She was sacrificed as a Jew for the good of her people. History has provided us with a list of shadowy Jewish women who acted in a similar fashion, becoming mistresses to kings, thereby protecting the Jews, for example, Raquel in Spain and Estherke in Poland.

Perhaps that is why I preferred Vashti, even as a child. This was a woman whose actions I could understand. Historians tentatively identify her as the daughter of the king conquered by Ahashverosh. In other words, she was a princess. In good Middle Eastern fashion, Ahashverosh married her partly to strengthen his own claim to the throne. Continuity would thus be provided at the same time that he started a new dynasty.

Vashti, as a person of royalty, knew what her duty was, and behaved properly until her upstart husband demanded something unforgiveable from her. "On the seventh day the king ordered his eunuchs . . . to bring Queen Vashti before him wearing her royal crown to display her beauty to the people and the officers, for she was a beautiful woman." This verse may be read, "wearing *only* her royal crown." In so doing, Ahachverosh probably knew that he would be pushing Vashti to the point of disobedience and no one—not even a royal princess/wife—could disobey the king. Did he really want to get rid of her? Probably yes, for if her response of standing up to him and refusing to obey such a demeaning order is indicative of her independent spirit, she probably had manifested this independence at other times, irking her husband who—to judge by his choice of Esther—preferred a passive obedient woman.

I always wondered what happened to Vashti. I prefer to envisage her banished from Shushan, living in a house on the banks of the Euphrates, free of her hated, crude husband, and able to enjoy a quiet life to the end of her days.

Opinion

Family Purity

April 2, 1992

Tazria is not one of my favorite Torah portions. It is very difficult for a thinking and educated woman to see the laws of ritual purification after childbirth linked to the laws of leprosy. Yet perhaps it is because I have had to wrestle intellectually with the laws of ritual purity for women that I am able to present the topics of *nidda* and *miqve* in a positive manner to my students. This positive approach was made clear to me ten years ago when I was preparing to get married in Jerusalem.

Marriage is part of the domain of "personal status" in Israel, and therefore, Israeli law places it in the control of the Chief Rabbinate (or church or mosque, depending on your religion). There is no secular "personal status." So, once we decided to marry, my husband-to-be and I had to register at one of the Chief Rabbinate's office and open a *tik ravakut*, or bachelor's file. The rabbi who interviewed us was most annoyed as he took our personal particulars, and when I caught the sense of what he was mumbling in Yiddish, I explained that we were not leaving things for the last minute, but that we had only met the previous week. Stunned, the rabbi said, "Why didn't you say so right away? Mazal tov! But how are we going to fit in all your classes on family purity and *miqve* into two weeks?"

Classes? Yes. In Israel every woman planning to marry must attend classes given by a *rabbanit* on this topic. Then she is given a *petek* (slip of paper) to be stamped by the *miqve* lady to be handed to the officiating rabbi as proof of having fulfilled her obligation to immerse before the wedding.

The rabbi personally took me into the *rabbanit*'s office, explained the need to rush and left. Smiling, the woman took a pile of books and pamphlets off a shelf, put them next to her on the desk, and began to read my file. Under profession, I had written "Professor," and she asked me, "Professor of what?" Normally I do not vaunt my knowledge or background to strangers, but I had no intention of spending hours in a family purity class. So I proceeded to explain what I taught as a professor of Judaic Studies, including a course on the Jewish woman.

After a moment of silence, she returned almost all of the books to the shelf. Then she quietly asked: "You teach the laws of *miqve* to religious Jews, irreligious Jews, and Gentiles?" Seeing my nod, she continued: "Do they react positively or negatively?" When I said that most had a positive reaction, she jumped up and agitatedly moved around the office.

"But how do you do this? I teach these laws and most of the women hate them!"

My turn to ask: "How do you teach them?"

She pulled out a couple of pamphlets to show me, and I had to restrain myself from shouting—"These are horrible! How can you?!" The pamphlets, loosely translated, said "Daughter of Israel, beware! If you do not go to *miqve* you will have physically deformed children (with illustration of unspeakable horror) or mentally deformed children (ditto), and you, yourself, will become sick!"

Quietly I tried to explain to this woman the differences between teaching positively and negatively, and the differences between performing a commandment out of understanding and performing it out of fear. As I spoke, I realized that my personal wrestlings with the unpleasant issues of family purity laws—whether philosophical or psychological or historical—had led me down the path to such a positive approach to the larger issues that I am able to convey this to my students. The *rabbanit*, who meant well and tried her best to teach Israeli women, could not understand me at all. But, after an hour's discussion, I was excused from taking classes. As I got up to leave, she gave me the pink slip for the *miqve* lady, and wished me well.

Opinion

Memories

September 2, 1994

Strange things happen around holiday times. One starts having flashbacks to childhood memories connected with preparations. Among the many things we did during Elul was go to make "special" visits to "special" relatives. One such visit was to my father's first cousin, Feigel, who at the time was living on the Lower East Side with her husband *HaRav* Heiman.

I loved and hated this visit. *HaRav* Heiman was gentle and kind, but my cousin scared the daylights out of me. She was huge, old and angry, and I knew—as all children know—that she really had no use for me. She always greeted my parents well, looked me up and down, uttering something in Yiddish (translation: "She is just like the others"). What others? Yet I went, year after year, for the trip included the purchase of pickles and challa and honey cake, or if the visit was before Sukkot, the four species.

On the long subway ride home I would ask how such a nice man could have married such a mean woman. My father told me that she wasn't mean; she just didn't know how to deal with children, since she was childless. "But," I said, "she was nice to my brothers." A brief silence, and then he would tell me a little about Feigel's background, how she had come from a small village to live with them in Brest-Litovsk after being orphaned. Her uncle—my grandfather—was to try to find her a husband. "How could anyone want to marry such an ugly angry woman?" I asked. My father responded with a quote from *Ayshet Hayyil*—"a woman who fears God shall be praised." The marriage was arranged, and her husband was a gem.

We moved to Montreal, Feigel's husband died, and by the time we returned to New York years later, she had moved to Israel and remarried—this time to Rabbi Unterman, then chief rabbi of Tel Aviv. I did not see her again until my first visit to Israel, when I was almost twenty.

I did not want to go on that visit, for my childhood memories were very clear, but my father insisted. My first reaction to her as an adult was that she had shrunk, for we were almost the same height. My next reaction was that she hadn't changed at all—she was still old and angry. She had barely greeted me, when I heard her muttering in Yiddish, the same thing she had said all those years before. But this time I knew more about her and was determined to at least try to find out what she was mumbling about.

We sat in her realm—the kitchen—and over a cup of strong tea I confronted her, telling her I really would like an explanation. The "others" it turned out, were my aunts—my father's four sisters. I pieced the story together myself. My cousin had arrived into a household of four attractive, lively, tiny sisters, who treated their cousin as a country bumpkin. She hated it and, as a good Litvak, remembered early insults forever. I reminded her of them, and so she had lumped us all together. But, I told her, I was not my aunts, but myself, and I told her to look at her two wonderful marriages—most of my aunts had had not-so-great marriages. She smiled in a self-satisfied manner and looking me straight in the eye, said: "A woman who fears God shall be praised."

Praised she was, for all the pieces of the story suddenly clicked into place, including my father's annual visits. During World War I, when the Jews of Brest-Litovsk left for safer places, Feigel had gone to Kremenchug (Ukraine) where my father's yeshiva had set up temporary quarters. At the end of the war two terrible things had occurred: a pogrom and a typhus epidemic. My father had disappeared. Jews didn't go out for fear of attack, but my great-grandmother prevailed on Feigel to do so. She donned a *babushka*, and armed with her large peasant-like appearance, she searched the morgue and the hospital. She walked up and down the rows of beaten Jews looking in vain for my father. Then she came to a cordoned-off wing of typhus patients. Undaunted, she opened the doors and looked at each patient, coming finally to my father, who described her as the vision of an angel to his fever-ridden brain. Day after day she came with soup and food until my father recovered and could be moved out.

He never forgot this act of *chesed*, and the story became part of our family history. Feigel may have had difficulties in her life, but her rewards included her two wonderful husbands and a first-cousin-once-removed who remembers her and her brave deeds three-quarters of a century later, praising her to the next generation.

Opinion

Prenuptial Agreements

December 8, 1995

When I got married almost fifteen years ago, I was as nervous and excited as I imagine anyone getting married would be. Yet, possibly because I was not of college age, I was also wary and wise—wise in the sense of my knowledge of the position of women within Jewish marital law and wise in the sense of having lived long enough to see certain realities of life. I had a friend whose mother had been a "modern" *aguna* for over twenty years—that is, her mother had a recalcitrant husband. I had a number of women acquaintances whose divorces were held up until they literally "paid off" their soon-to-be-ex-husbands. My Shabbat discussion groups focused on the pain of these women: on the unfairness of the situation and on our apparent helplessness. Then we started toying with the idea of prenuptial agreements.

It was not easy broaching the topic of a prenuptial agreement with my husband-to-be. He was initially offended—and I did not blame him—but when he saw my terror on this issue (I do not exaggerate the term—ask anyone who has personally witnessed the tragedy of a friend in an *aguna* status), he signed the paper (along with two witnesses) as a man in love who was sensitive to his future wife's needs. There was no set format. Each of my women friends marrying at that time worked out her own wording. Were these agreements valid contracts? We don't know since they have never been tested. In other words, all of us have good solid marriages.

But the issue of the prenuptial agreement continues, and the rabbis have finally concluded that we were right, that this is one way to prevent an *aguna* situation from developing. The Orthodox Caucus, a national group of rabbinic and lay leaders, has taken an important step toward achieving a standardized and universally utilized prenuptial agreement. Rabbi Mordechai Willig formulated the text and the caucus published a portfolio of marriage documents. The contract between the bride and groom obligates the future husband—if the couple no longer live under one roof—to provide his future wife with a daily dollar amount until the marriage is terminated by a *get*. This gives the husband an incentive to give the *get* promptly. A mutually acceptable *Bet Din* (specified in a separate document) supervises the actions of both spouses.

There will be resistance to this prenuptial agreement by the people who will say—"Oh, I don't need that! I trust my spouse-to-be-implicitly." There were many who reacted this way in the Classical Period of Jewish history when the *Ketuba* was first introduced as protection for women. Interestingly, it was the upper-class women in particular who rejected the *Ketuba* since they were already protected by their own style of contract, which went back to early Biblical times. Eventually, however, by rabbinic fiat, it became incumbent on all Jewish marriages to have a *Ketuba* with the basic formula of the contract identical for all.

This may happen sometime in the future for prenuptial agreements as well. Meanwhile, they are optional. I have a student whose sister went through the *aguna* torture for many years before her husband finally agreed to the *get*. She will be married in a few weeks, and I know that they will be using the prenuptial formula because I gave her a copy for their use. There is no doubt in my mind that this couple is in love; this document is proof positive of this love and their commitment to each other's happiness, no matter what happens in the future.

Opinion

Jewish Self-Images
April 12, 1996

The Jewish Museum on Fifth Avenue has on display a show entitled "Too Jewish?" There is a play in an off-Broadway theater entitled "Grandma Sylvia's Funeral." Both are exuberantly tasteless to many American Jews who are as mortified by them as they were by Philip Roth's various novels. Imagine a *hanuikyya* in which a gold Chanel handbag is the body and a row of lipsticks forms the candles. Picture a huge canvas with Barbra Streisand in profile, which is a takeoff on Andy Warhol's "Jackie O" series. The focus is most obviously on Streisand's nose.

Is there such a thing as a "Jewish nose"? There are large noses, medium noses, and small noses, in all groups and peoples. I don't think that anyone went out measuring noses (except for the Nazis in their so-called "anthropological studies") to prove that there is a real "Jewish nose." What did happen is that the "Jewish nose" became one of the fixtures of anti-Semitic caricatures over the past century or so, and we Jews unconsciously accepted this depiction. In all caricatures, there is a modicum of truth, and so what was true for a small group became expanded to all. That also holds true for the image of the Gentile nose as small and straight.

In the Americanization process, Jews imitated the Gentile image, and women in particular began to try to change their body images. The easiest thing to do was to start dressing in the perceived WASP style, i.e., tweeds, sweater-sets, and a single strand of pearls. Then came the hair color change for many, and—more expensive and drastic—the "nose job."

When I was in high school, I very much admired an older girl, who was, in my opinion, absolutely stunning. Then, on returning after a long vacation, I bumped into her in the corridor and pulled back aghast. She had changed her nose into a small button. What to me had been part of her beauty and had made her so attractive that people had turned around to continue looking at her, to her had been an ugly appendage. She had become just ordinarily pretty.

I thought that today's young women had better images of themselves. Imagine my surprise and chagrin to hear high schoolers talking about the "nose jobs" that they anticipated to have done at the age of sixteen. One of these fourteen year olds has her mother as an example, a woman whose recent operation was part of her just-turned-forty complex.

I'm not saying that there aren't some ugly noses out there. There are. There are also ugly chins, ugly mouths, ugly teeth, ugly skin, ugly hair, ugly bodies. Each of us has to come to terms with our basic looks and decide how to present ourselves to the world. It is a known fact that women are more discontented with their physical selves than are men. I can deal with that. What I can't deal with is the label "Jewish" to a part of our anatomy when one really should just say either "Semitic" (just look at the noses of Middle Easterners) or simply "big."

So, you say, what's in a word? A world of attitude and history. The words that we use should be our words, not words imposed from the outside, especially if that outside is of anti-Semitic origin. We called Sephardi converts to Christianity *marranos* for centuries, before this generation took a stand to call them *Conversos* or "Anusim," recognizing that *marranos* means swine and therefore was a label appended by the anti-Semites and not given to ourselves.

We are taught to think before we speak. That should apply to the words that we use to describe our self-images as well.

Opinion

The Dog in Jewish History

May 10, 1996

In the ancient Middle East, dogs were used to shepherd sheep and goats. They were also used for hunting, particularly the greyhound. A large mastiff-type dog was used for both hunting and guarding. There was also a type of dog kept as a pet, which we know of from excavations of the pyramids, for many pyramids contained the embalmed bodies of pet dogs meant to accompany their masters to the next world.

In ancient Israel, dogs performed similar functions. True, there are negative references to dogs in the text—for example, as a literary symbol for wildness—but there are many counter-symbols of the dog as the faithful and loyal servant of his master, guarding the home, the flock, and the city gate.

As the centuries passed, and the status of the Jew became that of a minority group living mainly in cities, the use of a dog as an aide to the shepherd disappeared. Since few Jews hunted, that function also disappeared. The guard dog and pet remained, but only as long as Jews were economically able to support them. As Eastern European and Middle Eastern Jews moved in the direction of poverty, fewer and fewer could support such a luxury. In addition, dogs were used in pogroms by peasants, police, and solders in Eastern Europe in particular, thus instilling fear of dogs in the Jews.

Then came modernization, Westernization, and the move of Jews to North America and Israel. Moving up the economic ladder, Jews were anxious to Americanize, and so pets started to become part of Jewish households once more. What we don't realize—those of us who buy dogs as pets—is that these animals become part of your life. In the dog, you have a kind of additional child, in the sense of having to provide all of its necessities—food, health care, exercise, love—but unlike a child, the only thing that is given in return is unspoken loyal devotion.

You sometimes get carried away and start to anthropomorphize your dog—it's normal for a human to do this. And when the inevitable happens, and the dog either gets painfully old or deathly sick, you agonize and finally put it to sleep. Can you believe that you even go through a mourning process, and you have to help your children go through it as well?

When my father was about eight years old, he and a group of his friends entertained themselves in the woods outside of Brest-Litovsk by playing a kind of stickball. The stick was a straight branch and the ball was a small rock. Once, when my father up "at bat," he accidentally slammed the rock into a bird, killing it. The boys were so upset, that they decided—in imitation of what they had all witnessed at one time or other—to make a funeral and bury the bird. They got so carried away that my father gave a eulogy, said Kaddish, and sang *Kel Malei Rachamim*. Seventy years later, in Jerusalem, at another funeral, a man came up to my father and said: "Are you Moshe Aron of Brisk? I remember the funeral of the bird."

My girls had to say good-bye to their beloved pet dog, and they will remember her passing just as that old man did so many years later. Is it worth having a pet? No, not in terms of the pain of parting, but yes, in terms of experiencing pure unadulterated affection. It is a humbling experience.

Opinion

A Question of Spirituality
January 3, 1997

Jewish men and women have a long history of searching for spirituality. The Bible recognizes this need by referring to the *Nazir*, the person who needed to do something extra for himself or herself to reach closer to God. The need was recognized, although the deed was frowned on as adding to the Torah's commandments.

This quest for spirituality continued through the centuries. Some expressed this through intense prayer, some through the writing of religious poetry, and some through fasting and self-abnegation. Judaism never allowed the search to lead to monasticism nor the formation of cults; those who moved in this direction were on the periphery of the Jewish people and disappeared from its midst.

The quest for spirituality took a uniquely feminine turn in the late Middle Ages. Women had been among the Nazirites as well as among the fervent worshippers, but now we get women writing prayers specific to women's lives. Most commonly known as *T'chinot* (*T'chines*), they addressed topics such as childbirth, pregnancy, infertility, the ability to nurse a baby.

Today the search for spirituality has led women in a number of new directions. Some have joined the Chabad movement, some have become more observant than their mothers, some have moved to communities in Judea/Samaria, and some have moved to women's prayer groups.

Not all women's prayer groups are the same. The most controversial ones for the Orthodox deal with the issue of chanting from the actual Torah scroll. The least controversial read the Torah portion from a printed book.

My daughter's *bat-mitzva* celebration was in the latter type group. Over fifty women and girls crowded into our living room to sing and pray aloud, sometimes very loudly indeed. *Hallel* was a joy because the twelve year olds led the way, singing the way they do in their all girls' class. The women got carried away by this youthful exuberance.

During the chanting from the Torah—each part read by a different woman—you could have heard a pin drop, and when my daughter's sweet voice sang the *Haftara* describing the prophet's vision of the high priest, the *menorah*, and God's promise that it was not strength that would determine the Jewish return to former glory, but God's will alone, there was a collective holding of breath until she was finished.

I had a number of concurrent personal reactions while she was chanting. I could hear my father telling me to look at the text and see what it was saying (he was a professor of Bible); to look at the *trope* marks which told which part of the word to stress (he was an avid Hebraist); and to study the musicality of the *trope* (he loved music), which should be combined with the text to produce a dramatic effect. I passed on this family lore to my daughter as we studied together, and as she reached the dramatic ending, I could hear the overtones of my father's rich baritone singing with her.

A number of the girls there tried to express their reactions to the women's service. It came out something like: "Cool, totally cool. Like, too bad I didn't know this could be done, or I would have learned *trope* too." A few of the women's comments were a little more lucid: "What a religious experience!" and "What a spiritual high!"

That is the point of the women's services. In good Jewish tradition, it is the quest for spirituality.

Opinion

Nechama: A Personal Comment

May 9, 1997

More years ago than I care to remember, I spent a half-year studying at Machon Gold in Jerusalem. It was not yet "the thing to do"—spending time in Israel studying Jewish subjects—and it took some convincing on my father's part to get me to go. What was the main attraction? Studying Torah with Dr. Nechama Leibowitz. We had classes with "Nechama," as she insisted everyone address her, three times a week, two to three hours at a time. Everyone remembers his or her first encounter with her, because within a half hour no one could tell you what she looked like, so overwhelming was her intellect.

She poked her head into our classroom, that first day, then her whole body was there, dressed in drab browns or navy blues or black, wearing her trademark beret. She went through the roster—she knew everyone's name by the first hour—and had us open our *Chumashim*. She called on a student to read the first verse and the first Rashi. "Baby stuff," I thought. Then came the first bombshell: "What is Rashi's difficulty with the text?" We looked, and we looked, and, at least at the beginning, most of us couldn't come up with an answer. After a few months she had trained us to study not only the words of the commentators, but their rationale as well. "Why did Ramban say that?" Then came my own personal crisis with her. I must have shown my dissatisfaction with a particular Rashi because, as the class ended, Nechama asked me to say behind. "Your Litvak rationalistic mind doesn't like when Rashi brings *midrashim* to solve his textual problem?" she asked. I responded that I couldn't understand why Rashi, the great legal commentator of the Talmud, kept bringing *midreshei aggada* to the Torah text. Nechama said: "This is your personal project. You will answer that as well as bring in commentators whose interpretation satisfies you more. Plus, you will explain to me why that seems more correct to you." What a half-year! What a mind-expanding time! What an approach to scholarship!

Over the years, as I came back to visit Israel, I usually ran into Nechama in the Hebrew University cafeteria. Over a cup of awful coffee, she would ask me casual questions, updating herself on my studies and then my career. She always remembered my name and the details of my life. She also always concluded our conversation with the query: "Any new ideas on Torah text and interpretation?" Guiltily I kept saying no, until our last meeting. By then I was teaching at Brooklyn College and had developed my course on "The Jewish Woman." Prepared now for Nechama's usual last question, I whipped out my Tanakh and shared some of my ideas with her. She listened quietly and smiled to herself.

"You see the value of teaching, Sara Reguer? When you have to explain the text and the commentators to a class, your entire approach changes. Your thinking sharpens because you are anticipating questions. And then you have to lead the students step by step to some sort of conclusion. The satisfaction at the end is worth it all." She sighed in satisfaction and patted my hand. "You will make a good *Morah*, maybe even a very good *Morah*." That was the highest accolade she could give, for that was how she viewed herself. In her will she asked that no inscription be written on her tombstone except for her name and the word "*Morah*."

Nechama Leibowitz died recently at the age of ninety-two, after having taught for close to seventy years. She taught everyone who was interested in Torah—right wing and left wing, religious and secular, men and women, old and young, beginners and scholars. Her intellect overwhelmed us all, along with her spirituality, piety, warmth, humor, gentleness, and modesty. She left no biological children, but since—to paraphrase the saying—your students are your children, she left thousands of spiritual children who will carry on her memory and her creative interpretations. May her memory be a blessing.

Opinion

The Challenges Ahead
January 14, 2000

In reading the overviews of the past Christian millennium, and especially of the last century, one is struck by the focus on technology. We have made incredible strides in science and in medicine, extending the average life span and unifying the world through Internet technology. We have also used technology to almost destroy each other.

The new century will present us with even greater innovation, along with difficult moral and ethical questions. Gene therapy, for example, can be applied to prevent birth defects, but it may also be used to engineer "designer babies." Will long lives be different, and will they change the balance of society? After all, living longer was a contributing factor to the major change in women's lives. Brain-altering drugs of the future will be used for treating Alzheimer's, depression, and schizophrenia, but they will also pose difficult moral questions if they are to be applied to enhancing cognition or personality. A new generation of drugs may force us to reexamine which aspects of our mental lives we consider essential and which we are willing to relinquish.

In the next five years alone, biotechnologists will make available to the public altered rice (enriched with vitamin A), altered milk (eliminating the most common allergen), altered produce (containing vaccines), eggs enriched with appetite reducers, and corn with conversion into polyester.

We stand in danger of being carried away by our abilities to gallop ahead with all of this new technology. We might fall into the same trap that snared the people of ancient times.

Everyone on earth had the same language and the same words. And they migrated from the east, they came on a valley in the land of Shinar and settled there. They said to one another, "Come let us make bricks and burn them hard" (Gen. 11:13).

The technological revolution then was brick-baking, which allowed more and more people to live in larger areas, to be able to settle in open plains away from caves, and to build taller and taller buildings. *Hubris* set in, *And they said, "Come, let us build us a city, and a tower with its top in the sky, to make a name for ourselves"* (4). Technical mastery gave rise to overweening pride, and the achievements of human skill were transformed from being a means, to an end in itself. Man, who had the power to reach technical heights, soon imagined that he was all-powerful, and he wished to build monuments to himself, likening himself to a god. By making himself "a name," he was deluding himself with a false sense of immortality.

It is within this context that Maimonides traced the decline of monotheism, from the time of Noah and Shem, and the growth of idolatry, symbolized in part by the tower of Babel, until the advent of Abraham, who reintroduced the pure idea of monotheism.

Technological advances can lead one again to overweening pride, and—in our case—self-worship. Technology certainly can enhance life, but only if it goes hand in hand with the constant reminder of God who created the world and the men and women in it. The moral and ethical challenges of the new century will be difficult ones but that must be met.

Opinion
___

Letter Writing

January 28, 2000

During intersession, I took a deep breath and began to read and organize my boxes of personal letters and documents. I was back in college, and even in high school. I found my father's Palestine passport with his visa to the United States. I read letters from both grandfathers, although I noticed that nothing existed from either grandmother. Some of the details of my letters I would have preferred not to remember; some I couldn't believe I had forgotten. My mother's letters from Jerusalem, after my parents made *aliya*, were full of the sunlight and smells of Israel in the spring but also full of longing for her only daughter.

The art of letter writing is rapidly disappearing. Nowadays, I would have either picked up the telephone or, more probably, sent e-mail to my parents. As a historian, this gave me pause.

Letters are a wonderful primary source. I read through thousands of them as I worked on my dissertation; most of them were written by Winston S. Churchill, but some also by his wife Clementine. Those letters opened a new perspective for me—a human one—on the subject of my research. The letters that passed between John Adams and his wife Abigail are sources of personal history as well as American history at the time of the writing of the Constitution.

The turn to the twenty-first century will not leave treasure troves of personal letters. E-mail messages, unless printed out, will fade into oblivion. The historian will be forced to look for primary sources similar to those that existed before the invention of paper, let alone papyrus and parchment.

But there was something else that struck this historian's notice as I started to read through the boxes of letters: there was self-censorship. I found no mention in any of my mother's letters to my father about the week that I spent in a Madrid hospital with a fever of 105 degrees. Nor did I mention in any of my letters from Russia, how many times the police had stopped me, or how my food had been doctored. Nowhere was there any comment on my "dates"-that-led-to-nowhere. My mother never wrote of her hypertension attacks, some of which landed her in the hospital. Neither parent ever wrote openly how worried they were about my future.

So, that means that personal letters, too, have to be read from the perspective of what may have been left out, just as we analyze autobiographies. And—since I had forgotten so many of the details of only twenty-five years ago—oral histories have to be treated very, very carefully. My father's memories of his life until the age of twenty-three, carefully written in Bialik-like Hebrew prose, are beautiful, but written some years after the events. Yes, they focus on what impressed him, but how much has been sugar-coated and glorified has to be taken into consideration as well.

I was apart from my parents for many years, as we lived in different countries or simply took very different vacations. At the time, it was painful and lonely as well as heady and exciting. In the end, it was worthwhile from the perspective of the letters—I would not have them had I stayed home.

Opinion

Public Humiliation

June 30, 2000

One of the many words applied to the incident in Central Park just after the Puerto Rican Day parade is "wilding." The detailed description of the actions of some twenty-or-so young men focuses on descriptions like hormonal, heat-induced (because of the ninety-five degrees Fahrenheit temperature), pack-like, gang-like, mindless. For the women who were groped and harassed, the final term used by all the reporters is "humiliated."

As a woman, I cringed when I read the reports and watched the television newscasts. Yes, even though this is the twentieth-first century, women still find themselves in vulnerable positions in public spaces. We do not create for ourselves—as veiled Middle Eastern women do— a private space in public, but are always aware and alert for possible danger. We walk the dog only where other people are to be seen, we walk hurriedly late at night from lighted door front to lighted door front, we live in apartments with doormen, and we teach our daughters to do the same. But Central Park was supposedly safe; it was an open space; it was late afternoon; there were crowds all around, and the police were on duty.

As someone immersed in Jewish history, the pack-attack on the women gradually percolated in my mind's eye as something entirely different. It must have been the repetition of the word "humiliation" time and again that finally set off the synapses in my brain. I could picture an eighteenth-century Jew in a Moroccan *mellah* setting off for the synagogue, wearing the distinct Jewish garb, suddenly finding himself the target of a gang of Muslim boys who were intent on humiliating him by showering him with small stones and animal dung. He was physically helpless to respond, and the Muslim adults would merely watch and do nothing.

In Italy before the Renaissance, Italian Christians entertained themselves on carnival days by having a race of the Jews. Selected leading members (including rabbis) of the Jewish community of Siena, for example, were forced to race through the streets, clad with very little, with the mob screaming epithets at them. Again, there was no one to turn to for protection, and the humiliation was absolute.

In Eastern European towns, villages, and even small cities, the word pogrom, which initially meant "an attack," came to be applied only to attacks on Jews as the Poles, Ukrainians, Letts, Lithuanians, and all the others perfected this form of humiliation of the Jews. In this case, however, people would be killed and the raping of Jewish women became part of "the fun." Again, there was no one to turn to for protection.

In the United States, minorities are legally protected. It is no longer acceptable for mobs or gangs to attack those who are racially, religiously, or ethnically different. Yet the one holdout seems to be attack on women. The homemade videos of those sub-human, leering males (calling them "animals" insults the animal kingdom) should be a wakeup call to all of us. The police will have to reassess crowd control and become more sensitive to women's cries. How dare they ignore the pleas of the female victims of that rampage (excusing the few who did respond positively). Women and men are finally joining together to do something to prevent such an event from ever recurring. As for punishment for the humiliators, I can think of a variety of very suitable suggestions, as can all of us.

Opinion
___

David's Prayer

September 22, 2000

Each year, as the month of Elul begins, we all recite Psalm 27 daily in the morning and afternoon prayers as a reminder that the High Holy Days are approaching, and repentance should be the focus of our attention. The Psalm is one of David's most profound expressions of submission, humility, supplication, and devotion. The depth of feeling cannot help but move us, and connect us to the long chain of Jewish history and tradition.

Prayer is a basic experiential category in Judaism, along with redemption, which Rabbi Dr. Joseph B. Soloveitchik defines as "a movement by an individual or a community from the periphery of history to its center" ("Redemption, Prayer, Talmud Torah," *Tradition*, Spring 1978, Vol. 17, no. 2, 55). *Halakha* views the two as inseparable, for the Sages considered them to be structurally identical. It is speech that enables redemption, and Judaism, continues the Rav, "wants man to cry out aloud against any kind of pain, to react indignantly to all kinds of injustice or unfairness" (65). Also, if an individual's own need-awareness is dull, he does not know what suffering is, and suffering is what makes us human. Suffering is not a sensation, like pain, but an experience, a spiritual reality.

Thus, prayer is bound up with human needs, drives, and desires. The *Amida*, the core of our prayers, is made up of requests for these needs—individual as well as communal. The happy person does not really pray, only the sufferer does, according to the Rav. God "wants to hear the outcry of man, confronted with a ruthless reality. He expects prayer to rise from a suffering world cognizant of its genuine needs" (66). Through the outcry of prayer, man finds himself and is thus redeemed.

David cried out to God, verbalizing his fears, beseeching protection in God's "Temple," "pavilion," and "tent." He petitioned his Maker not to abandon him, invoking the most awful of images, that of a child abandoned by his father and mother. There is no society which so values its family structure and its children as Jewish society, therefore by invoking such abandonment the poet causes the reader to shudder. Out of this ruthless reality, the person praying thus turns, as the poet intended, to the One who is his deliverer.

> Though my father and mother abandon me
> The Lord will take me in.
> Show me Your way, O Lord.

David concluded his Psalm by turning from the personal to the general, just in case the personal cry did not affect the reader as it should. He admonished or advised, depending on how the reader chooses to interpret the tone:

> Look to the Lord
> Be strong and of good courage!
> O look to the Lord!

Opinion

Two Concerts
December 29, 2000

This past December 3, a concert was held at Merkin Concert Hall honoring the winners of the Liberty Prize, an annual award to prominent Russian writers, poets, artists, musicians, or other cultural figures who made an outstanding contribution to American society. The performers were all young Russian-Americans, and the performances—with the exception of the vocalists—were outstanding. The music performed, naturally, was that of Russian composers such as Tchaikovsky, Rachmaninoff, and Skriabin, with a sprinkling of Verdi, Schubert, and Popper. Russians love to emote, and the cello and violin lend themselves to such emotionalism. But keep your eyes out for the pianist, Denis Matsuev, because his future is written in the stars. When he played Skriabin's "Two Etudes," the audience leaned forward in breathless concentrations, staring in disbelief at the speed and virtuosity with which he attacked the music.

We went to the concert because of Eugenia Pilyavina, winner of the Chopin Competition in New York, who was performing as accompanying pianist. She also has received a Brooklyn College Conservatory of Music award. We would never have known about this concert otherwise, for it was little publicized except in the Russian-American circles. It seemed that we were the only non-Russian speakers.

What is missing in all of the publicity is that most of these young musicians, as well as most of the winners of the Liberty Prize, are also Jewish. Somewhere along the road of Soviet history, these Russian Jews lost the "Jewish" part of their identity, similar to what has happened to other Jews living elsewhere in the world and at other times. The only thing Jewish about Felix Mendelssohn was his name; the same holds true of Yehudi Menuhin.

A very different concert was held at Brooklyn College's Levenson Recital Hall on December 10. The Conservatory Chamber Chorus, the Brooklyn College Chorus, and the Conservatory Orchestra performed a series of holiday songs. The performers or their families—in true Brooklyn style—came from all over the world. The instrumentalists and members of the chorus have Russian, Japanese, Chinese, Korean, Ashkenazi Jewish, Middle Eastern Jewish, Italian, Latino, African American, Greek, French, English, Irish, and Scottish names. The music united them all, and it did my heart good to hear *Mi Ye-Malel* and *Ha-Nerot Halalu* sung by such a variety of people and enjoyed by such a mixed audience.

The climax of the concert was Vivaldi's "Magnificat." Two African Americans, one Korean American, one Argentinian American, and one Yugoslav American solo-ed, singing in Latin, backed up by over sixty voices and fifteen instruments. The musical experience of being surrounded by all of this sound was a luminous one, even a spiritual one. Mulling this over afterward, I could understand perhaps why Jews were told not to go into churches in Europe, aside from the strict *halakhic* prohibition. It was not the Christian art, which usually depicts mother/child images or suffering men images, so Christian as to cause most Jews to automatically turn off. Nor was it the architecture, which, although impressive in its soaring space and stillness, was too alien from most Jewish experiences in the synagogues. It was certainly not the religion that was feared. It was perhaps the influence of the music, for music can speak directly to the soul.

Opinion

Word Play

August 24, 2001

The word "semantics" is defined as "the study of meanings in language." This study can be used by historians, psychologists, sociologists, and linguists. Words may not have the same resonance after centuries of use. Sometimes, words slip from one language into another in translation, but retain the cultural meaning of the first language. Some words carry religious attitudes, some carry gender attitudes, some carry racial attitudes, and some carry political attitudes.

Biblical Hebrew, for example, contains words that have changed meaning over the millennia. For example, in the book of Ruth (as well as in other places in the Bible), the phrase *am ha-aretz* means just that: "the people of the land"; in today's Hebrew, via Yiddish usage, it is a pejorative term for an ignoramus.

Examples of words slipping from one language into another in translation, but retaining the cultural meaning of the first are "girl" and "boy" as used by Ashkenazi American Jews in particular. "Girl" is ageless—she may be eighteen or eighty—as long as she is unmarried, a direct translation of Yiddish usage of *meidl*. The same hold true for "boy," the ageless unmarried *bochur*. Of course, the term "girl" also runs into sociological semantics of gender attitudes, as the fifty-something women go out to play bridge of mah-jongg with the "girls." In a youth-driven society such as America, this is one small attempt at retaining the fantasy of youthfulness. However, the flip side to this is that a "girl" (i.e., woman) is immature and therefore has to be treated like a child—protected, shielded from decision-making, and unable to understand finances.

Religious attitudes can be conveyed by specific word usage. For example, when Italians use the work "Christian," they mean Roman Catholic only. When they use the term the "Bible," they mean the Christian Bible. This is important for scholars as well as individuals merely having conversations, for ignorance of these usages blurs understanding. Middle Eastern Jews use the term *goy* for "Muslim," and *arel* (uncircumcised) for

Christian, whereas Ashkenazi Jews use *goy* for Christian and "Ishmaelite" (in medieval sources) for Muslim.

Racial attitudes can be conveyed by the American use of the term "boy" for mature black men. Ashkenazi Jews were ahead of the game of political correctness by using the term *shvartze* (black) for blacks; however, when it was used in the context of the cleaning woman, this crossed the invisible line.

Political attitudes conveyed by word usage are in the newspapers every day. If you are in Iran, the body of water between Iran and Arabia is the "Persian Gulf"; if you are in Arabia, it is the "Arabian Gulf," and if you are an American, it is just "the Gulf." Everyone knows where you stand if you refer to a section of land as the "West Bank," or "Judea-Samaria," or "the territories." That hold true for the use of the term "terrorist" versus "freedom fighter," or "activist"; or "preventative action" versus "assassination."

But some words, such as "shalom" or "salaam," cannot be twisted by semantics. You either have it, or you don't.

Opinion
___

Minimalism

October 12, 2001

The imagination freezes on seeing the unimaginable even if it is on television. It freezes even more when one physically witnesses the change in the New York skyline. Everything else becomes trivial. Yet as the mayor keeps urging, life must go on, and we all attempt to follow his lead. Therefore, I attended the opening of a new art gallery in the DUMBO section of Brooklyn (the up-and-coming Down-Under the Manhattan and Brooklyn bridges Overpass), called 5 + 5 Gallery. The gallery specializes in works on paper, and has, as its first show, art by two minimalist artists, the American Agnes Martin and the Australian Bruno Leti.

I have rarely appreciated minimalism. I like trees to look something like trees and people to look at least a bit like people. But standing in the gallery, which overlooks the Brooklyn Bridge and the damaged skyline of lower Manhattan, and then at the shapes and colors on display on the walls of 5 + 5 Gallery, I could relate intimately with minimalist art. It is as though, when one cannot find words to express one's feelings, this art form can take over, visually presenting what words cannot. The world is reduced to basic shapes and colors, the colors of nature, the colors of Creation. A feeling of tranquility and calm comes over the viewer, bringing with it a sense of comfort.

Comfort is what we are all seeking since rational sense is not there. During those days of sitting glued to the television screen, and reading column after column in the newspapers, I subconsciously noticed that in searching for comfort, most religious and secular leaders turned to the book of Psalms for inspiration. Perhaps the very personal nature of so many of the Psalms lends them to intimate comfort, or perhaps it is the soaring poetic power of so many of them. The divinely inspired Psalmist was able to do what so many of us cannot seem to do today—find the right words to express what our frozen imaginations cannot.

Inspiring as the Psalms are, I keep hearing—this Erev Yom Kippur 5762—echoes of the cantor singing the traditional Ashkenazi tune to *mi ba-esh u-mi ba-mayim,* "who (will be judged to die) in fire and who in water."

This is followed by the echo of *Avinu Malkeinu, ayn lanu Melekh ela Ata,* "Our Father, our King, we have no King but You." What a difficult Yom Kippur this will be as we concentrate on the meaning of the prayers, and have difficulty saying some of them. There is no question in my mind that most Jews will spend at least some time in a synagogue this year, even if it is just to have some minimalist moments of quiet reflection.

May this year bring us all peace.

Opinion
___

Limitations
December 28, 2001

Andy Rooney is one of the many commentators on the television program *Sixty Minutes*. I await his three- or four-minute sound bite because it is inevitably pleasing. He manages to be pithy and humorous while dealing with what many times starts off as a trivial point and then morphs into a scathing judgment of our society. How he manages to do this week after week is beyond me.

My mentor, Prof. J. C. Hurewitz, then director of the Middle East Institute at Columbia University, was the master of the three-minute commentary on any political issue connected to the Middle East. He was one of the most sought after experts to be interviewed by the major television networks during various Arab-Israel conflicts, and we, his students, always marveled at the seeming ease with which he was able to brilliantly answer difficult questions.

Prof. Bernard Lewis of Princeton University, one of today's leading specialists on Islam and the Middle East, on the other hand, refuses to be interviewed by the media because he says that after a twenty- to thirty-minute conversation with a reporter, what is ultimately aired is five minutes of statements taken out of context. So he remains true to the written word, or to the guarantee that he can preview what will be aired. I learned this the hard way, once on American television and once on Israeli television, when the reporters invited me to have a "conversation" before the show. These reporters then proceeded to repeat the conversations as if my points were their points, and I had to quickly come up with some new ideas. Always a quick student, the next time I politely refused the pre-show conversation and thus was more easily able to fill the time allotted to me.

Scholarly articles and encyclopedia entries often have word limits, as do scholarly presentations at conferences where you usually have twenty minutes. It is up to you to read your paper slowly or quickly.

We are all used to time limits of sorts: classes and examinations run for a set time, semesters are so many weeks, and applications to schools must be in by a certain date. The clock, the calendar, and physical space make their demands.

This holds true in the Jewish world as well. We have time-bound commandments such as morning prayer, Hannuka lights, and clearing leaven out of the house. Many synagogues demand that the rabbi's sermon not be longer than fifteen to twenty minutes. *Tircha de-tzibura* (a burden on the congregation) is an important concept that can be applied to lengthy sermons, or to splitting a Shabbat Torah portion into thirty *aliyot la-Torah* instead of the mandatory seven.

Space limitations may have played a role in the physical structuring of the scribes copying the Torah. It certainly played a role in the printer's decision, during those early days after the invention of printing, as to how large a book would be, how thick, and how dense the print. Expense always played a part in these decisions, for a rich patron could subsidize Immanuel of Rome's poetry, which could the fill a large volume, whereas a poor man such as Nobel Prize–winner V. S. Naipul's protagonist in *The Mystic Masseur* could only afford to print a pamphlet.

Some of my students inevitably ask me how long an essay on an examination should be; the same holds true for a term paper. All of us who are grading papers prefer the Andy Rooney style: terse, succinct, to the point, and without padding.

Opinion

Selective Memory

February 22, 2002

Every other week or so I go to the Lower East Side to buy *chalas* in Gertel's Bakery. I drop into the Iraqi-Jewish appetizer store for nuts, dried fruit, and Israeli pickles. On my walk to and from the subway I notice all the Chinese signs, the Chinese-owned fruit and vegetable stores, and all the Chinese people—even on Mulberry Street, that center of Little Italy. I think of the Jewish Lower East Side and do not miss it at all, for as an historian I do not become nostalgic about poverty, cold-water buildings, and one-toilet-to-a-floor apartment houses. Others do become nostalgic, filtering out the bad and only remembering the hustle and bustle, the Yiddish, and the smells of Eastern European Jewish cooking.

Nostalgia for *der heym*, the homeland, is a normal phenomenon. It is very hard for older people to move to a new country and a new culture. Some middle-aged people do fine; others have more difficulty. The younger you are, the easier to adjust. My father's nostalgia was based in part on youthful memories, connected with energy and optimism. Yet when prodded, he would admit to always being cold in the winter, as his boots had holes and were lined only with old newspapers. He also never had enough to eat. My husband's rosy *Casa Mia* is brought into clearer focus when he describes his mother's endless labor.

But memory is selective in other realms of life as well. This is February, i.e., Black History Month, and I was recently reminded that my father took a trip down south with a large group of rabbis who were sympathetic to the newly organizing civil rights movement. My brother remembers (and recounts) that our father marched with Martin Luther King Jr.; I remember that he took the long trip to express sympathies with the civil rights movement, but also to enjoy the long trip to the American South. The difference lies in the telling.

Selective memory is part of being human. Look at the Israelites in the desert complaining that they missed the meat and foods of Egypt. There wasn't even time enough for historic nostalgia to set in, yet this group of people who had suffered all the indignities of slavery and seen all the miracles of the Exodus was already yearning for something that they had left behind.

My older daughter just returned from an exciting ten-day Birthright Israel trip. As she detailed all of her experiences I had flashbacks to my own first trip, when I was her age. At first the images were all positive, but after a bit I remembered the barbed wire of a divided Jerusalem, the armed guard accompanying our organized tours, the burned-out storage facilities of the kibbutz in which I spent a month—burned by Palestinian infiltrators—and the constant wariness in public places like bus stations. Over the years I had chosen to forget these things, but now as a parent I can identify with my parents' fears over my own trip. I had conveniently forgotten the letters reminding me to be careful and to use my common sense. As I repeated these admonitions to my own daughter, I could hear overtones of the past.

Psychologists tell us that we need selective memory, for our brains cannot physically retain every experience. They also tell us that if we had traumatic experiences, selective memory enables us to overcome horrors and move on with life. The historian, on the other hand, has to deal with selective memory. We have to counterbalance all of this in order to try to recreate the larger picture.

Opinion

Rites of Passage
June 28, 2002

All societies have rites of passage. In traditional societies, these rites are connected with birth, coming of age, marriage, and even with death. Elaborate rules and ceremonies surround these rites of passage, and no one tampers with these traditions. They are passed from one generation to the next, either in written or in oral form, or in a combination of the two.

The best examples of rites of passage not connected with the cycle of life are those of inductions of new priests or holy leaders. The passing of clothing from Aaron before his death to Elazar his son is the oldest Jewish act of induction into the high priesthood. We Jews seem to be the only ones that have a ritual for the transference of symbolic crowning of new scholars, namely, *semicha*, rabbinic affirmation of a scholar's knowledge and readiness to offer *halakhic* guidance.

Modern rites of passage include graduations. At one time, it was only universities that surrounded their graduates with the pomp and ceremony of mortarboards, gowns, capes, tassels, and diplomas written by hand on sheepskin. High school graduates wore dark suits (boys) and pastel-colored or white dresses (girls). I have a framed photograph of my mother proudly posing in her hand-sewn dress holding her diploma to mark her graduation—the first in her family—from her high school in Montreal, Canada, 1930. I have a photograph of myself with my high school class, all in caps and gowns (boys in blue, girls in white), and I can still feel the sweat dripping down from under my cap as we posed in a non-air conditioned hall.

On June 19, my younger daughter graduated from Ramaz High School, and we all gathered to watch her proudly march down the aisle to end a major stage of her education and embark on the next one. This is a rite of passage for her, but it is also one for me and for all parents whose youngest child is leaving high school. This is a coming of age for both generations, for this is the step to adulthood.

In traditional societies in the past, the rite of passage to adulthood could have been a secret initiation including an act of courage like the killing of a wild animal. For Jews it has been and remains the public acceptance of the burden of responsibility of *mitzvot*. In Israel, for most, the next step would be army service. For all, the one beyond that would be marriage. But today, since education is such a lengthy process, societies have gradually created these modern rites of passage to express the need for ceremonial recognition of a new kind of accomplishment: high school graduation, then beyond that for whoever chooses to continue.

I have students who did not go to their college graduation. I myself did not attend the graduation ceremony at which I was awarded my doctor of philosophy, PhD—for me, the defense of my dissertation was my rite of passage, and I did not need to march in a cap and gown to receive my wings to prove it. However, no one misses attending his or her high school graduation, perhaps because it is so necessary for both the graduate and her parents.

Opinion

Jews of Arabia

January 10, 2003

PBS recently aired a two-hour program entitled "Muhammad." It is visually one of the best programs they have aired, and the editors deftly balanced interviews with scholars, American converts to Islam, and immigrant American Muslims with a narrative about the founder of Islam juxtaposed on images of Arabia. The end result is sophisticated and convincing. But is it historically accurate?

As a scholar of Middle East history, my reaction to the early part of the program, which dealt with Arabia's tribal setup, Muhammad's childhood and early manhood, as well as the social structure of Mecca, was positive. Even the somewhat apologetic tone of the scholars in dealing with the reason why Muhammad decreed that a man could take up to four wives if he could treat them equally—namely, to help the many women newly widowed by all the fighting—was acceptable.

The problem for me, as a scholar of Middle Eastern *Jewish* history, arose in the narrative about Muhammad's order to kill all the men of a Jewish tribe in Medina, the *Banu Qurayza*. First, the narrative was too simplistic, second, it was too apologetic, and third, it was not scholarly.

This is not the place to go through the details of the Jewish agricultural tribes of the oasis of Yathrib, later known as Medina, nor how they were in a confederation with the pagan tribes. Suffice it to say that there were three important tribes, all of which not only rejected Muhammad's prophethood but openly contradicted his teachings. As he felt with an unshakable religious certainly that his revelations were true, his logical conclusion was that the Jewish texts that they cited were corrupted and false.

In a deft combination of political, religious, and military savvy, Muhammad played off the tribal customs and rules against or with his new teachings, and managed to have two of the Jewish tribes exiled, confiscating their holdings. The third one—the Banu Qurayza—was attacked and conquered, but instead of letting the tribe go into exile, he manipulated the situation into having them accused of treason and beheading the men.

The scholars on the PBS show should have been more honest in their comments, saying that there is some disagreement among scholars about what happened. Instead, they simplified it, making it seem that this was what happened, period. Yet, even they knew that they were treading on dangerous ground, as Karen Armstrong looked straight at the camera and stated strongly, "This cannot be seen as anti-Semitism." No, it was not anti-Semitism, but neither blame nor vindication are proper here. We can't judge by present-day moral standards for, although the fate of the men of the Banu Qurayza was a bitter one, it was not unusual according to the harsh rules of tribal war at that time. So *say that*, and don't try to whitewash what happened: state, openly, that Muhammad, at that time only, took a political/religious chance, and it paid off richly for him.

Gradually, Arabia became *Judenrein* through exile, but never were the Jews killed again as the Banu Qurayza were in Medina. By the time the new Muslims were ready to invade beyond the borders of Arabia, a new system was gradually being worked out for monotheistic "Peoples of the Book," namely, second-class citizenship as *dhimmi* or "protected peoples."

Opinion

Topics for Discussion
May 16, 2003

Tonight I will be speaking at Hofstra University on the topic of "From the Maccabees to the Garden of the Finzi-Continis: The Jews of Italy." In the span of forty-five minutes, I will be giving a bird's eye view of most of my course on Italian Jewry. The lecture series is being given press coverage by *Newsday*, and the interviewer asked me how I got interested in the topic. It was not the question as much as the intonation that set me off—in other words, she implied, how did I get into such an exotic field?

First of all, the Jews of Italy are not an exotic group (and how does one define "exotic"?), and second of all, people become interested and even passionate about topics that resonate with them. I am one of the lucky people for whom many topics resonate. For example, I will be part of a round-table discussion of scholars of Jewish women's history tomorrow night, and there too, each of us is to address the opening question of how we got into our area of research. In this case, I am to address my publication of material on Middle Eastern Jewish women both of the premodern and postmodern periods.

On Sunday I will get a chance to lecture on that most fascinating of women, Dona Gracia Nasi, at the Spanish and Portuguese Synagogue. Dona Gracia, whose travels took her from Portugal to the Low Countries to Italy, and finally across the Balkans to Istanbul, allows me to interconnect the *Converso* experience of Portugal with Renaissance Italy and finally with the Ottoman Empire, the haven for Jews ruled by Suleiman the Magnificent. It also enables me to wax prolific on a superb example of women with political power.

Who knows what subject can turn a student on? Of the four students writing their senior theses with me, three found their passions fairly quickly—one student is writing on the end of the Jewish community of Iraq in 1949 and the role Israel played in it, one is focusing on the transplantation of the Bukharan Jews to Israel and America, the third is writing on a comparison between marriage customs of the Jews of Morocco, Kurdistan, and Yemen. But the fourth kept looking. I knew exactly what she meant when she said that she had not found "it" yet. Then, over Pesach she happened to see a Haggada of the community of northern China which no longer exists, and she e-mailed me that she finally had a topic—the connection between the Jews of the Middle East and those of China. Let us see what she finds.

It is wonderful to see the light go on. My older daughter is deep into a paper on women printers of the Renaissance (including Jewish women printers), and thanks to a scholarship from Brooklyn College, she will be able to travel to Italy to search for material. My younger daughter is reading so much about the sculptor Isamu Noguchi that she dreams of his artistic work. (If you have never heard of him, there is a museum in Queens dedicated solely to his work, and there is a sculpture garden in his name at the Israel Museum in Jerusalem.)

So, no field or topic of research is "exotic" to the person working on it. We professors hope that the experience of doing in-depth research that inspires passionate interest will be something that the students take with them into the real world and apply to future experiences.

Opinion

A New York Experience
April 16, 2004

Recently, after giving a lecture at the Frisch School in New Jersey, I took a car service back to Brooklyn College. I knew that the ride would be a long one, and after discussing the best routes to take with the driver, I settled back to catch up on some of my paperwork. It was probably because I was distracted that I ended up making the comment that turned what should have been a quiet ride into one of those "New York experiences."

Driver: "There will be traffic on the George Washington Bridge."

Me: "As always. That's an interesting accent you have. Where are you from?"

Driver: "Guess."

Me: "It's an Arabic accent."

Driver: "That's good. Yes, I'm Kurdish. Do you know Kurdish?"

For the next twenty minutes or so we discussed the politics of the Kurds as a minority group in three countries. We both agreed that a possible solution to their statelessness could be redividing Iraq into its three Ottoman Turkish *vilayet* (province) structures, giving the Basra *vilayet* to the Shiis, the Baghdad *vilayet* to the Sunnis, and the Mosul *vilayet* to the Kurds. Then we both agreed that it would never happen.

From there the conversation moved to Kurds in America, and the need for community structure to reinforce tradition. By this time we were crossing into Brooklyn.

Driver: "Professor, could I ask you something?"

Me: (Uh oh, to myself) "Sure."

Driver: "I was watching *Al-Jazeera* on television, and there was this Jewish rabbi being interviewed."

Me: "Mr. Ahmed, if he was on *Al-Jazeera* then most Jews do not agree with anything that he has to say."

But he told me of the interview anyway, and the last twenty minutes of the drive was filled with a polite confrontation over Islam's view of the Jews and my refutation of all of his comments, including his references to the Qur'an.

"But that is what it says in the holy book!"

"Show me."

He pulled out his trusty book (while driving) and found the chapter and verse (while driving). I said that since this is sacred text, it is open to interpretation, and if you put the emphasis on this word, and put a comma there, the meaning of the verse changes. It suddenly dawned on him that I could read the Arabic, and the intensity of the discussion increased.

We were on Avenue J. I pointed out that on one street there was a *halal* meat store and on the next there was a kosher butcher shop. There were women in two types of headscarves—Muslim and Jewish. This is America, where we live together and we discuss differences and respect other people's views, and most important, the right to have different views.

We were now right near Brooklyn College, and when we stopped at a red light, where Mr. Ahmed could see the large variety of ethnic groups crossing Bedford Avenue, I quickly left the car, wishing him good luck in America.

That was one intensive hour on the topic of Islam and Judaism. Then, a few days later, in the doctor's office, after watching an "Independence Day" DVD, I made the mistake of commenting to the women waiting with me that some of the movies today are so awful and so violent that I don't want to see them.

"I agree," said my neighbor. "But I took my children to see a wonderful inspiring movie on Sunday. We saw 'The Passion.'"

I kept my mouth shut.

Opinion
___

Natan Sharansky

April 1, 2005

In 1974, I was recruited indirectly by the Israeli government to make a trip to the Soviet Union. My task was to meet with as many *refuseniks* as possible, and to collect as many names and family particulars from as many Jews as I could. Those were the years when, according to the laws of reunification of families, Jews could emigrate from the USSR to Israel.

As an American student traveling with two British students, hiding in a Cook's Tour group, I thought I was safe. I was not. I was neither a female James Bond nor the star of "Alias," and by the time my three-week-long trip was over, I had had enough adventures to give me nightmares to this very day.

What made my trip worthwhile was the thought that I may have actually helped about a hundred Jews and their families get out of Russia. The Goldshtein brothers of Tbilisi, Georgia, were impressive, but the most impressive man I met was Natan—then known as Anatoly—Sharansky. This was before he went to prison, but he was already a *refusenik*, a Jew who had applied to emigrate from Russia to Israel to escape the persecution and prejudice of the Soviet Union, but was refused.

He and all other *refuseniks* lost their jobs and their rights. He was busy helping get information to the West through Americans like me, to be used by various Jewish organizations and the Israeli government.

Natan Sharansky is a short man physically, but a huge man spiritually. He repeated numerous times during our outdoor walking meetings—always outdoors and always on the move so that the listening devices used by the Soviets could be deflected—that he expected to be arrested. He expected to be sent to prison. How could I refuse to run the barricade of Soviet guards posted in front of the American Embassy in Moscow in the face of his bravery? So I did it, and felt part of a surreal spy movie as I leapt from the screeching cab and catapulted myself past the astonished guards. I then had to convince the consul to ship what Natan had given me out of the Soviet Union in a diplomatic pouch. Then I had to make it back to my hotel and my bus, which was leaving for the airport imminently. No wonder that when the pilot announced that we had left Soviet territory, I cheered my head off.

But Natan remained behind, and—true to his prediction—he was arrested and sent to prison in 1986 where he remained for nine long years. When he was freed in an exchange of prisoners with the United States, he went on to Israel to rejoin his wife Avital. As we all know, he became a politician, and created his own party, which has now merged with Likud.

His new book, *The Case for Democracy: The Power of Freedom to Overcome Tyranny and Terror*, summarizes his ideas and ideals, some of which have been picked up by President George W. Bush as akin to his own.

Natan Sharansky, always the idealist, has a deep faith in the power of freedom. No one can question his commitment to this ideal, for he speaks in the moral voice of a former "prisoner of Zion."

Opinion

The Task of Translation
April 28, 2006

A number of years ago I got involved in translating the Haggada. It was spurred on in part by some comments made by guests at the *seder* table, which made no sense to me until I realized that they were referring to the translation of the text. At our *seder*, we hand out a variety of *haggadot* in order to share the commentaries, the illustrations, and in some cases, the translations. Upon reading what our guests were using, I somewhat foolishly stated that I could do a much better job of it.

I had no idea how hard this translation would be. Until that time, I had translated documents in my research, and for most of that I only needed the sense of the document. If it needed to be literally translated, it wasn't that hard to do. However, in translating sacred text, any word chosen has to be weighed for exactness as well as the spirit of the meaning of the original words; otherwise you are writing commentary.

My respect for the role of Jewish translators of the Middle Ages (and earlier) grew apace. There they sat, for example, in southern Italy, especially under Frederick, King of Sicily and Apulia (who was at the same time Holy Roman Emperor), translating from Arabic and Greek into Latin and Hebrew. Some wrote dictionaries and books on philology as well. We take the availability of dictionaries for granted, but someone had to write the first ones. Jews in Spain played similar roles. The accuracy of the translations was especially important if the works were medical or pharmaceutical. Later translators were able to take poetry from one language and successfully transmute it into another language; that is an art form in itself.

I do not place myself anywhere near those translators, but I felt some of the frustration of searching for the proper word. This is happening to me again, but in a different form. I have been working on my father's letters from his family in Jewish Lithuania in the period before World War II. They are in Yiddish, and I have had to sharpen up my vocabulary, let alone my grammar. My grandfather's letters are the easiest to read as they are in Torah-Yiddish. My aunts' letters, on the other hand, are written the way they spoke—so I have to assume a Litvak-ear, like using an *aleph* instead of a *heh* at times. But then I found a treasure—a memoir written by my father in 1926, using beautiful literary Hebrew. Now the translation becomes difficult because the allusions and motifs are Biblical, Mishnaic, Talmudic, and Bialik-like modern. His style is Russian-Romantic, typical of his time, and so the translation has to take all of these things into account.

Why not just publish everything in the original Yiddish and Hebrew? Because what I am writing will be a time capsule of a world that no longer exists, and the primary sources are only part of the story.

So, back to the translations.

Opinion

Tracing a Career through Primary Sources
June 23, 2006

One of the biggest honors that a college student can receive is to be invited to join the Phi Beta Kappa Honor Society. It is a national organization with chapters in universities across the United States, although not every campus has a chapter. The invitation goes to students, who not only have excellent grades, but who have also achieved breadth of knowledge by taking challenging course outside of his or her discipline.

Brooklyn College's Rho Chapter had its initiation of forty new members the same day the college held its graduation. And for the first time in its history, the chapter invited a professor of Judaic Studies (myself) to appear as guest speaker. The ramifications of such an invitation are manifold, as the field is not held in high esteem by some scholars. This is true especially of those who feel that it should not be a separate department, but just a subsection of history, sociology, anthropology, literature, philosophy, economics, music, art, and religion departments.

The topic addressed was "Tracing a Career through Primary Sources," which would not only talk to the college graduates about to embark on their post-BA or post-BS lives, but would also talk to my many colleagues and show them of what my research consisted.

I started with my initial specialization, diplomatic history of the Middle East, and read a short except from Winston S. Churchill. It was written before World War I, when he was the First Lord of the Admiralty and interested in convincing the British Government to enter into the oil business through the newly created Anglo-Persian Oil Company (predecessor of British Petroleum). The second primary source was a letter to Churchill written after World War I, when as Colonial Secretary, he was in charge of mandated Iraq, as well as mandated Palestine. The document had nothing nice to say about the newly crowned King Feisal or about Iraqis in general.

From that, as teaching my course on modern Israel changed me, I moved to researching the Jordan River hydroelectric project of Pinchas

Rutenberg, which led to the Jordan River regional development plans of the 1950s and 1960s. The same thing happened as a result of teaching the course on "The Jewish Woman," and I read a phenomenally interesting deathbed letter from a woman to her sister, enjoining her to educate the dying woman's daughter. This was from the Cairo Geniza.

Finally, my courses, "The Sephardic Experience" and "Italian Jewry" reshaped my research projects as I worked on the Italianization of the two latest immigrant groups to Italy, namely, Jews from Iran and Jews from Libya.

Many people not connected with the university system think that professors teach, and that is it. No, that is only part of our jobs; if we do not continue our research and subsequent publishing, we will not be reappointed by our home department, nor will we be promoted. "Publish or perish!" is a fact of our lives. Yet, on campus—especially a commuter-college campus—we rarely know what our colleagues do. This was an opportunity for me to share my projects with a larger audience. It also enabled me to tell the graduates that *Man tracht und Gott lacht*—loosely translated as "Man proposed, but God disposes." We may have plans for ourselves, but life leads many away from the original youthful plan. That is not necessarily a bad thing, for it is the voyage itself that is exciting. How boring life would be if everything went exactly as planned.

Opinion

Small Kindnesses
March 16, 2007

The oddest thing happened to me the other week. The telephone rang, and a woman's voice asked for me, using my nickname. I said yes, and who are you? She responded that this was a call that was fifty years in the making. She proceeded to explain that when we were children, we had prayed together on Rosh Hashana and Yom Kippur in the auditorium of Yeshiva University. I had helped her pray, using my then new Birenbaum *mahzor*, explaining how to pray and why we said what we did. I vaguely remembered a younger girl who went to public school.

I didn't remember the praying part, only my reaction to what I thought was a bad thing that her parents were doing by not giving her a Jewish education. Sure enough, as she informed me, she left Judaism and tried every other religion that she could, searching for answers. Finally she ended up in Israel and ultimately discovered Hasidism and Chabad. She now teaches Judaism to other women. And whenever Rosh Hashana comes around, she always thinks of me, and the impression I had made on her.

Needless to say, I was speechless. How did she find me? She only knew my nickname and had no idea how to spell my surname. She had been in New York for a wedding, and the rabbi performing the ceremony was a Yeshiva University graduate, so she asked him if by chance, he had ever heard of me. He responded: "She is my cousin." Hence the telephone number and my updated history—and the long-planned call was put through. Her point was that small kindnesses truly can affect people and influence them, especially at times of vulnerability.

This got me thinking about whether I could have influenced other people, and how. The first topic to pop out at me was women saying Kaddish. Twenty-seven years ago, after my mother died, I faithfully said Kaddish every day at all three prayer times. It was an uphill battle all the way. My father's support was invaluable. Since it was almost unheard of at the time, I had to "fight it out" every time I went to a new synagogue. I always won because I was right to do it, but the constant fighting was wearying and wearisome. Five year later, after my father died, on his *shloshim* I gave a well-researched public lecture on women and Kaddish, citing all the sources and the conclusions of contemporary rabbinic scholars. It didn't matter how scholarly it was, for the fight continued.

My father was right. The advice he gave was just to do it and teach it, and if possible, publish it. I published a brief personal essay entitled "Kaddish from the Wrong Side of the *Mechitza*," which I expected very few people to read. I was wrong, for one referred it to another until the circle of readers can't be counted any more. But the scholarly lecture had little circulation.

Recently, this newspaper ran a two-part series on women and Kaddish; many of my sources are there, as well as some of my conclusions. How am I to interpret this? Perhaps it could only be published by a man with a rabbinic degree and not by a woman with a doctorate. To be more positive, my father was right, by doing it and teaching it year after year, and by offering the small kindness of helping a woman in pain over the death of a beloved parent. There can be lasting impressions on a widening circle of people that can lead to a positive refocusing of Jewish customs.

Opinion

The Roles of Animals
October 12, 2007

References to animals abound in the Tanakh, most in connection with domesticated types such as sheep, goats, cattle, camels, and horses. Many were used as food by the Israelites, as meat or producers of milk and its byproducts, or offered in the Temple, or used for transportation or war. One's wealth was often measured by how many four-legged animals one owned, and brideswealth was often paid in actual animals.

References to birds, especially domesticated fowl, such as chickens and doves, are also found in the Tanakh. The former were important for meat and eggs; the latter often used as offerings in the Temple. Wild birds such as eagles are referred to poetically, similar to the references to deer and other wild creatures.

What is not present is references to pets.

Cats were useful creatures, hunting rodents in the grain storage areas as well as in living quarters. Dogs were workers, trained to herd the sheep, goats, and cattle, and as guards for herds and homes to protect them from predators both animal and human.

But references to dogs are not positive ones. "You shall not bring the pay of a dog into the house of God" (Deut. 23:19). David, in confronting King Saul, asks why the latter is chasing him, comparing himself to a dead dog; in other words, more than useless. (1 Sam. 24:15). Earlier, Goliath had taunted David: "Am I a dog that you come against me with sticks?" (1 Sam. 17:43). Abner uses a similar phrase in facing Ishboshet, son of Saul: "Am I a dog's head from Judah?" (2 Sam. 3:8).

Offering up dogs as an image of disgust is described by Isaiah (66:3). David, too, does this in a number of Psalms: "Dogs surround me; a pack of evil ones close in on me" (22:17), and "Save my life from the sword . . . from the clutches of a dog" (22:21). "They come each evening, growling like dogs, roaming the city" (59:7).

And then, of course from Proverbs: "A passerby who gets embroiled in someone else's quarrel is like on who seizes a dog by its ears" (26:17). "As a dog returns to its vomit, so a dullard repeats his folly" (26:11).

Dogs ate dead things. "You shall be a holy people to me: you must not eat flesh torn by beasts in the field; you shall cast it to the dogs" (Exod. 22:30). Dogs ate the dead things in the cities and towns while the carrion-eating birds functioned in the fields (1 Kings 14:11). The dogs lapped up the blood of the murdered Naboth; Jezebel is therefore punished by being devoured by dogs as was King Ahab and his line.

Over the centuries the Jewish attitude toward dogs remained the same. It was made worse by the fact that solders in many countries used dogs as attack weapons. Jews did not hunt, so the many breeds used for this were also outside their experience, as were herding dogs, when most Jews became city and town dwellers. It seems that it was modernity that brought with it the change in attitude toward pets, especially toward dogs. My grandmother had a cat, but she was a mouser, not a pet. I had one aunt, however, in Brest-Litovsk, who had a large dog; she sent photographs of her three daughters with this dog to my father who was in New York City by then.

My parents absolutely refused any pets. We begged but to no avail. It wasn't until I married that this changed. Having had no experience with pets, I had no idea how they become part of the family. So my tricolor corgi moved in and took over. Walks, baths, hairballs, begging, snoring, more walks. He was there to greet you and to sulk when left home alone.

Walking a strutting show dog brings inevitable reactions: small children would light up, yelling with joy, making a beeline to pet, followed by frantic parents making sure that this was acceptable. Yes, corgis are bred to be gentle to children. Wall Street types would drop to the ground grinning from ear to ear, without asking permission to pet, but exclaiming, "Oh my God, how gorgeous! What is his name? Even the nutcases roaming the street would greet him: "Good morning, Mr. Corgi!" So, one of the functions of a pet dog seems to be to bring joy to people and to evoke praise of God for having created such a creature.

I don't think that people anthropomorphize pet dogs, for they really do have personalities. But, then comes the crisis: the death of the pet. And you really mourn. And anyone who says *Kappara* has never had a pet. So here is to Velvet, and to all furry pets that make this world a happier and more beautiful place.

Opinion

Professor J. C. Hurewitz
December 19, 2008

In May 2008, a very specialized group of scholars and government workers received the news that Prof. J. C. Hurewitz had died. E-mail announcements reached out to every Middle Eastern country, let alone to Washington, DC, and every department of Middle Eastern Studies across North America, that one of the founders of the field had succumbed to pneumonia at the age of 93.

Jacob Coleman Hurewitz had been the director of Columbia University's Middle East Institute from 1970 until 1984, teaching and often supervising the dissertations of what were probably hundreds of students. I was among that number.

His most influential scholarly achievement was collecting primary sources, such as secret papers and treaties, government communiqués and legislation, each with an incisive explanation, documenting the history of the Middle East from the sixteenth century to the mid-twentieth century. From my perspective, his most important interpretive work is *The Struggle for Palestine* (1950), which is still the best study of the mandate period.

Prof. Hurewitz was a stern advisor, without (to many of us) any sense of humor. To me, despite his last name, he was the epitome of the WASP. Imagine my surprise when my father told me that he was the son of the leading orthodox rabbi of Hartford, Connecticut. When during one of our many unpleasant student-professor meetings, I asked him about it, he very quickly changed the subject, but did not deny it.

During World War II, Prof. Hurewitz was recruited to work in the Near East section of the Office of Strategic Services, the wartime intelligence agency, because of his language skills — skills that he insisted that all of the PhD students obtain. He then moved on to the State Department as one of the advisors on Palestine, and on to the United Nations Secretariat; he accepted the job at Columbia University in 1950.

When I came to Columbia University in 1967, the serendipitous-ness of life made its presence felt. I was sitting in the waiting area, which served five professors, and I was on the list to see two of them. Prof. Gerson D.

Cohen's line was shorter, so before I knew it, I was writing my master's thesis under him instead of under Prof. Hurewitz, even though the topic was more the latter's field. However, as Prof. Cohen was planning on leaving Columbia, he escorted me into the next-door office, and Prof. Hurewitz, the slave driver, became my thesis supervisor. But the upside of Prof. Hurewitz's attitude to his students was that those of us who "stuck it out," actually finished our theses and in an acceptable time frame.

I remember on specific incident. Prof. Hurewitz wanted me to go to Iraq for "a couple of years" to read their archives and write about the formation of the Iraqi mandate after World War I. I informed my parents of his plan, and the next day, to my chagrin but also to my relief, my father marched into Prof. Hurewitz's office, introduced himself and asked him if he had any daughters. Nonplussed, Prof. Hurewitz replied, "Two." My father asked: "Would you send either of them to Iraq for two years?" That was the end of that dissertation topic for me.

He taught us to be objective, a most difficult task in Middle East studies. He taught us how to really "read" the primary sources. He was also a master of the two-minute sound bite, as he appeared on countless television programs as one of the American experts in his field. I loved witnessing him nailing William Buckley during one interview. His memory was prodigious.

At the memorial held for him on November 12, the majority of the speakers focused on his career. Rashid Khalidi, the present director of the Middle East Institute, and not a good heir to Prof. Hurewitz's objectivity, was smart enough to regale us with memories of how his father had been one of his first PhD students. No one mentioned his Jewish connection until one niece got up and spoke of her memories of "Uncle Ya'acov." Good, I thought to myself, he didn't escape his past completely.

Opinion

Cruelty to Animals

2009 [rejected by the press]

I was appalled and acutely embarrassed at the same time, on reading an article in the *New York Times* on the internal report from the Department of Agriculture that found that AgriProcessors Inc., one of America's leading kosher slaughterhouses, had violated animal cruelty laws. Also, some of the plan's inspectors had failed to correct unsanitary conditions. I remember when the scandal broke over a year and a half ago, but I had subconsciously suppressed the memory.

The violators had not only broken American laws abut had broken at least two basic Jewish precepts. One is *tza'ar ba'alei haym* (animal cruelty), and the second is *chillul ha-Shem* (desecration of God).

Judaism attaches particular stress to respecting the needs of animals. The Talmud counts cruelty to animals as one of the most serious offenses. We are enjoined not to slaughter an animal with its young, and not to discomfort beasts of burden by yoking two different-sized animals together. We do not hunt for pleasure. We feed our animals before we eat. The principle of kindness to animals is extended to how we slaughter them.

The laws of *shekhita* are part of the Torah's oral law. They are detailed and precise with regard to the slaughterer, the knife, and the animal. The principle of prevention of cruelty to animals, of inflicting as painless a death as possible, dictates these laws.

So why did workers at AgriProcessors Inc. of Postville, Iowa, pull out the tracheas of the steers with hooks, causing them to stagger around the pens for a couple of minutes before they lost consciousness? To increase the speed of the bleeding. Why? To move on to the next animal in order to speed up the process and make more profit. AgriProcessors is the country's largest producer of meat certified *glatt* kosher; it sells under the brands of Rubashkin's, Iowa's Best Beef, and Aaron's Best. The irony is the stress on the non-necessary aspect of *kashrut*, namely, *glatt*, a term unknown and unheard of by the Jews of Lithuania, Poland, Russia, and Western Europe in the pre-World War II era. Why stress *glatt* kosher when the basic law of preventing cruelty to animals is being broken?

Yes, the Agriculture Department, the Orthodox Union, and Israel's chief rabbinate pressured AgriProcessors to change its practices and therefore no legal action was taken, but the publishing of the report re-awakened the second transgression, that of *chillul ha-Shem.*

Defamation of the Divine Name through an act performed in defiance of religious or ethical principles is a serious transgression of Torah law. Every Jew upholds the honor of Judaism and the Jewish people. I teach non-Jews that the laws of kosher slaughtering are ethical and kind, and that Islam took over our attitude to apply it to *halal* meat. The actions of AgriProcessors make it more difficult to defend our laws and to claim—which we always have—that our trait of compassion, nurtured by centuries of tradition, has protected animals and therefore we never had a need for organized societies for the prevention of cruelty to them.

Opinion

Hebrew Language Instruction
May 21, 2010

One of the things that I have to do, that is not in my "job description," is deal with Hebrew language exemptions at Brooklyn College. About twenty years ago, when Hebrew language and literature was taken from the modern languages and literature department and placed in the Department of Judaic Studies, this became part of our responsibilities. Usually this means writing a letter to the administration that the student's Hebrew Regents was never recorded and to please take care of the oversight. Other times it means actually giving and grading a level three Hebrew examination. A third instance would be a native Hebrew speaker who had graduated from an Israeli high school. But there is a very sad small group that also shows up: children of Israeli parents who moved to America, speak Hebrew at home, but never educated their children to be literate in the language. They are illiterate Hebrew speakers, similar to many Yiddish speakers of earlier generations.

Hebrew education in general is declining, even in the really good Jewish day schools. The generation of teachers who were so enamored of the language that it was almost raised to the level of a religion are almost all gone. I could see the difference even in the education that both of my daughters received at the same high school that I had attended. Grammar? How boring. Memorizing? Old-fashioned. Linguistics? A field for total nerds.

About a month ago I received an email from a member of a kibbutz asking if I was related to a Rabbi Reguer who had taught in Yeshiva University. When I replied in the affirmative, he told me that he had wonderful memories of my father, both as a teacher, and as someone to whom Hebrew was so important that he supervised a Hebrew-speaking club for the student Zionists who were dreaming of making *aliya*.

Two weeks after this exchange of emails, a meeting was held in my office by one of my colleagues on the topic of Holocaust survivors' oral history. One of the older gentlemen came rushing back after leaving the office. He had just seen my name on the bulletin board. Was I related to a Rabbi Reguer who taught at Yeshiva University in the 1940s? When I said yes, he got all excited about how his knowledge of Hebrew was directly connected to my father and that he still knows his grammar better than his grandchildren who are studying in a Jewish day school. I told him about the emails from Israel. He asked for the name of the kibbutznik. They were classmates.

How can we address the decline in instruction of Hebrew language? In my department the answer is relatively easy: we need a line in Hebrew language and literature to teach the advanced courses. For years we have had to rely on an adjunct who taught only the three basic courses. It is astonishing to those in my department that there is no money for a full-time instructor in a borough which contains more Jews than most Israeli cities do.

As for high schools and grade schools, the pedagogical questions need to be discussed. Foreign language instruction is actually a national issue, as the American attitude seems to be, "Let the world learn American!" And for most Jews in this country, foreign language acquisition is an historical anomaly, for never before in our history have we only spoken one language, with just a very basic knowledge of Hebrew.

Opinion

A Dangerous Cult

June 4, 2010

A number of years ago I had a very bad personal experience with a student. He had taken one of my classes, done very well in it, and was sitting in my office discussing his desire to major in Judaic Studies. As I went through the list of requirements and possible courses that he could take, he suddenly became very quiet. When I looked at him questioningly, he became very pale, and the warning signals went off in my head. "Uh oh, I'm about to hear something personal and private that I don't want to know," my little voice told me. "Professor, I want to be totally straight with you, because I have only told you half of my story and I know that you know all about my Baghdadi Jewish past. I'm a different kind of Jew now. I'm a member of 'Jews for Jesus.'"

I did know about his illustrious family, and I thought that I knew him. My professional persona disappeared, and I reacted like a Jew and cried: "Why? How?" I heard the story that is repeated across the United States, as well as in Israel, Russia, Germany, France, and South Africa, of a lonely young Jewish person drifting along, being warmly embraced by a group that pretends to be Jewish—i.e., "Come to Shabbat services and dinner!" or "We have a wonderful Pesach *seder*—come! Join us!" The warmth and camaraderie and lack of Jewish education leads to friendship, belonging, and brainwashing. They number perhaps 200,000.

The founder of Jews for Jesus just died, and my reaction to the news was that I hoped it was a long and painful death, and that "Moishe" Rosen goes to that special place in hell reserved for those ex-Jews who spend their lives trying to convert Jews to some form of Christianity.

Martin Rosen was born in Kansas City, Missouri, into an Orthodox Jewish family. He married a fellow Jew at a young age, and, when she was attracted to Christianity, he read about it and they converted together. Like many converts throughout history, he went overboard in his new identity and was ordained a Baptist minister, working with evangelical groups. Moving to San Francisco in 1970, then in the midst of countercultural ferment, he founded the "Jews of Jesus" cult. Its central tenet is that it is possible to be Jewish and also simultaneously to accept Jesus as the Messiah.

Mainstream Jewish organizations have sued them, not for practicing their religion, but for misrepresentation. The United States has truth in advertising and truth in labeling laws, and the handout literature of Jews of Jesus should state that they are Christian missionaries out to convert Jews. Mainstream Jewish organizations around the world also began to take steps to actively counter their activities. My last run in—and a very loud one at that—was at last year's Israel Independence Day parade where I was handed a flyer and lost my cool completely. They did not argue with me, but moved across the street to stand near the anti-Israel groups, where they belonged.

I have no idea what happened to my student. I do know that he dropped out of Brooklyn College a few semesters later. What a sad story.

And "Moishe" Rosen made it into the *New York Times* obituaries section, where it was reported that he had left instructions that he wished to be buried in his *tallis*. No comment.

Opinion

A National Treasure

November 5, 2010

I have a confession to make: I have been in Washington, DC, numerous times but I had never entered the Library of Congress until October 25, when I delivered a lecture there. The building is incredibly attractive outside, overwhelming on the inside, and the main reading room is just astonishing. I came early in order to take a guided tour, and the numbers that kept being repeated were in the millions—millions of items including books, documents, cartoon, films, and other things.

In the main hall, on the left side, a Gutenberg Bible is on display, as is a Mainz Bible on the right side. I happened to be standing next to a boy of about ten who was there with his class, as they all approached the Mainz Bible. I overheard him say to his friend that the Bible would be in Hebrew, and I saw his surprise when he saw that it was not. So I said softly that when the Gentiles say "Bible," they mean the Christian Bible, which may or may not include a translation of *our* Bible. He smiled conspiratorially at me and said "Thanks," waving good-bye as the class moved on.

Yet, there were Jewish-themed statues and Jewish-themed decorations, and Jewish names intermixed with the motifs depicting the world's wisdom. And there is a wonderful Judaica collection of books, including *incunabula* (books printed before 1500), artist's books, illustrated Hebrew poetry, and Bibles. I saw a German-Hebrew Passover *Had-Gadya* printed in Germany in the early 1920s, with illustrations that made my hair stand on end, as they seemed to evoke a prediction of the horrors to come, in the graphic dog biting the cat scene, for example. I saw an illustrated Hebrew poem attributed to the wife of Dunash ben Labrat, of the "Golden Age" of Spain. There were more contemporary things too, printed by the Jerusalem workshop and as well as other Israeli printing workshops, and a *Mashal ha-Qadmoni* printed by Pardes Rimonim Press with reproduced woodcuts from the Venetian edition of 1542. I did not see the Hebrew *incunabula*, but I know of them.

My lecture attracted about fifty people, many with PhDs, and looking at the interested faces, I was inspired to go "all out." Unlike what often goes on at scholarly conferences, these people took time out to listen and learn and not to critique. That in itself is exhilarating. Many stayed after the lecture, so I met Israelis, a couple of Brooklyn College alumni, someone who was related to one of my Mexican cousins, and an old college friend who lives in the Washington area. I also met many of the impressive administrators and staff of the Library of Congress, who run that complicated organization. As the introductory video seen by visitors reminds us: "This is your library, but this is also Congress' library. Use it, learn from it, visit it."

The topic of my lecture was "The Cairo Geniza: The World of Jewish Women," and it was sponsored by the Hebraic Section of the African and Middle Eastern Division of the Library of Congress. I urge everyone to not only visit the various museums on the mall, the White House, and the Capitol, but also to cross the small park on the backside of the Houses of Congress, cross the street, and visit this national treasure.

Opinion

At Your Parent's Knee

November 18, 2011

Educators have long debated how much influence parents have over their children's formal education. In other words, when a child is young, is it the school learning that makes a bigger impression or is it what the child sees at home? I am of the school of thought that both are important.

I was reminded of this when we read both *Bereishit* and *Lech Le-cha*. I pictured myself during my first-grade performance, at the Talmud Torah School of Montreal. Six of us were chosen to recite the proper verses for the six days of Creation. I was given day six, the longest, probably because I was "the Rabbi's daughter." There I was, a first grader, facing the audience of parents and students, and I did what any normal first grader would do—I panicked and went blank. I looked at my parents, sitting in the front row, and my father stood up and lifted a "pretend" *Kiddush* cup, mouthing *Yom ha-Shishi*. I immediately picked up my own little "pretend" cup and proceeded to sing the verses at the top of my lungs. The teacher wisely stepped up just as I reached the blessing, which was not in the script, and held my hand, thereby silencing me.

The following year the teacher was smarter, and for the second-grade performance on *Lech Le-cha*, the whole class sang together.

The point is that specific family customs are taught by parents, and not by formal teachers. How to put on a *tallit*, how to hold your hands while lighting and blessing Shabbat lights, how to wave the *lulav* and *etrog* during *Hallel*, how to divide up the challa after the blessing, how many times to dip in the *miqve*, tunes to sing for *zmirot*. This is in addition to all of the special family recipes for all kinds of occasions.

School is for formal Jewish study of Torah, Hebrew, Jewish history, Talmud, law. If a child is lucky, he or she will have a teacher who inspires, but, as we all know, there can also be a teacher who does the opposite. I remember most of my teachers in grade school and high school fondly. Many of them were of the generation that almost idolized the Hebrew language. We may have hated those grammar lessons, but we ended up really speaking Hebrew, and appreciating the writers and poets. We memorized entire poems, along with selected chapters from the Tanakh. That methodology is gone, for better or for worse.

So who we are, as far as our Jewish identity goes, is a complex matter. Parents cannot do the job of educating alone. I see children of Israelis who emigrated from Israel to Brooklyn, who speak to their children in Hebrew but did not send them to Jewish day schools or even to afternoon schools. Their knowledge of Hebrew is purely aural—they can neither read it nor write it. Their parents did not realize the realities of the Diaspora. But, on the other hand, just sending children to the day schools and keeping nothing Jewish at home, often creates ambiguity in the child, who, as an adult will drop everything Jewish and feel that the parents are hypocrites. However, the child can have both the proper Jewish education as well as the proper informal education at home, and, as an adult, make the decision to either uphold everything or to leave everything behind.

The bottom line is that it is not easy to be a Jewish parent. We have to try our best on all levels—and hope that our children will turn out well.

Appendix

"Kaddish from the 'Wrong' Side of the *Mechitza*." In *On Being a Jewish Feminist*, edited by Susannah Heschel, 177–81. New York: Schocken Books, 1983. Reprinted in *Norton_Anthology of World Religions*, Vol. 2, edited by Jack Miles and David Biale, 631–34. New York: Norton, 2015.

Today is the first anniversary of my mother's death. She died suddenly, in the prime of her life, and the void left in my life is immeasurable as well as indescribable.

Jewish laws and customs concerning death are infinitely wise. Without knowing the psychological terminology, the laws teach the need of facing the reality of death—hence in Israel, in particular, no coffin is used for the burial, so that you cannot pretend that the shrouded figure is not what it is. The laws first recognize the need to have time alone during the immediate aftershock of death as well as the need to have people come to comfort you so that you do not feel totally alone; and then the laws gradually push you, first after seven days, then after thirty days, and finally after eleven months, to rejoin the world.

But what if you are, as I am, an Orthodox Jew as well as a feminist? How do you deal with the dilemma of burying your mother outside Jerusalem where the burial societies, the *hevrah kadishah*, are run by men who still think they are living in the ghettos of the late Middle Ages? Let me add one more personal note. I stem from an Orthodox family of note (i.e., I have *yihus*); therefore, what I do tends to have wider ramifications than if I were merely acting on my own. I can also get away with what some consider outrageous behavior because I have the backing of my father, a man well trained in the rational Lithuanian *yeshivot* of the previous generation.

There we were, in our grief—my father, one of my brothers, and myself—standing in front of the body of my mother. Without even thinking, I joined the two men as we mumbled through the first choking Kaddish of the funeral service. After about three repetitions of the Kaddish, as we moved from the chapel toward the grave, the head of the *hevrah kadishah* suddenly realized that I was saying it aloud with the men. Before the next one, he ordered the men only to say it, repeating this order in Hebrew, then in Yiddish, and finally in English. I looked straight through him and continued in an even louder voice. At the grave site, the same thing happened. He handed the shovel to my father to shovel some dirt into the grave, then gave it to my brother, and then pointedly gave it to a male cousin. I ignored the man, bent down to scoop up some dirt with my hands, and threw it into the grave, as is required of all close relatives of the deceased, in keeping with the traditional attitude toward the reality of death. By now the man was livid, especially as he saw he had no backing from any of my family.

After the body is buried, Jewish custom dictates that attention then turns from the dead to the living, and the process of comforting begins. This is traditionally symbolized by the formation of a double row of people through which the mourners pass. The head of the *hevrah kadishah* cornered me as the lines were being formed and said that I was absolutely forbidden from passing through the two rows. Why, I asked. Because it was not modest for women to go between two rows of men. (Until that point I had not even noticed that the lines were male.) I retorted that this had nothing to do with men or women but with mourners, and if it bothered him so much, he should have two rows of women for me. The logic of the statement, I later found out, made the rounds of the ultra-Orthodox communities in Jerusalem, with many rabbis agreeing with my statement. Unfortunately, many of my sister-Jews do not have the internal fortitude to follow what I did, but remain cowed by the *hevrah kadishah* and "custom," that old excuse for not allowing women to follow ritual.

During the week of sitting *shiva* I continued to say Kaddish with the *minyan* that came twice daily to the house. I studied laws of mourning with my father, and he backed my resolve to continue the practice for the required eleven months. Yes, daughters too should say Kaddish for their parents. The rabbis, in their wisdom, knew the psychological benefits of going to the synagogue daily to perform this duty, and they did not discriminate against women. What seems to have happened—here as with a long list of other practices—is that certain *mitzvoth* (commandments) have luck and others do not. An example of a lucky *mitzvah* is candle lighting. The law states that a house must have candles lighted in it in honor of Shabbat: if there is a married couple in the house, the wife lights the candles, and if a married woman is not there, then a man lights them.

This *mitzvah* regarding candle lighting has been expanded by certain sects of Judaism to include all females, young and old, with all sorts of mystical overtones given to it. Few women attending Brooklyn College have not been accosted by Lubovich men who ask them first whether they are Jewish, and if so, whether they are willing to light the free candles in the holders Friday night.

An unlucky *mitzvah* is Kaddish. Too bad. It was saying Kaddish for the past year that enabled me to keep my sanity. If I had not *had* to get out of bed at 6:30 a.m. in order to be on time for the beginning of services, I can guarantee that I simply would not have left my bed at all. Depression is a terrifying experience partly because one is virtually unable to fight it.

Did I mean what I was saying? Was I really reaffirming my belief in God's greatness (which is the meaning of the words of the Kaddish prayer)? Not for the first few months. Rather, I battled God every inch of the way. Catharsis came suddenly, violently, but it took almost the full eleven months before I again really meant the words I was pronouncing— meant them of the internal level.

Externally, there were some very interesting aspects to my Kaddish-saying career. I had my "home synagogue," the one that I attended most often, and after the initial shock of my appearance wore off and the old men agreed among themselves that I was right in saying Kaddish, I became one of the gang—or almost. For I sat behind a separation, in the corner. My anger at this particular *mechitza* grew to the point that one rainy day, when a man came in and unthinkingly draped his wet coat over the "cage," I growled aloud. He jumped at the sound and looked at me questioningly. I said, "If you treat me like an animal, why the surprise if I growl like one?" He excused himself and removed his coat. I later found out from some of the men that this particular man did something unusual a few days after that incident. I was away for five days or so, and each morning during my absence the old gentlemen I had growled at sat behind the *mechitza* to see what it felt like. He agreed with my dissatisfaction and frustration, but neither of us could come up with a solution to the problem.

Most daily services are not held in the main synagogue but in a small room either downstairs or to the side of the main hall. Since women do not usually come to weekday services, most synagogues do not have facilities for them. When I appeared, the solution to the problem this posed was usually my standing to pray outside the room through the open door. Inevitably, there would be a scramble to get me a *siddur*, a chair, a Bible, and an embarrassed apology for the lack of a women's section. Inevitably, also, there would be a moment of stunned silence as I would rise to say Kaddish out loud. Some would come and ask if I had a brother. I would reply that it made no difference if I did or did not, for all children were obligated to say Kaddish for parents. Some would offer to say it for me. I repeated what I said about brothers. I also said that if it offended anyone for me to say it alone, they were welcome to say it with me, but not for me. A rush to the books, or to the rabbi, brought the usual—albeit sometimes reluctant—affirmation of my deed.

In one Hasidic synagogue, one man shouted at me to say Kaddish silently because my chanting aloud was against the injunction of *kol ishah*; the singing voice of a woman is considered by some to be sexually arousing to men and therefore is forbidden. I asked the man whether he spoke to women in public. He said yes. I said that I was merely speaking in public also, but to God. And if it still bothered him, he had no business setting right near the *mechitza* to start with.

Then there was the time I visited Boston and was praying in an Orthodox school attended by one of the most outstanding Jewish scholars and rabbis of our day. (i.e., Rabbi Dr. J. B. Soloveitchik) The sexton was nervous because I had already told him what I would be doing. He insisted on saying Kaddish with me. But I saw a flurry of activity in the corner where the rabbi sat, and when it came time to say it, I said the Kaddish along and all answered, as they properly should have.

It has not been easy. This past year has been the worst of my life. It has been eased somewhat by my Kaddish-saying and by the positive reactions of most of the men I met at the services. On Sabbaths and holidays, women often came over to ask about what I was doing, usually adding that it was too bad they had not known about this during their own year of mourning, when they too had needed desperately some sort of ritual to lean on.

After much soul-searching, I decided at the end of the past semester to share my ideas and thoughts with my class at Brooklyn College, where I gave a course on "The Jewish Woman." At first I had hesitated: even though I felt strongly about the validity of my actions, I did not want to influence my students, who tend to be very much impressed by what I do. But if someone like myself is not going to teach this, who will?

Index

A
Aaron, 93, 144
Aaronsohn, Aaron, 110
Aaronsohn, Sarah, 110, 111
Abner, 282
Abraham, 22, 74, 75, 77
Abramovitch, Ilana, 148
Acqua de Canicare, 124
Ad De-Lo Yada, 15
Adoniyahu, 96, 100
Aguilar, Grace, 230
aguna, 161, 165, 166, 167, 238, 239
Ahaliav ben Akhisamakh, 44
Ahashverosh, 232
Akiva, Rabbi, 168, 170
Altneu Shul, 1
Amida prayer, 170, 254
Amnon of Mayence (Rabbi), 190
Anna of Rome, 124–1
armies of Rome, 58–59
Armstrong, Karen, 269
aron kodesh, 227
Ascarelli, Deborah, 114
Ashdod, 38
Ashkelon, 38
Ashkeloni, Joseph b. Isaac, 113
Ashkenazic *trope*, 31
Ashkenazi Jews, 41,
Ashkenazi Orthodox Jews, 16
Ashmedai,

auto-da fe, 20
Avishag, 96
Avtalyon, 170
Ayshet Hayyil, 236

B
babushka, 237
Babylonian exile, 4
Balfour Declaration, 16
Banu Qurayza, 268, 269
Bar Kochba, 34, 132
bat-mitzva, 244
Bat-Sheva, 75, 96, 97, 100
Bay of Naples, 202–203
Beersheba, 111
Benjamin, Rabbi, 54, 55
Benzion Meir Hai Uzziel, (Rabbi), 18, 19
Berger, Aliza, 142
Bezalel ben Uri, 44
Bialistok, 134
Bible, 41, 134
  Deut. 21:14, 102
  Exod. 22:30, 283
  Exod., 90
  Exod. 18, 92
  Ezekiel, 98
  Ezekiel 27, 200
  Gen. 25:5, 75
  Gen. 50:15, 88
  Isaiah (66:3), 282

1 Kings 14:11, 283
Lev. 22:32, 106
Num. 12:1–16, 92
Psalm 27, 254
Psalm 119, 69
Book of Ruth, 258
Kohelet, 100–101
Biblical women
    Avishag, roles of, 96–97
    Bat-Sheva, 75, 96, 97, 100
    Bilha, 72, 80–81
    Bilha and Zilpa, 80–81
    captive woman, 102–103
    Chana, 72, 230–231
    Deborah the judge, 94–95
    Dina, 82
    matriarchal legacy, 86–87
    midwifery, 90–91
    Miriam, thoughts on, 92–93
    Noah's wife, 70–71
    Ruth, lessons from, 98–99
    Tamar and Judah, 84–85
    Vashti, 232–233
Bienvenida, Dona, 202, 203
Bilha, 80–81
Bilha's sons, 72
Blackburn, Robert, 44
Bleich, J. David, 167
blessings, 188–189
Bolshevik Revolution, 52
book of Ruth, 258
Borromeo, Cardinal Federico, 212
Braham, Randolph, 137
Brianda, Dona, 89
Brown, Erica S., 143
Brynner, Yul, 144
Bulaffi, Michele, 30
Burton, Richard, 58

C
Caesar, Julius, 58, 59, 208
Cain and Abel, sibling pair, 88
Cairo Geniza, 22, 37

Capristo, Annalisa, 162
captive woman, 102–103
Carlebach, Shlomo, 30
Carnivale, 14
carrela de sos Ebreos, 217
Castiglioni of Trieste, 115
Cayam, Aviva, 142
censorship, 42–43
Chabad movement, 244
Chafetz Chaim, 160
Chaim Ber Gulewski, Rabbi, 53
Chafetz Chaim 160
chalutzim, 120
Chana Senesz, 230
Chayim of Hameln, 108
Chevra Kadisha, 198
chillul ha-Shem, 286, 287
cholent, 161
chol ha-mo'ed, 172
Chumashim, 246
Churchill White Paper, 157
Churchill, Winston S., 38, 250, 278
Cleopatra (movie), 58, 59
Cohen, Gerson D., 284–285
Confucianism, 51
Conversos, 20, 21, 88, 104, 112, 217, 241
Courter, Gay
    Flowers in the Blood, 140, 141
Cross-Israel Water Carrier, 38
cruelty to animals, 286–287
Cum Nimis Absurdum, 204

D
dancing, 62–63
dangerous cult, 290–291
Darwish, Nonie, 158, 159
David, 170
David's poetry (Psalms), 40
David's prayer, 254–255
David ben Zakkai, 61
Dead Sea Scrolls, 136

Deborah, 94–95
DeMille, Cecil B., 144
Deut. 21:14, 102
dhimmi, 269
Dina, 82
dog in Jewish history, 242–243
Dona Gracia Nasi, 104, 112, 113, 230, 270
Don Joseph Nasi, 112, 113
dress code, 26–27
    Jews, 27
    women, 26
Drew, Charles, 151
Duke of Naxos, 112
Dulcia, 106, 107
The Dybbuk, 230

E
East Ghor Canal, 38
Eidelman, Jay
    Jewish Press, 148
Eliach, Yaffa, 137
Eliezer, 71, 80
Elimelech's land, 99
Eliyahu, 120
Elkana, 72
El Maleh Rakhamim, 139
Elul, A Lesson in Tolerance, 220–221
empty nest syndrome, 54
Enayim, 85
entrepreneur, 28–29
    Webster's Collegiate Dictionary, 28
Erev Ba, 30
Erev Yom Kippur, 260, 261
eruv, 161, 196–197
Esau, 76
Estee Lauder, 29
Esther Kiera, 104
Exodus, 90
Exodus 18, 92
Ezekiel, 98

Ezekiel 27, 200
Ibn Ezra, Abraham, 66

F
family purity, 234–235
Feingold, Henry, 137
Fez, 226
The field of food, 32–33
Finzi-Continis, 270
Finzi, Roberto, 162
Firestone, David, 158
firzogerin, 126
Frederick, King of Sicily, 276
Friedlander, Henry, 137

G
Galen, 150
game of chess, 66–67
Garzia, David, 30
gastronomical Jews, 225
gastronomic Judaism, 32
Gaza, 34, 158
geirei tzedek, 171
Gen. 25:5, 75
Gen. 50:15, 88
Geniza records, 91
Gentiles, 14, 17, 235, 292
Geonim, 60
German Jews, 116
ger tzedek, 98, 170
ger ve-toshav, 182
ghetto Jews, 204–205
Gideon, 170
glassmakers, 200–201
Glass, Philip, 42
glatt kosher, 160, 286
Gluckel, 86, 87, 108–109, 126
Goitein, S. D., 90
Gomez, 24
Gracia, Dona, 89
Great Synagogue of Livorno, Italy, 30
Greek culture, 170

Gregory IX (Pope), 20
Gregory the Great, 209
Grossman, Susan, 126
Gutenberg Bible, 292

H
Habakkuk, 98
Haberman, A. M., 106, 112
Had-Gadya, 292
haftara, 41, 74, 95, 98, 110, 245
hagana, 154
haggada, 45
haggadot, 276
Haidt, Frances, 136
Ha-Kalir, Elazar, 180
halakha, 16, 18, 19, 142, 179, 196, 254
Halpern, Micah D., 142
Ham, 70
Ha-Makom yenahem et-chem, 173
Hameln, Haym, 86
hanuikyya, 219, 240
HaRav Heiman, 236
Harrison, Rex, 58
Harvey, William, 150
Ha-Shomer, 120
Hasidic movement, 127, 134
Hasmonean tactics, 59
Haut, Rivka, 126
hazzan, 180, 181, 208
Hebrew education, 226, 288
Hebrew language instruction, 288–289
Hebrew literature, 134
Hebrew poetry, 41
Hebrew printing, 112
Hebron, 68, 74
hekhsher, 172
Henkin, Chana, 143
hevrah kadishah, 296, 297
High Holy Days, 207, 254
history
    American Jews, 24–25
    armies of Rome, 58–59

the blessing of water, 38–39
censorship, 42–43
dancing, 62–63
dress code, 26–27
entrepreneur, 28–29
The field of food, 32–33
game of chess, 66–67
Judaic Studies, explaining, 46–47
Kaifeng, China, 50–51
learning languages, 56–57
the power of poetry, 40–41
The Purim Play, 14–15
a question of art, 44–45
Roman roads, 34–35
sacred music, 30–31
saying good-bye, 54–55
setting the calendar, 60–61
Shanghai, 52–53
The Spanish Inquisition, 20–21
stereotyping, 64–65
synagogue decorum, 22–23
tombstones, 68–69
the traveler, 36–37
tribal divisions, 48–49
women's suffrage, 16–19
holocaust museum, 130–131
holocaust studies
    annual conference, 134–135
    busy week, 136–137
    fifty years later, 132–133
    holocaust museum, 130–131
    Kristallnacht Seventy Years Later, 138–139
House of Sforza, 14
hubris, 248
Hurewitz, J. C., 146, 262, 284–285

I
incunabula, 292
inquisition documents, 21
Irish Catholic church, 152
Irving, David, 134
Ishboshet (son of Saul), 282

Israeli War of Independence, 59
Istanbul, 226
Italian Jewish communities, 14
Italian Jews
   completing a course, 210–211
   ghetto Jews, 204–205
   Italian Journal, 212–215
   Jewish symbols, 206–207
   Megillat Antiochus, 218–219
   synagogue history, 208–209
   View from Naples, 202–203
Italian Journal, 212–215
Italian *trope*, 31
Italy and the Holocaust, A Reappraisal, 162–163

J
Jericho, 128
"Jewish" food, 224–225
Jewish Law and Custom
   blessings, 188–189
   decisions, 172–173
   endless summer, 174–175
   eruv, 196–197
   glassmakers, 200–201
   Kashrut laws ramifications, 178–179
   local custom, 176–177
   love of parents, 168–169
   in memoriam, 184–185
   modern day aguna, 165–167
   moving prayer, 190–191
   presentation, 186–187
   social justice, 182–183
   special relationship, 194–195
   the synagogue service, 180–181
   Tefillat Ha-Derech, 192–193
Jewish Legal Writings by Women, 142–143
Jewish nationalism, 41
Jewish Press, 126
Jewish self-images, 240–241
Jewish symbols, 206–207
Jewish women, 27
   Anna of Rome, 124–125
   first woman publisher, 112–113
   Gluckel, working woman, 108–109
   Kiddush HaShem, 106–107
   lady was a spy, 110–111
   modern Zealot, 120–121
   realities of widowhood, 122–123
   second thoughts on Rahav, 128–129
   stereotypes and, 116–119
   travelers, 36
   of Turkey, 104–105
   Ugav Rahel, 114–115
   women and synagogue worship, 126–127
Jews hats, 26
Jews of Arabia, 268–269
The Jews of Brooklyn, 148–149
"Jews of Jesus" cult, 290
Jordan River, 38
Joseph, 79
Joseph, Saadya ben, 60, 61
Joshua, 68, 110, 111
Judah, 78, 84–85
Judah Maccabee, 218, 219
Judenrein, 269

K
Kabbala, 98
Kaddish, 184
Kaifeng, China, 50–51
kasher, 33, 37
kashrut, 117, 225, 286
   laws ramifications, 178–179
Katz, Maidi, 143
kedeisha, 78
kedusha, 30
kehilla, 118, 222

Kel Malei Rachamim, 243
ketuba, 66, 239
Khalidi, Rashid, 285
Kibbutz movement, 121
kibbutznik, 289
kiddush, 224
Kiddush HaShem, 106–107
Kiera, Esther, 29
kindertransport, 154
Kineret, 38
King David, 78, 96, 97
Kochavei Yitzhak, 114
Kohanim, 68
Kohelet, 100–101
Kook, Abraham Yitzhak Ha-Cohen (Rabbi of Jerusalem), 16–19
Kristallnacht, 138–139, 154
Kurosawa, Akiro, 84, 85
Kurtzer, Sheila, 158
Kuzari, 66

L
Ladino poetry, 134
Lattes, Moshe, 213
learning languages, 56–57
Lech Le-cha, 294
legacy, 222–223
Leibowitz, Nechama, 246–247
Leonardo da Vinci, Master Draftsman, 44, 45
Leti, Bruno, 260
letter writing, 250–251
Lev. 22:32, 106
Levi, Primo, 210
Lewis, Bernard, 262
Libyan and Iranian Jewish immigrants, 32
Lipstadt, Debora, 134, 135
Lishansky, Joseph, 110
Lithuanian Jews, 220
Lithuanian *yeshivot*, 296
Litwak, Olga, 146
Luria, Isaac (Rabbi), 68

Luzzatto, Samuel David (Rabbi), 83, 114, 218

M
Maccabee, Judah, 218, 219
machzor, 190, 212, 213,280
Maimonides, Moses, 22, 66, 170, 171, 228, 249
Mainz, 226
Malchi, Esparanza, 29
mamzerim, 166
Mandarin Chinese, 54
Manoach's wife (mother of Samson), 70
Manya, 121
marranos, 20, 241
Martin, Agnes, 260
Masechet Purim, 14, 15
Mashal ha-Qadmoni, 292
Materia Hebraica, 69
Matityahu, Yochanan Ben, 218
matriarchal legacy, 86–87
Matsuev, Denis, 256
mechitza, 25, 126, 127, 298, 299
Megillat Antiochus, 218–219
Mehmet, Sultan III, 104
Meir, Aaron Ben (Rabbi), 60, 170
Mendelssohn, Felix, 256
Mendelssohn, Moses, 56
menorah, 69, 245
Meshullam, Kalonymus ben (Rabbi), 190
mezuzot, 188
midrash aggada, 144
midrashim, 70, 71, 94, 246
midreshei aggada, 94, 144, 145, 246
midwifery, 90–91
Millen, Rochelle, 142, 143
Ming dynasty, 50
minhag, 196
minhag ha-makom, 177
Minhagei Lita, 160–161

minhag ha-makom, 177
minimalism, 260–261
minyan, 69, 196, 228, 297
miqve, 188, 234, 235
Miriam, 62, 92–93
Mir Yeshiva, 52, 67
Mishkenot Sha-ananim, 186
Mishnah Berurah, 160
mishnayot, 220, 222
Mishne, 184
mitzvot, 267,297
Mizrachi, 16
modern day aguna, 165–167
modern Zealot, 120–121
Modigliani, Amadeo, 210
monotheism, 129
Morais, Sabato, 115
Moroccan Jews, 185
Moroccan *mellah*, 252
Morpurgo, Jacob, 114
Morpurgo, Rahel, 114, 115
Moshe, 92, 93
Moshe's Song of Triumph, 40
Musaf, 22
Musica Sacra di Livorno, 31
Muslim Cordoba, 22
mysticism, 134

N
Na'amah, 70
Naftali, 72
Naipul, V. S.
  The Mystic Masseur, 263
Naomi, 99
Nasi, Dona Gracia, 88
Naso, 23
Natan Sharansky, 274–275
  *The Case for Democracy:
    The Power of Freedom to
    Overcome Tyranny and
    Terror*, 275
Nathan the prophet, 97
Nazis, 131, 132, 139, 222

Nechama, personal comment,
  246–247
New York Times, 42, 138, 158, 286, 291
Nidal, Abu, 175
NILI, 111
Nissan, 60
Noah's wife, 70–71
Noamzara. see Noah's wife
Noguchi, Isamu, 271
Numbers 12:1–16, 92
nusakh Sfard, 176

O
oasis of Yathrib, 268
Onan, 84
Operation Barbarossa, 52
opinion
  challenges ahead, 248–249
  cost of being Jewish, 226–227
  cruelty to animals, 286–287
  dangerous cult, 290–291
  David's prayer, 254–255
  defense of Vashti, 232–233
  dog in Jewish history, 242–243
  Elul, A Lesson in Tolerance,
    220–221
  family purity, 234–235
  Hebrew language instruction,
    288–289
  Hurewitz, 284–285
  intertwining links, 228–229
  "Jewish" food, 224–225
  Jewish self-images, 240–241
  Jews of Arabia, 268–269
  legacy, 222–223
  letter writing, 250–251
  limitations, 262–263
  memories, 236–237
  minimalism, 260–261
  Natan Sharansky, 274–275
  national treasure, 292–293
  Nechama, personal comment,
    246–247

New York Experience, 272–273
personal Chana, 230–231
prenuptial agreements, 238–239
public humiliation, 252–253
question of spirituality, 244–245
rites of passage, 266–267
roles of animals, 282–283
selective memory, 264–265
small kindnesses, 280–281
task of translation, 276–277
topics for discussion, 270–271
two concerts, 256–257
word play, 258–259
   At Your Parent's Knee, 294–295
"Oriental" traditionalism, 19
Orthodox Caucus, 238
Ottoman Turks, 110

P
Perani, Maruo, 69
Perlman, Itzhak, 156
personal Chana, 230–231
Pesach, 127
Pharaoh, 91
philanthropy, 183
Pinchas, 120
Pius XII, Pope, 211
piyyut, 40, 218
Poliakoff, Menachem Mendel
   (Rabbi), 160, 161
Pontercorboli, Giuseppe, 30
Pope Pius XII, 211
Potiphar's wife, 79
prenuptial agreements, 238–239
prophet Elisha, 70
Psalm 27, 254
Psalm 119, 69
Psalms of David, 181
Pu'ah, 90
public humiliation, 252–253
Purim of Cairo (1524), 14
Purim of Syracuse (1425), 14
The Purim Play, 14–15

Purim "rabbi," 14
Purimspiel, 14
Pyrenees, 40

Q
Qing dynasty, 51
Queen Esther, 232
Queen Vashti, 232
question of spirituality, 244–245
Qur'an, 181

R
rabbanit, 234, 235
Rachel, 72
Rahav, second thoughts on,
   128–129
Rashi, 94
Rashomon, 84
refuseniks, 274
Reguer, Sara, 247
Reguer, Simcha Zelig (Rabbi),
   172, 288
Renaissance, 14, 22, 112, 124
Renaissance Florence, 22
Reviews
   Biblical Films, 144–145
   Book Day, 158–159
   "Dr. Ruth," 154–155
   intellectual stimulation,
      146–147
   Italy and the Holocaust, A
      Reappraisal, 162–163
   Jewish Legal Writings by Women,
      142–143
   The Jews of Brooklyn, 148–149
   Minhagei Lita, 160–161
   protecting women, 152–153
   The Story of Blood, 150–151
   visions of Israel, 156–157
   a woman of enterprise, 140–141
Reyna, 113
Rhineland, 40
Ricchetti, Rav (Rabbi), 214

rites of passage, 266–267
Rivka, 75, 76
Roe vs. Wade, 130
Rokeah, 106
Roman roads, 34–35
Rooney, Andy, 262
Rosen, Martin, 290
Rosh Hashana, 60, 72, 190, 280
Roth, Cecil, 114
Roth, Philip, 118, 240
Rovina, Anna, 230
Ruth, 98–99

S
Saadya ben Joseph, 60, 61
Sachs, Jonathan (Rabbi), 126, 127
sacred music, 30–31
Safiyeh, 104
Safrai, Chana, 142
Sages, 87, 98
Samson, 170
Samuel, Don, 202
Sara, 72, 77, 111
Sarna, Jonathan, 24
Sassoon, Flora, 140, 141
Sassoon, Solomon, 140
Saul, 170
Schechter, Solomon, 212
Schiffman, Lawrence H., 136
Schwartz, Ezra (Rabbi), 196
Screen, James T., 158
Scroll of Esther, 14
Sea of Reeds, 62
seder, 21, 276
Sefer ha-Mo'adim, 61
Sefer ha-Zikkaron, 60
Segre, Vittorio, 210
selective memory, 264–265
Sephardic communities, 62
Sephardi Jews, 56, 68
setting the calendar, 60–61
Sforza archive collection, 124

Sforza, Catherine, 124
Shabbat, 22, 37, 64, 117, 127, 195
Shabbat Hannuka, 218
Shabbat laws, 117
Shabtai Zvi, 86
Shanghai, 52–53, 67
Shapiro, Robert M., 138, 139
Shavuot festival, 98, 127
Shechem's house, 83
She'erith Israel, 24, 25
Shelah, 84, 85
She-lo Asani Isha, 143
Shem, 70
Shema, 22, 51
Shifra, 90
Shi'i Fatimids, 60
Shimon, 83
Shlomo Carlebach's music, 30
Shmaiya, 170
Shmone-Esrei, 180, 230
Shoah, 137
shofar, 69
Shu'a, 70
Shunamite, 96
siddur, 36, 126, 127, 212
Siegman, Henry, 146
social justice, 182–183
Solomon, 97, 100, 101
Solomon, Haim, 24
Soloveichik, Haym, 146
Soloveitchik, J. B. (Rabbi), 228, 254, 299
Song dynasty, 50
The Spanish Inquisition, 20–21
Spanish Jews, 21
Stanislawski, Michael, 146
stereotypes, 64–65, 116–117
stereotypical Jewish jobs, 28
Stern, Mendel, 114
The Story of Blood, 150–151
The Struggle for Palestine (1950), 284
Struth, Thomas, 44
Sukkot festival, 127, 206

Sullam, Sarah Coppio, 114
sultan's harem in Istanbul, 29
Sunni Abbasids, 60
Sykes-Picot Agreement, 157
synagogue decorum, 22–23
synagogue history, 208–209
synagogue service, 180–181

T
Tabernacle, 48
tallit, 174, 196, 215, 222
Talmud, 42, 140, 184, 246
Talmudic passages, 134
Talmudic period, 40, 60
Tamar, 78, 84–85
Tanakh, 282
Tawil, Ralph (Rabbi), 85
Taylor, Elizabeth, 58
T'chinot, 244
Tefillat Ha-Derech, 192–193
tefillin, 36, 172, 196
9/11 terrorist attacks, 159
Thanksgiving, 33
"The Game of Kings: Medieval Ivory Chessmen from the Isle of Lewis," 66
tircha de-tzibura, 180, 263
Tisha B'Av, 54
Titus, 207
tombstones, 68–69
Torah, 17, 18, 23, 74, 76, 78, 87, 88, 90, 98, 99, 102, 103, 114, 122, 123, 127, 168, 169, 184, 234, 244, 263, 294
   Bereishit, 294
   Lech Le-cha, 294
   Matot, 122
   Naso, 23
   Tazria, 234
   Toldot, 76–77
   Va-Yishlach, 82–83
Torquemada, Tomas de, 20
tza'ar ba'alei haym, 286

U
Ugav Rahel, 114–115
Umma, 48
U'Netaneh Tokef, 190
Unterman, Rabbi, 236
upsherren, 161
Uzziel, Benzion Meir Hai (Rabbi), 18, 19

V
vaporettos, 215
Va-Yishlach, 82–83
Venice, 226
Ventura, Moise, 30
Vesalius, Andreas, 150
vilayet, 272
visions of Israel, 156–157

W
Washington, George, 24, 150
water desalinization, 38
Westheimer, Ruth, 154–155
   Heavenly Sex: Sexuality in the Jewish Tradition, 154
widowhood, realities of, 122–123
Willig, Rabbi Mordechai, 238
woman publisher, first, 112–113
women
   dress code, 26
   and synagogue worship, 126–127
women of valor, 71
women's suffrage, 16–19
   Converso traditions, 21
   Judaism, 21

X
Xu Xin, 50
   The Jews of Kaifeng, China: History, Culture, and Religion, 50

Y
Ya'akov, 76, 80
Yadin, Yigael, 35
Yafet, 70
yahrzeits, 69, 184, 185, 220, 221
yayin nesekh, 134, 147
Yehuda, 85
Yehudi Menuhin, 256
yeshiva ketana, 226, 227
Yeshiva, Slobodka, 160
Yeshiva, Telshe, 160
Yibum, 84
Yiddish, 126
Yiddishe Mama, 117, 118
Yigael Yadin, 136
Yishuv, 16
Yitro, 92
Yitzhak, 75, 76

Yochanan Ben Matityahu, 218
Yom Ha-Sho'ah, 132
Yom Kippur, 21, 22, 190, 191, 280
Yotzer of Hannuka, 219
Yuan dynasty, 50

Z
Zakkai, Exilarch David ben, 61
Zichron Ya'akov, 111
Zilpa, 80–81
Zimmerman, Joshua D., 162
Zimmerman, Mary, 42
Zionism, 17, 19, 120
Zuccotti, Susan, 163